Suits

Suits

A WOMAN ON WALL STREET

Nina Godiwalla

ATLAS & CO. *New York*

Atlas & Co. *Publishers*
15 West 26th Street, 2nd floor
New York, NY 10010
www.atlasandco.com

Distributed to the trade by W. W. Norton & Company

Printed in the United States

Atlas & Company books may be purchased for educational, business, or sales
promotional use. For information, please write to info@atlasandco.com.

LIBRARY OF CONGRESS CATALOGING-IN-PUBLICATION DATA
IS AVAILABLE UPON REQUEST.

ISBN: 978-1-934633-95-3

15   14   13   12   11   1   2   3   4   5   6

Note from the Author

I have based this book on my recollections of my life, and my experiences in the world of investment banking. However, some characters are composites; events have been compressed, rearranged chronologically, or otherwise altered; and the names and identifying characteristics of companies (other than JP Morgan and Morgan Stanley), deals, and individuals (other than my own) have been changed. All of the dialogue is a recreation on my part based entirely upon my current recollections, and should not be mistaken as an actual transcription of what people said. At times, instances have been embellished.

To my mom and dad,
for giving us everything

Contents

CHAPTER 1

Training

As I walked to JP Morgan, I didn't see anyone around except the sidewalk food vendors. At every third corner, a massive semi would drive up to a street corner and a vendor would hop out, open the back of the truck, and push his little rectangular steel food cart down the ramp. I kept pace with the ColdSoda-WaterSnapple guy, the Shish Kebab guy, and the Nuts 4 Nuts guy. They were a global collective—Pakistan, China, and Guatemala—who had adopted New York as their new home, paving the way for their kids' futures. I was on my own journey from Texas, off to conquer Wall Street.

Before I arrived in New York, my dad impressed upon me that subways were places where people could get knifed in broad daylight, so I walked from Thirty-fourth Street and First Avenue to Wall Street. In Texas, I had never been on any public transportation, other than a Greyhound a few times, so the New York City buses with their transfers and the trains with theirs were so intimidating that I decided to walk. It made me feel more in control. Plus, Manhattan's 2.3-mile width was less than the width of my suburban neighborhood outside Houston. Looking at the map, I estimated it would be an hour's walk, but I left three hours early just in case. "It's always better to play it safe," my dad had said.

A purposeful walk four miles to work solved this issue of navigating the daunting subway system and also gave me an outlet for my nervous energy. I was an hour and a half into my trek when my Payless heel got stuck in a steel grille. I'd spent at least a half hour at Payless Shoes choosing these sensible heels—not too high, not too low, not too thin, not too thick. *How could they be the precise size of a hole in a New York City grate?* It was lodged so tight that I could not get it out. *Not now, heel. Not today.* I struggled desperately, and now I was covered in the sooty smoke that angrily erupted from the drain. Leaving the shoe in the grate, I hobbled into the only store open, Larry's Fish Market, and was instantly hit by the smell of fish guts. The first three guys in white aprons splotched with blood never looked up from gutting fish. There were no smiling faces welcoming me with, "Good morning, miss. What can I do to help you this morning?" I guessed what they said about New York was true.

"Can someone help me? My shoe's stuck in the sidewalk grate," I said, walking across the cold tile floor on my tiptoes. I anxiously waited for a minute before repeating myself. At first I thought they might not speak English, but it soon became apparent that they were blatantly ignoring me. "My shoe's stuck!" I shouted. "I can't go anywhere until I get it out!" The fourth man wiped his sweaty forehead with his arm. I waited for several minutes before he looked up and took in my pathetic state—one pantyhosed foot standing in fish blood and the other foot wobbling in a heel made for a grown-up. *Someone, please help me.* He shook his head. "What!" he screamed at me with an accent that reminded me of a Corleone from *The Godfather.* "You really can't get your shoe out?"

"I can't!" I whined desperately. "I came all the way from Texas. And I'm going to miss my first day," I said, balancing on one foot—one shoe on, one shoe off—and squinting so that he wouldn't notice that my eyes were starting to water.

He rolled his eyes and slammed his sawtooth knife against the fish table to let the excess blood fly off. "Where is it?" he said, sprinting out of the store.

I hobbled behind him like someone who was just coming off an all-night bender.

With one sharp slash, he took his knife and sliced off part of my heel, letting it fall through one of the slits in the grille. The heel splashed into a pool of black sewer water. He threw the shoe toward my feet, splashing blobs of fish juice and blood onto my left calf. He walked off with his stiff arms swinging side to side, his shiny knife splashing blood and fish juice onto the sidewalk.

"Thank you, sir!" I said in my sugariest Southern hospitality pitch. "Thank you!" I yelled out to him. "Thank you so very much, sir!"

Thirty minutes later, the JP Morgan skyscraper towered over me. Outside the building, stock exchange traders stood sucking on cigarettes, anxiously pacing back and forth. They wore bright-colored vests and jackets labeled with investment bank names. Just being around their intensity excited me. With the confidence of an everyday Wall Street banker, I fiercely pushed the full-glass revolving door and was instantly faced with two people at a desk who looked like miniatures in front of the two-story deep green marble panel towering behind them. *Is that real marble?* "I'm here to meet with Gail Grover," I informed a woman wearing a CIA headset at the desk.

"That's 60 Wall," she corrected me.

"Okay," I said standing, waiting with a friendly smile. *I can't wait to get an ID card.*

She repeated, "It's 60 Wall."

"Which way do I go?" I asked, overwhelmed by the numerous elevator banks.

"Out the door," she said, pointing to the revolving door.

"But I'm working for JP Morgan." *What is it with these New Yorkers?*

"Congratulations," she said with a smile. "So am I. But, honey, we're in 15 Broad. You want 60 Wall Street. JP Morgan is a big company with many buildings. Go out the door and take two rights."

I shook my head at my reflection as I pushed the revolving door. The New York soot clung to my sweaty face, and loose strands of my low, tightly pulled ponytail were hanging messily. *Don't forget to pull back your shoulders and smile when you walk in.*

I had only seen the New York Stock Exchange on television. I felt minuscule as I stood before it. I covered my mouth to contain an uncontrollable smile and wished someone could take a picture of me. My parents, who were both of Persian descent but had grown up in India, would take it to a Parsi — Persian-Indian — function and pass it around before dinner as the samosas were being served. A magnet from Manic Uncle's law practice would hold it to their fridge at home, and my grandparents would get a blown-up five-by-seven-inch copy in India that they would carefully protect in a quart-size plastic baggie and pass around at friends' dinner parties. All of this would confirm my success on Wall Street — or at least that I'd gotten there.

I'd researched so much about the history of Wall Street and JP Morgan that snippets of information ran through my head like a built-in tour guide. The old JP Morgan building on the corner of Broad and Wall Street still bears scars from the 1920 terrorist bomb that exploded and killed many people. Broad Street is so narrow that just to see the building's familiar ornate triangular pediment supported by the white Corinthian columns, I had to bend my head way back like a howling coyote. I stared at the central female figure, Integrity, with her arms outspread, dressed in a flowing gown and winged hat. To her left and right are nude males who represent Work. "*Integrity Protecting the Works of Man*," I mumbled, suddenly remembering the name of the sculpture. As I rocked on my butchered heel, I wondered why work and integrity were represented separately.

Though I was familiar with the iconic stock exchange building, it was unclear to me what these Wall Street people actually did. *Why are so many of them wearing fancy sunglasses?* I had a curiosity that many of my friends from Texas, content to stay close to our small suburban community, didn't quite share. It seemed only right to escape to be part of something bigger than Texas. Popularity throughout school and being one of the best students in college were only small victories—Wall Street was much bigger than that. There was an importance to these suited characters who walked in fast, measured strides. Later I'd learn that their crinkled foreheads and scowling faces represented nothing more than the expressions of busy people lost in their thoughts. Even though I enthusiastically tried to make eye contact, they were oblivious to my smiling face. I didn't understand what they were screaming about on the stock exchange floor, or the meaning of the flying papers and the mechanical hand gestures that looked obscene, but I knew I was exhilarated by the idea of being that important.

My childhood ambitions never involved Wall Street. But I did know that money and prestige would raise my status in my family and my Persian-Indian community. Growing up, I made all kinds of lists that I hoped would impress them one day. I added "Become quadrilingual" after I heard Natasha Aunty say there was no greater sign of brilliance than knowing a lot of languages. I added "Get a 'Dr.' title" since I'd often seen aunties and uncles turn to this highly educated group first after I asked random questions like "Where does our tap water come from?" But all these credentials were common in our community. I wanted to stand out from the crowd just like when Zareen Aunty's brother, who worked in finance in New York, visited Houston. When he came to our Persian New Year's party, all the uncles clustered around him. Fali Uncle, who worked at a local Houston investment firm, would ask, "Do they work much harder in New York?" Zareen Aunty's brother spoke much faster than us and constantly kept looking around the room as if someone were missing. We all stared at him, eagerly awaiting his every response. Other than a trip to India, I'd hardly left Texas, so New York sounded more like a place where they filmed movies rather than a place to call home.

"Wow," my dad said, eyes glassy with admiration, after only a five-minute conversation. "Those New York finance guys are really something."

Toward the end of my long walk, I briskly turned right onto Wall Street and was immediately bombarded with tourists' video cameras. Today I smiled as they all eagerly recorded my conservatively suited body. By the end of the summer I would impatiently dodge them like my other colleagues did.

After finding the right building, I entered the boardroom,

crooked, salmon-spiced, and salted in sweat. I was immediately intimidated by the high ceiling, the forty-foot gleaming mahogany table, and the twenty or so heads that turned my way, eager to check out the competition. The table sparkled with the reflection of bright ceiling lights and was neatly lined with green bottles that I'd later learn to recognize as Perrier. By the heavy scent of musk cologne, I assumed I wasn't the only one trying hard to make a good impression. Even so, I got the feeling of walking into a fancy restaurant and sensing that others realize you don't belong. Less than a year ago I'd been a cashier at a rundown grocery store in Houston.

Before I could fully take in the scene, I was greeted by someone who looked my age and yet walked up to the door to meet me like a butler. "Hello, I'm Alan."

"Hi! I'm Nina," I said with a broad smile. *Is he an intern or one of them?* I gave him the firm handshake I had practiced in career training sessions many times. *And now, the small squeeze.* Career service representatives told us in their hearty Texan voices that "soft, slimy fish handshakes" wouldn't do.

"Do you work here?" I asked, confused by the aggressive greeting.

"No, I'm an intern," Alan replied. Later, one of the other interns explained to me that he was a hard-core networker who was certain that we were being videotaped. Alan stared at the blood splatters on my pantyhose, and in smooth downward motions, he stroked his tie with the delicacy one might use to pet a rare Persian cat. He then abruptly flipped his tie briskly, yet carefully enough to advertise Armani. "From Princeton," he clarified.

"Nice to meet you," I said, self-conscious about my

appearance. *Why is he the only one standing? And so close to me.*

"It's a pleasure to meet you too," Alan replied. "Where are you from?"

"Texas," I said as I looked across at the closely packed interns already seated at the enormous shiny boardroom table. I must have been the last one there, but luckily there were no JP Morgan representatives to note it.

"I've never met anyone from Texas," Alan replied.

"Me neither," another intern said, tapping her JP Morgan pen. "I don't think I've been friends with anyone south of Pennsylvania." *Seriously?*

"So you went to school close to home?" Alan asked.

"Yes," I answered. "Isn't anyone else from Texas?" I asked hopefully, feeling an urgent need to belong. *Were we told to only wear black? I don't remember them writing that in our welcome letter.*

"And you went where?" Alan asked, ignoring my question.

"UT Austin," I said. After seeing vacant stares, I remembered I was no longer in Texas. "University of Texas."

"That's a good school," Alan said, nodding his head. He turned around to face the others, who started to join him in nodding.

"Oh yes, UT is a great school," another intern informed me.

"So you must have a good GPA?" suggested an intern who had her hair pulled back in a tight bun and wore a black cameo brooch that reminded me of my grandmother.

I shrugged my shoulders and smiled politely. *"Don't we all?"* might sound too obnoxious.

"So, Nina," Alan asked in a talk-show-host tone, "what year are you?"

"I'm a freshman," I said, unaware that I might be the only one.

"How did you get here?" one guy in an all-black suit at the far end of the table demanded.

"I just interviewed," I responded.

"Interviewed through connections?" Alan suggested.

"No," I said. "Through recruiters." *Why so many questions? I already had my interview.*

"You don't even have a Texas accent!" the guy at the far end of the table said as he stroked his chin and squinted his eyes. "Hey, I thought everyone from Texas had big blond hair. Were you born in Texas?"

"Born and raised," I said, wanting to be proud. "I'm from Houston. It's a big city with all different kinds of people," I said, hoping he wouldn't press it any further so I could avoid the whole "you don't look Indian" conversation. No need to stand out even more.

I only had four suits, just short of one for each day, and two pairs of shoes for the whole summer. I'd already devised a schedule as to when to wear each suit so that my shortage would not be so obvious. My Texas friends said no one would know the difference, but it was already clear that these people would. My 100% polyester houndstooth TJ Maxx suit stood out like sweatpants at a wedding.

I sat down at the far end of the board table, where interns mingled, talking nervously to one another, trying to look busy, as we all anxiously waited to be greeted by a JP Morgan representative. To my right were three Yale students talking about their operations professor and to my left were two Dartmouth students reminiscing about their annual Polar Bear Swim. I rummaged through the Kmart briefcase my parents had bought me as an "our daughter is going to Wall Street!" gift. I was about to take out my binder before I realized that some might find the plastic burnt orange folder out of place on the table neatly lined with Italian leather notebooks. While I was fumbling, a little note that had accidently stuck to my binder fell to the floor. Written in all caps in perfect English was a note my grandmother had written down from an advertisement:

FAST, EASY, HEALTHY.

FAGOR PRESSURE COOKERS THE SINGLE MOST IMPORTANT PIECE OF COOKWARE YOU'LL EVER OWN.

FOR A STORE NEAREST YOU CALL 1-800-207-0806.

BEST POT EVER!

She had a habit of making notes like this and absentmindedly leaving them around. Nothing slowed her down. Even though she rarely ever left our house, she always found little ways through watching television shows to become a better cook. I suddenly felt very grateful that I had the opportunity to sit at this boardroom table.

Exhausted by the long morning, I leaned my forehead, which I had carefully waxed the previous night, into my cupped right hand. I stared past all the eyes and Armani ties and focused on the three enormous paintings that hung on the wall. Each was a six-foot-by-six-foot monochromatic canvas—one red, one orange, one yellow. How odd for them to be in this room; they belonged to the Texas warmth. I hoped to meet some friendly Southern faces soon, even though just weeks ago I'd been eager to break away from them in search of something new and exciting.

Sitting at the boardroom table, I thought back to the JP Morgan recruiter who hired me in Texas. Six months into college, while all my classmates were spending their free time trying to find ways to fly home to visit their families, I was spending my time at career fairs. As usual, my mother was at the forefront of making things happen. She reminded those in our Persian-Indian community how brilliant I was and sent me contact information for aunties and uncles who might be hiring business interns in Houston. My PR queen advertised at the Parsi dinner parties she and my father attended every weekend: "She's very studious now. Not at all like her high school years of fun. Top of her class at UT."

At one fair I spoke with a JP Morgan recruiter who was hiring a few juniors for jobs in New York City. Assuming I was a junior, she enthusiastically described the challenging positions in vibrant New York City. She sensed my eagerness and was disappointed to find out that I was a freshman.

"This is really out of the question," she said. "Come back in two years."

I followed up by reading *The House of Morgan, J.P. Morgan: The Financier as Collector*, and *How to Read the Wall Street Journal for Pleasure and for Profit*—all 1,053 pages. Money *and* prestige? I was sold. I sent the recruiter an essay explaining why I was as capable as any junior. "It's less about my specific finance knowledge and more about my ability to thrive in a fast-paced, frenetic environment. With my natural curiosity and unparalleled determination, I have no doubt I can do this just as well as a junior." She replied that in the past they had only hired freshmen who attended Ivy League schools and had family connections. I had neither. Months later, she returned to campus and was surprised to see me at her information session. After her session, we had a long conversation about my leadership positions on campus, and my top standing in classes infamous for failing students. She said to me, "You are going to be very successful, and JP Morgan would hate to lose you. Let me see what I can do." After a month, an offer showed up in my mailbox. I was the only freshman in the department hired that year.

In due time, I found out that my fellow interns were mostly from Harvard, Wharton, and Yale. I was entirely unfamiliar with many of the other schools' names, including Brown, Amherst, and University of Pennsylvania. But I would learn that these names were clearly as important as JP Morgan and Morgan Stanley.

One intern mentioned she was from Williams, a school I had never heard of. "Where is Williams?" I asked. Was she talking about her high school?

"You've never heard of it?" she asked as she toyed with the pearls strung around her neck. She then turned to the two people sitting next to her to see if they, too, were surprised by my ignorance.

"No," I said.

"I've heard of your school," she said, adjusting her black-rimmed glasses and pointing a finger at me like a reprimanding teacher. "And my school has the best economics department in the country!"

After another intern informed me he was from the University of Pennsylvania, I leaned over, eager to make a connection with anyone, and said, "Thank God—I thought I was the only one from a public school." He glared at me as he fingered his

Penn-engraved cuff links and informed me, "Penn is definitely not a public school." He clarified: "Ivy League."

My first impression of my fellow JP Morgan interns was as startling as theirs of me. Initially they judged me harshly since I wasn't one of them. But I'd learn soon that it wasn't personal. Most of them were used to being around people just like them, and so their natural tendency was to box outsiders into categories before they could get to know them better. Once I got to know them, I met several with whom I got along well, but only during the workday, mostly over lunch at JP Morgan's free cafeteria. After one dinner with this money-is-no-object crowd, I learned that this was where the real bonding took place, but I couldn't afford it. Our evening started at Harry's, a café and steakhouse and a self-described "Wall Street institution." Once I saw that most of the entrées were well over twenty dollars, I opted for an appetizer and purposely drank only tap water even though multiple bottles of Perrier and wine were ordered for our table of twenty. When the bill arrived, a guy at the far end shouted, "A hundred and thirty dollars a person." "I didn't even drink," I announced in shock. The intern next to me said, "I only drank two glasses of wine, but let's not make this complicated." "Yeah," another fellow intern agreed. This was my first lesson: In these crowds bills would be split evenly—not like the Texan practice where the bill is passed around and each person pays his or her own portion. While everyone else headed to a dance club with a thirty-dollar cover, I went home.

My team at JP Morgan was unlike any other investment banking group I'd work for in the future. I told the human resources department that I wanted to major in management so that they would place me in an appropriate group, but they just placed me with several senior officers. As a freshman, I had only taken a handful of classes, and the only one I liked so far was psychology. After I explained to the career counselor that my dad wouldn't be thrilled about psychology as a major, she advised that I major in management, "the closest thing to psychology in the business school."

My JP Morgan team was small—two women and three men—mostly older, senior officers who analyzed operational processes. None of them was your stereotypical banker. They'd worked in more frenetic divisions of the bank and then moved on to this more analytical, almost academic group. They valued their personal lives and were eager to get home to their families before 9:00 P.M. I was their first intern, and they were determined to make sure I had a good experience. They paired me with a mentor in another group, with whom I'd meet weekly to make sure my experience was going well. They were impressed by my ambition and charmed by my innocence. Peter, the head of the group, told me that he'd worked there for twenty-five years, and he was amused when I blurted out, "That's before I was even born," mistakenly thinking he'd feel like an expert rather than just old. Almost immediately after I arrived, there was a ticker-tape parade to celebrate the Rangers winning the Stanley Cup. I stood at the window in awe for hours as more than twenty tons of paper snowed down from our Wall Street skyscrapers. Peter laughed as he watched me frantically run between floors to see the parade from all angles. In moments like this, New York's inconveniences of no free Coke refills or easy-to-find public restrooms vanished. That day, I announced gleefully, confident that

I was now part of history, "I can't imagine anyone would want to live anywhere other than New York!"

My first two weeks at JP Morgan were slow since the team was scrambling anxiously to pull together my intern projects, so I went to the company library and watched the videos that were made for training post-MBA employees. Though I had not even taken a business class in college yet, I watched hours of videos on derivatives, fixed income, bonds, capital markets, commodities, etc. My whole team was shocked since they didn't even know there was a company library. Throughout the rest of the summer, I'd give them lessons on the different financial assets that I learned about through the videos. "She's as smart as a whip," Peter would announce before introducing me to others.

Since my group had been studying mundane planning processes for so many years, Peter welcomed a fresh pair of eyes. I'd challenge many of the processes they used that seemed obviously inefficient to me but tested and established to them. "Be the solution" was Peter's response to me. By the end of the summer, I had redesigned and automated several of their processes. What seemed basic to me was revolutionary to them. "She's a high-tech whiz, too," Peter said, shaking his head with pride.

While my group at JP Morgan considered me a young dynamo, I still had to work on fine-tuning myself in networking situations. Early on in the summer, we were at a lunch event. Three interns were invited to the top floor, to the elite private dining room available only to a select group of senior bankers. We were surrounded by walls of windows that left us with no place to hide. We towered over Wall Street, reducing it to the width of an Excel spreadsheet cell. The dining room was filled with artwork. Behind me sat a large horse sculpture from the second-century Eastern Han dynasty. Our host, Mr. Stevens, the head of one of the bank's major divisions, informed us that we came at a good time since the Louvre had just returned several of JP Morgan's works.

I was relieved when Mr. Stevens steered the conversation from art to the firm's history and future strategy, since I had done a lot of extra reading about JP Morgan. For the other interns, it was expected that they, as the top students in their economics classes, would work at the top Wall Street firms. For me, this internship was a chance of a lifetime that I couldn't screw up. I could hear my dad reminding me, "A solid American job, with good benefits. Plus, prestige. Be loyal to them!"

"One of the conversations we as senior managers are having," Mr. Stevens began, "is how to take advantage of the potential repeal of the Glass-Steagall Act. Now, you are all too young to know about the 1933 regulation, but loosening it could have a major impact on the banking industry."

The other interns stared at him, waiting for him to explain the act, but I jumped in. "The current regulation is far too strict and can be loosened without compromising the safety of consumers' deposits." I paused, taking a moment to explain to the other interns, "The act restricts commercial and investment banks' affiliations, and loosening restrictions will allow banks to offer a much broader range of services."

Mr. Stevens and I debated the issue back and forth, dominating the conversation. I was at my peak by the time my poached pear with champagne cream and lavender shortbread arrived.

"So," I went on excitedly, "do y'all see . . ."

Before I could finish, Mr. Stevens choked on his port wine

and spurted it onto his napkin. "Wow!" he said, "I didn't know *y'all* really said that." He shook the entire table with a sudden thunderous guffaw. On command, the other two interns followed. Between Mr. Stevens's lulls, each intern would try to give out the loudest hoot, rocking the table, eager to be the best supporter. Mr. Stevens stomped his foot and let out a piercing scream, which attracted all the other diners, who were now jealous of our table's fun. To be part of the team, I too joined in their laughter. But as they watched each other, I looked down at the champagne sauce spilling out of my violently joggled pear.

Mr. Stevens stopped as abruptly as he began, and, following protocol, our last chuckle was in unison with his. He took a sip of his port and looked at me. "Sorry, go on and ask your question."

After we left the dining hall another intern patted my back sympathetically, leaned in, and whispered, "Nina, why did you do that to yourself?"

With the exception of Mr. Stevens, I'd learn that my team at JP Morgan was much more tolerant of differences than other bankers at the company. But I only had to slip up at a few events like this to learn very quickly what to lose—anything Southern or middle class. Luckily, I was a quick learner. It was the same skill that made me popular in high school—copying other people's behavior to fit right in. Since my friendly Southern demeanor could easily be interpreted as flirting in this emotionless atmosphere, I lost it. I used the right lingo, like *i-banking* and *B-school*. At the close of a phone call, I now said "take care" instead of "talk to you later." I began talking much faster and with a more serious tone that commanded attention. I walked the halls with purpose. And my "middle-America" habit of happily eating at chains like Olive Garden or TGI Friday's was quickly scrapped. The small dangling pearl earrings and the few more suits I invested in enabled me to look as much like them as possible. At the time, all this felt like quite an adjustment for me, but I had no idea how small an adjustment it would be until I gave up so much more to fit in at Morgan Stanley.

My JP Morgan team gave me an offer to return my sophomore summer as well as an outstanding review, which would be sent by my mom to my grandparents in India to be passed around at family dinner parties in a protective plastic cover. "Our little Nina," I could hear them say. My status on campus rose too, given that—as far as career services knew—I was the first freshman to intern at a top-tier Wall Street firm. They requested that I give résumé workshops and recommended that I join the dean's advisory council. Suddenly, I became more of an advisor than a student on campus.

After my summer at JP Morgan, I knew I enjoyed the ambitious Wall Street crowd and the fast pace. More importantly, I loved that my group valued my opinion.

By the time I started my second summer internship at Morgan Stanley, my junior summer, I was much more polished. It was easier to impress this Wall Street crowd once I had a better idea of what to hide. I could have returned to JP Morgan, but Morgan Stanley had started a minority program a few years earlier that provided a scholarship in addition to my salary. Plus, Morgan Stanley's investment banking division was considered stronger than JP Morgan's. After an intensive application process and many long grueling interviews, I was accepted into the Morgan Stanley Scholars Program.

Like JP Morgan, Morgan Stanley spent an extraordinary amount of time wooing their interns. While JP Morgan focused on treating us to Broadway shows, Yankees games, and elaborate meals in order to seduce us with a certain lifestyle, Morgan Stanley matched these fringe benefits and then took it to another level. As corporate events, we took field trips to our executives' summer and fall mansions. Their vast homes were outfitted with golf courses, tennis courts, vineyards, and nearly Olympic-size pools. There, we met their families, who seemed to dwell on all their other homes around the globe that they tried so desperately to visit. They would explain how little time they spent at this mansion while showing us pictures of their Italy and Fiji homes, "which are much bigger than this one." Like skilled game-show hosts, they played to our hunger.

I was in awe. Everything I was experiencing was foreign to me. It was as if someone had flung me into one of my grandmother's soap operas, but unlike her, I didn't believe Americans *really* lived like this. I found myself looking at their children, wondering what it was like to eat fresh-baked chocolate-filled croissants for breakfast instead of Pop-Tarts; have your own nanny to treat like a servant; and spend weekends ordering banana splits with chocolate, vanilla, *and* strawberry ice cream at country clubs that didn't allow you to wear shorts. With every new place we went, I knew I was out of my element, but my curiosity and excitement for the extravagance I wouldn't see otherwise kept me hungry.

At the time, most of us didn't realize we were being sold something. We believed what they chanted: "You're here because you are the best of the best." Who wouldn't want to believe that? In some way or another, most of us had worked hard to get there, and, finally, we were hearing what we had been trying to prove to ourselves and others for years. Even many of the interns who had grown up wealthy hadn't experienced such extravagant childhoods. They, too, were taken in by this opulence.

It was irrelevant to my teammates or officers that I was a Morgan Stanley Scholar, since most of them weren't familiar with the program. To them, I was just another intern. Through an extremely competitive process, the Scholars Program chose about twenty minorities in the country and provided us with a two-year scholarship as long as we interned with them. As Scholars, we got to meet senior officers for lunches over the summer, most notably the chairman of Morgan Stanley. There weren't many University of Texas alumni available for networking, so Morgan Stanley became my alumni register.

The few senior-level minorities had been at Morgan Stanley for most of their careers and had learned to conform to the rigid corporate culture. Their years spent fighting to succeed left many of them hardened, yet they realized the need to offer a hand to those who would follow them. At the beginning of the summer they collected us for a meeting in conference room 32A. "As a minority you will be scrutinized. And if you are a woman, expect ten times the challenge. If they drink, you should drink less. Don't think you can do whatever they do. They look at you differently than they do themselves. You will be required to prove yourself. You DO NOT get the benefit of the doubt. One slipup can cost you years of hard work." Their faces were fixed with stern grimaces, but you could see in their eyes that they were speaking from painful experience. We interns looked at one another with fearful brown eyes: *Are they sure they want us here?*

During one of our lunches, one intern made the mistake of complaining to a senior officer about the cafeteria food. This prompted another collective meeting so we could all witness his public humiliation by one of the senior minority officers. "These are not the people you whine to about mundane things. Use every minute you have wisely. And remember, if one of us looks bad, we all look bad!" she announced, furious that she had to spend more time stressing something that she'd already made evident. It was lesson enough for me to carefully script what I said. Before we had lunch with the chairman, there was another meeting where we were groomed with rehearsed conversations. As I looked around the room I noticed that a good number of the minority Scholars could pass as white. I'd heard officers say, "We get so many bright people during interviews that it's less about their résumé and more about a good corporate fit." *Did lighter skin help with the good corporate fit?* I wasn't dark-skinned enough to be asked, "Did you grow up in America?" like other Indians were. And officers seemed to be comfortable saying many unflattering things about minorities in front of me, as if I were one of them. This voyeurism was new to me: In Texas it was clear I was a minority and wouldn't be privy to such comments.

I still remember the chairman's charismatic smile as he welcomed us into the formal dining room. "Tell me all about your experience here at Morgan Stanley," he said. "I'm dying to hear about you all. Please, just relax and be yourself!" But we were all too scared to ask the questions we really wanted to ask: *Why do we have to be like everyone else to fit in? Why are you so much friendlier than everyone else? Were you once like them?* Though the chairman was genuine, his casual demeanor read like a trick. We minorities weren't naïve enough to slip up and ask embargoed questions. Instead, the half-white, half-Spanish guy started off in a shaky voice asking one of our scripted, approved questions: "Given talk of a potential merger, what is your vision for retail banking?"

The chairman was the only powerful person I remember who seemed interested in knowing how he could make our experience better rather than in telling us what we needed to change to fit into their culture. He even looked like he was interested in what we had to say on the topic. To him, we were a gesture toward diversity; the burden fell on those who organized the program to justify its existence. The Scholars Program was quite new and was just beginning to establish itself. While few knew about it, those who did were aware of its prestige. Even today, the program is still going strong.

During the summer, most of the minorities hung out together, partly because we had more in common: immigrant parents or middle-class lives. Maybe twenty percent of our class was composed of minorities, which was considered a lot, since there were hardly any senior officers who were minorities or women. At the end of the summer, one of my fellow Scholars told one of the program directors that she didn't have a good experience because she couldn't deal with the condescending way analysts, especially women analysts, were treated. She went on to tell me about her conversation with that director: "Instead of asking me what made my experience bad, she just stared at me with annoyance. She may as well have just screamed, 'You are so ungrateful! Do you know what I had to put up with fifteen years ago? You are lucky to be here. No one singled me out and offered me a hand up.'" But this Scholar, along with many others, wouldn't get an invitation to return for a full-time job. In fact, some of the Scholars didn't perform well, but it was hard not to notice that several of them were the more outspoken ones who tried to change the culture rather than conform. Again, I made this brutal cut.

It wasn't until my full-time experience in corporate finance that I began to understand why women and minorities didn't seem to stay in the department very long. It often felt like there was more to give up than to gain.

My education as an intern soon turned into the real thing. A five-week training course provided the bridge between that world and the world of a full-time employee at Morgan Stanley. All the Morgan Stanley analysts worldwide—about two hundred new bankers fresh out of college—gathered together for this training, but only about half would stay in New York City for the real Wall Street experience, while the rest would disperse throughout the world.

Three of us—Luis, Michael, and myself—would join a group that conducted major financial transactions (initial public offers, mergers, and acquisitions) for the country's largest blue-chip companies. We interacted with CEOs and CFOs from the most prestigious corporations. Competing for groups was difficult, but my performance during my prior year's internship landed me in this group. I was thrilled when I was told that I performed so well that I could choose any group I wanted. However, I didn't realize until I started working in the corporate finance division that I'd be the only woman in a group of about twenty-five men. I guess no one felt the need to let me know the demographics. Were we beyond such briefing at Morgan Stanley?

Even though I had the extensive advantage of my varied internships, I still felt a little threatened by Michael. I knew that each group had an unspoken star analyst and I had a hunch that he was the chosen one. His credentials were all too perfect compared to my Southern public school pedigree. Since the age of ten, he had been groomed by his parents to fit into investment banking culture. His upbringing included a prep school whose alumni would cringe at anyone who referred to it as a "school" rather than an "academy" and required students to wear their shield on their cuff links; tuna tartare appetizers; a deft backspin onto the green; friends whose names ended in III or IV; and a place in Yale's most prestigious secret society. Every evening by 6:00 P.M. the vodka would be adequately chilled for his parents' gimlets, and after dinner they would all go into the study and debate the issues raised by that morning's *New York Times*. Given this education, Michael knew to laugh before a superior even made the joke and how to discuss a 1966 Balvenie single malt's complexity. When people mentioned they were spending the weekend at their summer home in Bar Harbor, Nantucket, or Martha's Vineyard, Michael knew to befriend them immediately, whereas to me, these names didn't register at all—they sounded more like hokey generic grocery store brands.

To top off his credentials, Michael was as good looking as he was smooth. Many of our colleagues found his face as attractive as his chest—a combination we all agreed was hard to find. Typically, you get one or the other, and at Morgan Stanley this was definitely the case. He highlighted his lacrosse player's chest by wearing thin white dress shirts without an undershirt, revealing just enough to confirm his nipples had a healthy pink shine.

Our second colleague, Luis, was from Johns Hopkins. He had studied in American International schools and spent his childhood in gated expatriate compounds around the world. Since his parents were both diplomats, he had no distinct sense of home. From his heavy-handed application of spicy cologne and unique mix-and-match suit style, I got the feeling he spent a good amount of time in Europe. It was a challenge for him to be conservative in the office, especially if an officer was around, but at heart he was a metrosexual, spending extra attention on riding the line between aristocracy and Eurotrash. He was hired by one of our nostalgic senior officers, Ken, who wanted to relive his college years at Johns Hopkins. Like Michael, Luis would make it a priority at work to enjoy the luxuries it afforded while making sure his friends remembered where he worked. His thin face and overly visible cheekbones were remedied by his carefully styled hair, but his emaciated body was hardly saved by his stylishly loose suits. Growing up in Texas, I had learned to appreciate the bodies of linebackers. In sunny practice fields, they worked out so much that their efforts made them look bloated. Early on I knew I never wanted to see Luis without clothes. His jutting pelvic bones would soon discipline my eyes to not wander any lower than his shoulder blades.

Lack of attraction aside, there was something about Luis's lack of identity that connected with me. He had picked up bits and pieces from all the countries where he'd lived, but he was hard-pressed to settle on a hometown; he couldn't pinpoint a place where he belonged. In New York, I was considered a Texan.

In Texas, I was an Indian. In India, I was a Persian. All the labeling felt isolating. Not everyone needs to fit in, but I wanted to. My family believed in an almost extinct ancient Persian religion, Zoroastrianism, which has fewer than two hundred thousand followers left in the world. There was still a small population of Zoroastrians in modern-day Iran, but they were culturally very different from our Persian-Indian community, which had spent the last thousand years in India. When I tried to get a visual feel for where we came from through BBC documentaries or research online, I'd find ancient ruins in modern-day Iran and the former Soviet republics—nothing that satisfied my curiosity. Not having a real sense of where I fit in, I tended to blend into new environments, hoping to find somewhere to belong.

After five weeks of crantinis, Tahitian crème brûlées, and front-row *Rent* tickets, we Morgan Stanley full-time analysts found it hard to believe that we had all been college students just a couple months ago. The courtship was over and the transition from our training to working was abrupt—from late nights of clubbing to late nights of number crunching. Soon we would begin our long, two-year analyst program.

Early in our training, Michael, Luis, and I stopped by our new group to mingle with our numerous soon-to-be bosses. "Training is secondary," they assured us. "Just have a great time! Drink and enjoy life as much as you can," they warned.

"Sweet!" Michael said, lifting his hand to Luis for a high five. He took a moment to pat down one of Luis's hairs. They always kept an eye on each other's sticky hairdos. "Is that for real?" Michael asked, trying to confirm that we didn't have to take it seriously.

"We have tests," I said, tightly grasping my Morgan Stanley training manual.

"Trust me," our future colleague, only a year ahead of us, said. "It doesn't matter."

"Are you sure?" I clarified. "I don't want to screw up."

The veteran looked at his co-worker, and they laughed at the conscientious novice. "Have fun!"

Almost every night of our training was spent at a dinner or a party hosted by the firm. That night we were at Au Bar. A place that described itself as "more than a nightclub—an institution," Au Bar looked like an old castle library; its main clientele consisted of nouveau-riche Russians who sat at bottle-service tables dropping at least three hundred dollars a sitting. Huge mirrors and European paintings covered the walls. The large club was divided into several smaller, cavernlike rooms in an attempt to create multiple sitting areas with an intimate setting similar to a living room. It was decorated with Victorian flowered velvet couches, sprawling Persian rugs, chandeliers, and countless fireplaces. High arched ceilings were supported by roman columns, and the walls were full of rare books on tall mahogany bookshelves. In a forced attempt to create a sensual aura, the lighting was so dim you had to squint to see; I had come to learn that this was a trademark of New York–chic.

A dozen half-finished dirty Chopin martinis and French cognacs were sitting at our table. Most people kept forgetting where their drinks were, so they would return again and again to the open bar to order another two or three. The women were more cautious: There were fewer drunk women than men. I was overly careful. At the University of Texas we were instructed to politely decline drinking at any meeting, party, or business anything.

"It is a test!" the career services office representative, Ms. Spencer, warned us with her bright red roller-curled hair and slight drawl. "It is always a test. They will try and make you feel comfortable and assure you it is okay," she said as she paused to look around the classroom of unseasoned future corporate executives. She explained all this in the same cautionary tone we Morgan Stanley interns would get from officers prepping us to meet with the chairman. "But," she went on, "just like adding salt to your food before you taste it, and having your fingernails too long, or worse, too short," she railed, "it is a test!"

But after a few internships in investment banking, I was acclimated and knew not to fall into the "no thanks" trap. Having already learned these lessons, I was now an advisor to those who were completely new to the world of investment banking. At Au Bar, Scott followed me around like a curious monkey. Like Michael, Scott had graduated from Yale, but he had none of Michael's airs. These two were a couple of the better-looking guys in our analysts' class. Scott was naturally striking, while Michael was a mass-market product. At first sight, they were similar—copper skin, bright blue eyes, and light brown wavy hair with blond highlights. However, Michael's glowing skin was airbrushed on by technicians at Bliss Spa, his eyes were enhanced by FreshLook two-week disposables, and his hair was highlighted and waved quarterly by different salons. If you were standing close enough, you would choose Scott, though they were both second-glance guys.

If you knew Michael well enough, you would learn that he used his charming *buddy* and *pal* labels to flatter. Everyone who could get him anywhere was a "close buddy" and anyone who had potential was a "pal." On our first day of training we got an Analyst Facebook, a spiral-bound notebook with each analyst's picture, background information, and personal interests. Morgan Stanley copied the concept from schools like Phillips Exeter

Academy and Harvard. It's been said that these print editions inspired the founder of Facebook.com to take these booklets to a larger, web-based level. Michael listed his favorite magazine as GQ. Next to most, especially Michael, Scott came off as naïve. He looked white despite the fact that his mother was half Cherokee. Though they were wealthy, it was her idea to teach him the value of money by lending him tuition for college that he would eventually have to pay back at the prime interest rate discounted by two percent. I related to Scott. He asked all the questions I wanted to ask when I started, though I didn't have anyone I trusted to turn to.

"So did anyone scream at you?" Scott asked me.

I stared at his thin black leather strand bracelet covered in red and yellow beads. It reminded me of jewelry sold on the Drag in Austin's outdoor market. I could hardly see it, yet it was visible enough to show that he wasn't familiar with this environment.

"What's that?" I asked.

"Oh, thanks," he said, smiling as if I'd complimented him. "I worked for a program teaching future environmental concerns, and one of my students gave it to me," he said, so caught up in his fond memories that he needed human contact. He reached over and touched my arm and said, "I haven't taken it off since he made it."

"Sounds like an interesting program," I said, touched that he had something he was passionate about but concerned that he didn't understand how quickly officers would label him. "But the bracelet looks a little voodoo," I warned. The word *voodoo* was what my summer associate used to describe my Persian necklace. "Be careful with that," my associate said helpfully. "It looks like a marijuana symbol, and we wouldn't want our clients to think we condone that." You'd often see colleagues policing each other, hoping to save one another from later embarrassments in front of senior officers.

"Voodoo?" he said, crinkling his nose so that his freckles squelched each other. "What does voodoo look like?"

"Like that," I said, pointing at his bracelet, trying to help him but not exactly sure how to explain the requirement of conformity that was expected if you wanted to do well. "You don't want people to get the wrong idea about you. Officers really want us to look very corporate," I warned. "Anyway, I haven't had anyone yell at me, but I've heard stories. If they scream at you, they're doing it because they want you to get better. Last summer I didn't use the right font on one of our presentations to our clients. We only use Times New Roman 21 for the headings— memorize that." I paused and took a long slow gulp of whiskey. "I'd been there pretty late that night. The head of our group took my presentation and circled all of the headings and left me a note saying, 'This is not a small mistake.' At first I got really upset about it, but then I realized the importance of Morgan Stanley as a brand. You have to be perfect here, but that's part of the challenge." As I spoke, I nodded my head, surprised at how I had already come up with stories to justify all the actions I had originally found appalling. *Did I just say "Morgan Stanley as a brand"?* I'd spent hours during my internship in a conference room on the phone calling friends and saying, "You wouldn't believe what just happened."

As I spoke to Scott, I was trying to convince myself of everything I was saying. I looked down with a smile, distracted by the clashing powder blue and maroon Persian rug. I looked as if I was engrossed in thought, but I couldn't control my relief as I watched Scott anxiously play with his bracelet. I could already imagine officers ripping him to shreds because of his polite demeanor; the bracelet would just be an excuse for them to attack him. I looked up and went on: "Over the summer, I worked in capital markets on the trading floor, where the desks are lined up right next to each other like a cafeteria table. A senior officer sat next to me who was always getting upset. He would lift his phone receiver and hurl it across the trading floor at the slightest frustration while screaming, 'Fucking idiot!' The people in the row in front of him quickly vacated their desks whenever he got on the phone, but the row in back soon learned to jump up and get out of the way too, since the phone's cord might boomerang back. After a while, most of us just looked up when he started screaming, to make sure that we weren't in his line of fire. Over time, you just got used to it. You'll learn." I glanced at his gaping mouth. But I was torn between my calm explanations and the twinges in my gut. The more money people brought in, the more the company seemed to tolerate their bad behavior. They became invincible, and they knew it.

"Although I'm sure this doesn't happen often, this happened to me last summer, so I should warn you. There was a bomb threat in the building. They announced it on the speaker several times, and they asked everyone to evacuate immediately. My advice is, don't go. It sounds crazy. At first, you panic and want to leave. But you need to watch everyone else's lead. Almost no one left on my floor. Business went on as usual. A pregnant woman left and so did another intern. That intern wasn't invited to return full-time. You just want to watch yourself because they are watching you."

"Wow!" Scott said. "This is going to be so weird! I turned down an environmental organization to come here. This is totally different. Hard-core," he said, tapping his fingers against his lower lip while twisting his tongue in a nervous rhythm. "They did warn us," he reminded himself, as he raised his lean hand to his face and rubbed a closed eye with his moist fingertips. "Over and over, they said it would be exciting, thrilling, and challenging."

"Don't worry. It will be, Scott," I said, enjoying this authoritative role. "Plus, my summer was in capital markets. Who knows, corporate finance may be totally different," I added with a hopeful smile, even though we both knew corporate finance was considered one of the most brutal divisions in investment banks, mainly because of its hazing culture and long hours. I'd chosen corporate finance because a senior officer had told me during my internship, "You haven't really experienced investment banking until you've worked in corporate finance, where you get real CEO and CFO interaction." It was my curiosity that brought me to corporate finance. How different could it be? Was it harder? How much harder?

"What did you think overall about capital markets?" he asked.

"Over the summer I worked late sometimes, but I never had to stay all night. My team was small and very supportive—two women, two guys. Tammy was my direct manager and she went out of her way to look out for me. Overall it was a great summer—fast-paced, but totally manageable. People were pretty decent. I was challenged and there were some jerks, but my manager did her best to shield me from any real drama."

"I've heard corporate finance people aren't nearly as friendly as capital markets because it's so hierarchical," Scott said. "But you seem really put together. I'm sure you'll be fine."

"Probably," I said, shrugging my shoulders. "What does hierarchical mean anyway? It's not like they can put a leash on us."

"It can't be that bad," he agreed as we both laughed.

As Scott and I continued chatting, Michael staggered over to our table in a drunken-looking state. "Oh my God!" he said, "The bar just gave me two glasses of Cristal Roederer. Nina," he said, sitting close to me on the couch and offering me a glass, "celebrate with me."

"That's okay," I said, shaking my hands in front of me so that he couldn't force a glass on me.

"You don't like it?" he said, sounding as offended as if he'd harvested the grapes himself. He leaned his elbow on the headrest of the couch and turned his face toward me. His stare was accompanied by a smirk that he must have thought was irresistible. "Ninaaa," he whined.

"I just don't want any right now," I said, looking over at Scott and raising my eyebrows. I had to balance looking like a bore and looking too wild. I knew not to say I had never tasted such a champagne or, worse, to admit that I had never heard of it.

"I'll take it," Scott said, trying to pacify his drunken colleague.

"You *have* to have it," Michael said, handing me the glass. "Let's get Luis and make a toast to our group's new analysts."

"Luis!" Michael screamed several times. Finally, he got up and went to get Luis off the dance floor.

Two of our colleagues walked by—Daniel and Bryan. We had hung out a few times the night before, and Bryan had made a much better impression on me than Daniel. I couldn't place it, but there was something about Daniel I didn't trust. There was a consistent nervousness to him that made me feel like he was hiding something. Earlier in the week, I'd heard him crunching loudly on chicken bones during one of our dinners. It didn't bother me because when I was little my mom would crack meat bones open and tell my sisters and me that it was a treat to suck out the marrow. But when I looked up at Daniel, he gave me the weirdest look, as if I'd caught him red-handed. Unlike Daniel, Bryan had a very composed, calm nature. He was a caretaker, which was so refreshing in this corporate atmosphere. During most of training, Bryan took it upon himself to ride home in cabs with the drunkest person to make sure they got home safely. I automatically gravitated toward him, surrounded as I was by people who I wasn't too sure I could trust.

"Cheers," Bryan said, holding out his bright blue drink. We all haphazardly clinked our glasses.

"Nina," Daniel said, pointing his glass toward me, "we were just talking to one of the officers in your group."

"Which one?" I asked. "There are about fifteen of them."

"I know," Daniel said, "and they're all good old boys. I'm pretty sure every officer over forty who's spent his whole life at Morgan Stanley is in your group. You're screwed! With those two clowns," Daniel said as he laughed and looked toward the dance floor at Michael and Luis, "and that many officers generating a bunch of bullshit work." He paused and shook his head. "Just so you know, most teams have about four officers. I expect that the next time we see you will be in about two years."

"Yeah, that schmoozer in your group," Bryan said, moving his head in Michael's direction, "thinks he's a celebrity here. And I'm sorry to say that even though he's not Rockefeller's son, he'll get away with it because he is *crazy* connected. I hung out with him last night and he knows everyone. There must be one of those guys in every class, because we had the same kind of dude at Merrill last summer." Bryan shook his head. "It sucks because the rest of us will be working our asses off. Didn't you intern here last summer?" he asked me.

"Yeah," I responded as I shifted in my seat, suddenly much less confident as I realized how little I knew compared to them. "But I was in capital markets. Corporate finance sounds like it will be different."

"Take capital markets and raise it to the tenth power. Don't worry, I'm screwed too," Daniel said. "I've got a *real* celebrity on my team," he said, pointing to the son of one of Morgan Stanley's biggest clients. "While he's off at dinners with the Kennedy family, I'll be covering his ass."

I'd later learn that they spread out these celebrity kids across groups since it was understood that they wouldn't do much work and the other analysts would have to pick up the slack.

"I interned in corporate finance at Merrill last summer," Bryan said. "Money trumps everything. Because corporate finance officers have the relationship with the client, the company lets them get away with murder. If they lose the officer, they may lose the client's millions." Bryan looked at Daniel and they both laughed.

"Cheers," Daniel shouted in a loud, sarcastic voice as they both walked away.

I let out my breath after realizing I'd hardly been inhaling while Daniel spoke. I was losing my confidence, and the more Daniel said, the more I realized that even though I had interned before, this corporate finance department switch was more than I had banked on. I could feel Scott staring at me with a small smile. "Scared?" he asked.

"A little," I said, even though I looked at him with eyes that were clearly fearful. *I'm a fighter. Plus, I used to stay up all night talking on the phone to friends in high school—sometimes two nights in a row. A little sleep deprivation never killed anyone. How bad could it be?*

Michael finally came back with Luis, who was sweat-sopped. "Oh, man," Luis said, still on a dancing high, "this music is outstanding. I think I heard it in Ibiza." He unbuttoned his fitted Euro shirt, revealing his thin, freshly waxed chest, and took a deep breath. "Seriously, why are you pulling me off the dance floor? We should be dancing," Luis said, thrusting his emaciated hips from side to side.

"Because," Michael said, "we're drinking to our future!"

"Michael, we are going to have tons of work to do," I said, laughing at his idea of fun.

"Oh my God, it is going to be so intense," Luis added. He wiped his forehead and looked down as if just thinking about it exhausted him. "Did you guys even understand that LBO model they showed us today? Because I have no idea," he said, swiping his hands across each other, then opening them wide with so much enthusiasm he looked like a baseball referee calling safe. "None!" he reiterated.

"Well, at least one of us should make sure we understand it," I suggested. "Last summer, when I was going up to the word-processing floor at about 3:00 A.M. to drop off some work, I saw this analyst from the chemicals group who was completely freaking out because he had a mini-merger that was supposed to be ready by 7:00 A.M., and he had no one there to help him. Of course, the chemicals group is tiny, so he was the only analyst. There are three of us, so in the middle of the night we'll be lucky that we can help each other out."

"That's cool," Michael said. "But we aren't going to learn anything now. We've got to just hit the ground running when the time comes."

"I didn't even get that Treasury method stuff they were doing,"

Luis said. "Does the Treasury really buy back the shares?"

"Yeah, I pretty much got that stuff," Michael said. "They don't really buy it back. I'll show you later. Don't worry about this now. We are going to have such a great time over the next couple of years. My secret-society buddies totally helped me out during the interview process. They'll make sure we're taken care of," he said as he slapped both of us on the back. "You guys, we're going to have such a sweet time! This is so amazing. Luis, did you see that they have Cristal Roederer?"

"No way, dude. I love that shit," Luis replied.

"Here, take Nina's. She's not drinking it."

"Seriously!" Luis said. "Nina, are you okay?" he asked and looked at me as if taking note of my early symptoms of insanity.

"I'm fine," I said. "I just didn't want to mix it with whiskey."

Luis took a long sip as he used his other hand to stroke his chest. His Barneys shirt clung to his sweaty totem-pole figure. While looking at Michael, he nodded his head and said, "Niiiice."

Ken, one of the VPs from our group, came around with a tray of tequila shots. I knew I shouldn't turn them down since those who did were silently eyed as non–team players. "These are my new kids!" Ken announced loudly as he approached the three of us. "Come on. We're the toughest! Three shots for each of you!

"Luis," Ken said, caught up in a college drinking memory, "do people still go to Charles Village Pub? Do they still have that big sign behind the bar?"

"I don't think so," Luis replied slowly while he considered lying to appease.

"I'll be back," Ken said as if forgetting he'd asked a question.

"Only take two tequila shots," he instructed us. "I'm going to go get Goldschläger and Jägermeister."

I looked down at my watch and tried to remember what time we had class the next day. I knew my limits—five gin and tonics or three vodka martinis or two and a half whiskeys straight up or three tequila shots before I would buzz. I made a mental note to check the alcohol content of Goldschläger and Jägermeister, which I hadn't planned on drinking. Estimating, I tried to translate how many gin and tonics would equal two tequilas. As I calculated, Ken interrupted me.

"Nina, can you handle it?" he asked, touching my shoulder in a fatherly way.

"Of course," I answered, embarrassed at being singled out.

We each took four shots in the order that Ken demanded: tequila, tequila, Goldschläger, and Jägermeister.

"Ken," Michael called out after his last shot. "Can you get a picture of us?" he asked as he ran his fingers through his crusted hair.

Luis nervously looked across the room at a mirror and squinted, trying to make sure his hair was styled properly. "Oh God, I've been dancing for hours, Michael. I'm drenched in sweat," he complained, giving himself leeway for an unflattering shot. Luis often got away with comments that most American guys wouldn't have, reminding us of his Euro origins, which demanded that men have style.

"So what. Smile!" Michael demanded, taking out his new palm-size handheld camera. I sat in the middle and put my arms around their necks.

Michael pointed across the room in the mirror's reflection, "Hey, look, we're a perfect team!"

"Okay," Ken said. "Say MORGAN STANLEY!"

On command, all three of us smiled. Even though I tried to fight it, I soon felt the alcohol. My head grew dizzy and my body slowly started to go numb. In unison, we screamed out, "Morgan Stanleeeeeeeeeyyyyyy!"

CHAPTER 2

Good Enough

From an early age I learned that nothing is ever good enough. In kindergarten and first grade I used to come home with straight Es, for "Excellent." I never received anything less. I was even quiet and obedient in my classes. Every time my mother saw my report card she would announce to my uninterested father, "Did you see Nina made all Es, just like her two older sisters? Perfect," she'd say to me with a kiss on my cheek that would make me self-conscious in front of my father.

My father thought my grades were a fluke since I was not as obedient as my other two sisters. He considered me "a wild tongue that needed to be leashed."

"Good," he would say to my sisters. In an attempt to be affectionate, he would smack their heads—a gesture easily mistaken for a whack—and say, "Next time too, Mickey Mouse." My sisters' heads would jerk down from the blow, but as they scurried off, they were always smiling. My dad's brother once explained to us that when they were little, going to the movies in India was a rare treat and the Mickey Mouse cartoon that played before each film was more exciting than what followed. It was one of their few glimpses into the thrill of America.

We lived in a suburb north of downtown Houston, which many residents considered a small town. It was far enough outside of the city that we saw beautiful mockingbirds in our yards and parents felt safe letting their kids ride their bikes all around the neighborhood. Unlike in central Houston, there were few minorities in the area, and hardly any Indians. Aside from attending Parsi events, our family rarely left the suburbs. We were isolated from the other Parsi families, most of whom lived in central Houston. Our suburban entertainment consisted of mall, movie, and bowling alley visits.

Each time my mother pestered my father about my grades, it played out like a trial. The day before my seventh birthday, it was 90 degrees in our clammy suburban Houston home, only 5 degrees cooler than outside since my father didn't like to waste money on unnecessary luxuries such as air-conditioning. "People are comfortable in 120 degrees in India," the Indian immigrant informed his pampered, American-bred kids. "Get used to it. It takes discipline." He shook his head at what he saw as our fragility. Sapped of energy, we collapsed on the floor in front of the television.

Our comfortable home was covered in beige, aged carpet coarse enough to give me rug burns when my sister Farah and I took turns dragging each other by the legs during our "fish for sale" game that my grandmother frowned upon. With a full-time job, my mother rarely had time for homemaker-type work, and my father couldn't be bothered with it, so our house was sparsely decorated with a few wall hangings—two Indian wooden figures—that had been part of the home décor ever since my parents arrived from India and a pair of gold-etched vases on the mantel that were gifts from one of my parents' Parsi dinner parties. The vases were one of the few items my mom chose not to regift. She decorated the living room with pictures of all four of us, but none of her or my dad, as if that would be too egotistical of them. I appreciated our house's simplicity. It didn't have the frilly country, flowery theme that many of my American friends' moms created, with ornate vases, candles from the Yankee Candle Factory, and potpourri from Pitty Patch's Porch at Willowbrook Mall. Nor did it have the raw immigrant feel, with sofas still covered in plastic, of some of my Parsi friends' homes.

This evening Farah and I clung to the carpet drenched in juicy sweat. She was one year older, and when we walked around together others thought we were twins, even though my mom always let her keep her hair much longer than mine since Farah was tidier. After my father, she had the biggest forehead in our family, with a pair of bangs that could only half-cover its expanse. Farah and I sat in front of the television watching *The Brady Bunch*. We were both doing splits, a stance our ballet teacher seemed to think we should assume whenever we were idle. To become more flexible, we lay with our stomachs flat on the ground in front of us. The bases of our palms forced our cheeks so high upward that they practically obscured our view. We lay like two neighboring wineglass stems, our upper bodies much longer than our stubby legs. We were almost linked together, but we kept enough distance, as squabbling neighbors might. Our toes were less than half an inch apart, but we were very careful not to touch each other.

When Farah accidentally touched me, I screamed, "Nasty! Get your feet off me!" and then jumped up and cleaned my foot thoroughly by wiping it against the carpet several times, screaming, "Yuck!" all the while. Unfazed, she kept watching television. Even though she was only a year older than me, she had a calmness and maturity about her that made me feel years younger.

"Would you kiss Bobby Brady?" she asked without looking at me, careful not to make any unnecessary movements.

"You know we aren't allowed to date an American," I replied. "That is so stupid."

"I know, but I'm just saying, would you if he asked you?" she persisted.

"He'd never go out with an Indian girl. You don't even have light eyes."

"You don't know who he'd go out with," she said, shaking her head. "Anyway, his eyes are hazel, so sometimes they are brown and sometimes green," she rationalized. She smiled, thinking about him. "Plus, if I told him I saw a UFO, like the ones him and Peter saw in their backyard, I bet he would at least be interested in talking to me."

"You're being an idiot," I said, borrowing one of my father's favorite nouns. I studied her inferior face in detail and repeated what I'd heard one of the boys in my class say about me: "Bobby would never go out with a hook-nosed, hairy girl." I was one of those kids who believed the mean things kids would say. Instead of ignoring their comments, I worked to change all the things about myself that separated me from the other kids. Farah tended to look for friends who just accepted her for what she was, but those kids were rarely the popular ones.

"He might like it that I'm different," she said with a dreamy smile, as if she were experiencing the pleasure of Bobby's tongue. "You don't know," she said.

"I do," I said, bewildered by her inability to see that different was not valued.

Our hands propped up our chins. Our heads were uncomfortably angled upward, bent back as far as they would go, just so we could see the TV from such a low position. Farah wore her favorite long-sleeved black leotard with a slight V scoop in the back, pale pink tights, and an elegant sheer pink ballet skirt. I wore a sleeveless red leotard with opaque black tights. We both wore our leg warmers even though they caused thick sweat rings around our ankles. Like a perfect ballerina, Farah kept her feet pointed throughout all three of our TV programs: *Brady Bunch, Fame,* and *Three's Company.* Her toes were astute followers. I would begin with mine pointed, but soon after, I would laugh at Bobby Brady's stupidity for letting a girl who had mumps kiss him, and my toes would involuntarily release. My dad's voice would echo in my head—*"You have no discipline"*—reminding me to point them again.

"*Fame!*" we screamed together. The start of the show was the highlight of our evening. Farah and I had a whole routine choreographed for the sixty-second theme song. We screamed the lyrics as we did split jumps and pirouettes. "I'm gonna live forever. Baby, remember my name!"

Dancing was our passion and our only hobby. We were the two most flexible students in our dance studio. Everyone referred to us as "Rubberband One" and "Rubberband Two." We spent every weekday after school in dance classes—ballet, tap, and jazz. Since Farah was only one year older than me, we were usually grouped in the same classes. My mom made sure we never missed a class—she had always dreamed of becoming a ballerina. It was a great disappointment to her that my other two sisters—one was five years older and the other was four years younger—never cared for dance. Because of our closeness in age, Farah and I did almost everything together.

Dance was our savior since my father discouraged us from doing anything that involved sports. While I found school terribly boring, dance channeled some of the restless energy my teachers couldn't handle. We didn't talk about passion in my family. We did things because we were supposed to. Dance offered me one of the few opportunities where I felt I could enjoy life and be myself.

"These are girls. Are you going to take them to the hospital when they break their legs?" my father retorted every time my mother suggested we needed hobbies.

Dance was just another reminder to him that we were only girls. I imagined he wanted two children—two boys. "Boys and girls are like assets and liabilities—very different." After the first two girls, he thought it would be impossible to have yet another one. He was resigned to having an extra kid since it would be a boy. The third girl was shocking. And the fourth was a family tragedy.

It wasn't until the day of the fourth's birth that we found out the sex of our sibling. Before my mom left for the hospital she yelled out, "While I'm gone you all should be praying for a boy!" She chanted as she left, "Pray! Pray! Pray!"

"I promise I'll make sure it is a boy, Mom!" I yelled out, wanting credit.

Under my grandmother's guidance, my two sisters and I sat in a small circle as though we were about to play Duck, Duck, Goose. But there were no smiles.

"Five *yatha ahu vairyos* followed by three *ashem vohus*," my grandmother commanded as she walked around our huddle, listening to our pronunciation of ancient Persian prayers. Anything to bring blessings to our house of failure. With our heads covered in scarves, we all looked at the floor in shame. Every couple of minutes each of us would feel her sly eye, sharp with the wish that one or the other had been born a boy. Disappointed again, my parents returned home with another daughter, not a son. With four girls, my father was overburdened with irregulars. He would never be able to turn over his damaged inventory fast enough.

＊

This evening, both my parents had just returned from work. My mother spent her day as an administrative assistant at a major company in a skyscraper downtown, and my father was a civil engineer who designed roads and runways for the city of Houston. Though my grandmother, who lived with us, would often cook beautiful elaborate meals, we rarely ate together. My father ate dinner in the kitchen and my mother sat behind us reading the mail on the sofa in the living room. She created two stacks, one to throw away, which sat on top of the large coffee-table book filled with photos of the streets of Bombay, and another stack, which sat on top of my grandmother's *National Enquirer.* Upon opening my report card, she joyously exclaimed, "Nina, you got straight Es again! Very good, *beta*," she said, and walked up to me, leaning down to caress my head. "Just as perfect as your sisters."

Without moving to acknowledge her, I responded, "It was easy, Mom. It's only first grade."

"Still, *beta*, this is very good." she said. She began walking to the kitchen in pursuit of my father. "Zal!" she hollered.

As she walked away, I gleefully pointed my toes sharply, forcing my big toe to strangle my index and middle toe. Anxious with excitement, I watched all three turn bluish purple. *Look how disciplined I am.*

Eager to hear my parents' exchange, I grabbed the remote from between my sister's upright arms. "God! Why do you have to turn it up so loud! Now I have a headache," I said, while turning down the volume, anxious to hear my parents' conversation.

My mother walked into the kitchen, just off the living room, and stood over my father while he ate.

"Zal," she said, with one hand on her hip.

He sat at the dining room table ladling curry and rice into his mouth with a serving spoon the same width as his mouth. His plate looked like an eruption. The rice was completely hidden under the bright orange lava, ready to overflow onto the table.

"My God, what are you doing!" she exclaimed and shook her head in irritation.

"The plates aren't big enough," he said calmly with his mouth full.

"You are eating too much!" she said in a tone he called nagging.

"One of my colleagues told me today that coconut milk does not have bad cholesterol, so I can eat as much as I want."

"You don't even have high cholesterol," she said with annoyance.

"I don't have a problem with cholesterol because I'm watching it. If I don't control it, then I will have a problem. That's the law of science," the engineer told his uneducated wife. "You should be thanking me for saving us money by cutting back on potential health problems."

After his lesson, he leaned his head over the plate, only a few inches away from the mound he'd created. He continued scooping each bite and ladling it harshly into his mouth. He made sure that with every bite his teeth clung tightly to the spoon, causing a high-pitched grating sound with each forceful shovel.

She stared at him in dismay. Then she responded to his habits as she usually did: She ignored them. "Did you see Nina's report card?" she asked.

"It doesn't matter, Mom," I screamed from the living room.

"All Es, again," she continued, ignoring me.

Still, he didn't look up. "I saw."

"She's doing just as well as her sisters," she added.

"Mom!" I screamed even louder, my toes pointed so hard I began feeling dizzy. "I told you, it's only first grade!" Already I was convincing myself that I hadn't accomplished anything worth notice so that I wouldn't have to be disappointed by my dad's inevitable reaction.

He put down his mini-shovel and pointed at her with his index finger. "In this house, your daughter doesn't get an E for discipline!"

After he finished dinner, he walked through the living room, which lay between the kitchen and his bedroom, on his way to change out of his suit. Though he walked behind us, I knew exactly where he was positioned based on the clinking keys in his pocket. He carried them on the DAD'S KEYS key chain that was my birthday present to him.

"Hi, Mickey Mouse," he said in the unusually high voice he used when he was excited to see us. He gave us his signature hello hand motion, lightly digging his fingers into our scalps, which felt like a one-second head massage. "Dad, stop!" I squealed. "You always mess up my hair."

As he walked away he realized how close we were sitting to the television. "Hey!" he barked. "Back up! You kids will spoil your eyes."

Without moving any other part of our bodies, we both scooted back slightly by using our pelvic bones to inch backward like worms.

He stood over us in silence. Though I stared straight ahead at the television, it was invisible. All my senses were reserved for anticipating his next move.

"What kind of way is this to sit?" he asked and paused as if waiting for a response. But he was used to us ignoring him. "Is this what those people teach you in dance?" He shook his head,

"You people will break your bloody necks."

We both continued looking straight ahead as if unfazed. He remained standing over us and then, aggravated, continued his journey to his room.

Within three seconds, he was back. "Nina," he said in the gruff voice he reserved for his rebellious child, "your mother says you got all 'E'ggheads again." Before he could fully finish his words, he broke into a loud guffaw.

Still staring at the television, watching *Fame*'s closing credits, I began softly mouthing the theme song with the television: "Fame! I'm gonna live forever. . . ."

For the closing song, normally Farah and I would yell out together "Fame!" and "Remember!" each time the chorus played, but it was impossible to sing with him there, ready to interrupt us with his mockery. He moved closer, as if it were only an accident that I was ignoring him. Now he stood only a few feet away, slightly in front of me and to my right. Out of the corner of my eye I could see his belly quivering with excited laughter. He grabbed his waist, which held up his plaid polyester pants, to control his joggling, curry-filled belly from indigestion.

Though I stared straight ahead, I knew exactly what he looked like. Every three seconds his face would increasingly stain red and his torso would vibrate thunderously as if he were being shocked.

From my left, I sensed Farah's judgment. Her eyeballs jabbed me with her sideways stare. She was careful not to turn her head. Though I felt a terrible sting in my stomach, I shrugged my shoulders, trying hard to convince myself that none of this bothered me. I started to sing louder and carefreely bounced my feet, toes pointed stiff, to the rhythm of the television song:

"Baby, remember my name. Remember, remember, remember, remember."

The next morning was my seventh birthday. My mom woke me by singing "Happy Birthday" in my ear. Farah slept just a few feet away and woke before me. She threw off her Blueberry Muffin comforter and sat up in bed, joining in the song with add-ons that I could tell my mom didn't appreciate. "Happy Birthday to you! And many more! On channel four! And Scooby-Doo! On channel two . . . !" Once Farah had finished singing, my mom surprised me with several gifts from both my father and her. Farah was as eager as I was to see my gifts. My birthday spread included a new birthday outfit—a pair of Jordache jeans, leg warmers, and a bright blue T-shirt that said on the front:

Check one:
☐ Smart
☐ Adorable
☐ Cute
☐ Loveable
☑ All of the Above

"Turn it over," my mom said proudly.

I looked on the back and in rainbow metallic, glittery letters it said, NINA. "Mom, you got it custom-made!" I said in a weak, stunned voice. I lost my breath for a moment, shocked that I had actually gotten something I wanted so desperately. "Mom!" I cried out loudly as I threw my head in her lap.

"Don't be so dramatic, Nina," she said as she played with my hair and smiled proudly. Gifts tended to be moderate in my family. My parents thought it was absurd to buy something for themselves. Money was meant to be saved or spent moderately on the kids. We spent much less than our neighbors. My father was particularly protective, insisting that it would be best for our family if he stayed in a government job his whole career so that we'd never have to risk a corporate layoff. He never considered it a sacrifice but rather his duty.

"But how did you get my name on the back?" I asked my mom. I knew how expensive it was to have names printed on shirts. At school everyone had at least two shirts with their names on them, but I never expected even one. Anytime we asked my parents for the newest fad, they'd respond, "Do you want to go to college?" In India there were school uniforms and there was no such thing as prom queen.

Sitting on my bed, I caressed my shirt and thought of all my friends who would admire it at my Pizza Hut birthday party that night. My choice was Pizza Hut, where my uncle got his first American job, or an Indian restaurant. Whenever we celebrated something, my father insisted that we patronize the Indian community or anyone else who helped us prosper in the United States.

"Well," my mom said, "Kmart just started doing it too, and I saw this shirt that is perfect for you, *beta*." She tightly cupped my chin with her hand. "After all those terrific grades, you deserve it."

Abruptly, I stood up on my bed and shouted, "Look, Farah!" We would constantly share clothes with each other. So we closely ogled each other's gifts, knowing we'd soon share. Farah's birthday had just passed, and I'd saved up my pocket money for four months to buy her a fancy Tinkerbell perfume set that I hid under her pillow the night before her birthday. She had a hard time saving her money so I knew not to expect a gift from her, but it didn't bother me since I always got a kick out of seeing her cover her gaping mouth with her hand every year when she'd find my gift.

"Ohhh," Farah said, jumping out of her bed to touch it. "Rainbow colors," she said in awe, touching the soft, silky letters. Eager to play with it, she pulled at the shirt. "Look with your eyes, not with your hands," I said, pointing at her as if she were a naughty pet and laughing. "Just joking," I said. I grabbed her hand, helping her jump onto the bed. We held hands and, as if choreographed, we began dancing perfectly in sync. We thrust our necks forward and backward and then from side to side like two Indian dolls as we high-kicked like Rockettes.

I held my new leg warmers and wondered whether to debut them along with my new shirt or spread out the compliments. We wore our leg warmers everywhere—dance class, school, the mall, even to bed. Wearing them comforted me; it made me feel like someone was snuggling up to me. "Second pair," I said to Farah. "I'll let you borrow them if you let me borrow your black scoop-neck leotard." She grinned back at me. We had our secret clothes swapping that sufficed for a new wardrobe. We believed that no one in our dance class would know that it wasn't new.

"Thanks, Mom," I said. "I love the gift, especially the shirt. I love it!" I rested against her thick, warm arm, grateful to her for feeding my hunger for attention.

I ran around frantically making sure my family had appropriate outfits to wear for my Pizza Hut party. I arranged my new shirt, leg warmers, and jeans on the bed with a note for Farah's eyes that said "DON'T TOUCH." My mom said I could only have ten guests, including family. Since there were already seven of us—my mom, my dad, my grandmother, my two older sisters, me, and my two-year-old baby sister—I could only invite three friends. But I had convinced my mom that my little sister didn't count as having a personality yet, so I was able to invite a fourth friend.

At Pizza Hut, I sat at the head of the long rectangular table, ecstatic that I was in charge. I took every opportunity to get out of my seat, conspicuously and inconspicuously, so that all my friends could see the back of my shirt. Even though there were only four friends present, I kept insisting that I needed to tell something private to each one so that I could prance around while everyone marveled at my shirt and smelled the Love's Baby Soft perfume that I'd borrowed from my older sister's second drawer while she was in the shower.

I was hyperaware of all my differences and did whatever I could to maximize commonalities. My friends were mostly white, native Texans, as was the majority of our neighborhood, who found my cultural differences to be abnormal rather than intriguing. It was clear we weren't white, but what we were wasn't clear. Our ancestors were Persians who had moved to India over a thousand years ago, so we didn't exactly look Indian. But who knows what a Persian looks like? Outside of my family and community, I'd never seen any others.

I often felt different, but never quite got used to it. In fourth grade, in Ms. Manor's English class, we had a smorgasbord. Everyone was supposed to bring in something different. Ms. Manor wrote on the board the night before: "Smorgasbord—medley or a rich variety."

"Please bring in different types of food so we can try new things," she told us. She announced the smorgasbord weeks ahead of time and I excitedly went home and asked my grandmother if she could make *burfi*, my favorite Indian sweet. Farah and I would sit on a La-Z-Boy, squished next to each other like we were one overgrown body, and stuff mouthfuls of the vanilla and cardamom fudge in each other's mouths while we watched soap operas. In our Persian-Indian community, we would give *burfi* to others whenever good fortune came our way, especially for a birthday or holiday. "It wouldn't feel right to accept good fortune if you couldn't share your joy with others," my mother would say.

"I'm the only one bringing something from India, so make it pretty, Grandma," I said eagerly. "With that Indian silver stuff you put on top to make it shiny." I tried to think of improvements, "And will you make it a pretty color, like green? And in leaf shapes?"

"I'll make a pistachio *burfi* with the silver *varak* on top," she said, so pleased to be able to share Indian sweets with Americans. She imaged their lives as being perfect as Lily's from *As the World Turns*, and her eyes glowed to imagine that she could create something they would actually enjoy. When I was born, my grandmother was imported to this country as if she were a curry leaf. She left her bustling life and came to take care of her grandchildren in the United States. She could not drive anywhere, spoke in broken English, and remained trapped in our suburban Houston home. She was fascinated by the Americans she only saw on television and on her weekly outing to the grocery store.

"Grandma, you have to make enough for everyone. Ms. Manor said so. There are twenty-five kids in my class. Can you do it?"

She prepared the Parsi way. "Let's say fifty people. You don't want to run short," she warned me. "This way everyone can have. And it looks bad to do less."

A week before the feast, my mom took my grandmother

to the Indian grocery store to buy all the ingredients. It took my grandmother a full day to make it. She insisted it be fresh and would only start her mission at 4:00 P.M. I went to bed at 8:00 P.M., but I still heard her in the kitchen at 2:15 A.M. I jumped out of bed to check my alarm for the fourth time. "Why is she up?" I whispered to myself, worried that something had gone wrong. I came downstairs in a panic. "Grandma, I have to be in school in five hours." I looked around the kitchen covered in bright silver vessels that looked like they belonged in a restaurant's kitchen, each filled with different colored ingredients. Her scarf pulled her hair back tightly, and she stood over a pot, pouring a green liquid into a yellow substance with eyes as focused as those of a mad scientist.

"Go to bed," she said calmly. "Everything will be ready in time."

I saw my face in one of the pot's reflections and gave myself a secret smile. "Thank you!" I said. Then I kissed her on her cheek and ran out of the kitchen.

The morning of the smorgasbord I woke up and found a gold platter with generous blocks of green *burfi*. Each piece was shaped like a leaf and decorated with a paper-thin layer of silver, individually etched with a different Indian design. The pieces were stacked high in a pyramid.

Dearest Nina,

Make sure you share with everyone. If there is extra you give it to another class. Never be stingy with food.

Have a nice day. I love you.

Love,
Grandma

I picked up the bejeweled tree and proudly carried it to school.

It was in our last period that we had the smorgasbord. I anxiously tapped my ruler on the desk, eagerly awaiting the feast, and paid little attention to our double-digit multiplication lesson. I was confident no one in the room had tried Indian food. This would be their first opportunity. I imagined that later they would tell others how they first tried it from me. At our feast, we each had to place a card next to our dish with our name, the name of our dish, and the country it was from. Dishes included fried rice (Chinese), sausages (German), tacos (Mexican), chips and salsa (Mexican), fried chicken (Southern), pasta and cheese (Italian), cheesecake (French), and Toll House cookies (American).

Shelley was one of my closest friends from dance class; she could pick up dance moves faster than any of us. She wore black-and-white-striped leg warmers and stood in front of me piling mounds of pasta onto her plate. I was disappointed by the food selection since I'd already tried these foods before. I became less interested in eating and more focused on having other people enjoy my dish. I kept a close eye on the mound of leaves, which I now stood across from. Two girls behind me began nudging in line, fearful that the food would be gone by the time they got there.

"That looks like green puke," Fred said to Jeffery. Jeffery responded to him with gagging noises. "*Barfi*? Barf! Barf!" he said as he gagged. They walked around the table with their tongues dangling out of their mouths like panting dogs. Everyone around them watched silently, then stared first at my green-and-silver leaves, then at me. Plates were filled with everyone else's food. Not even one piece of *burfi* was taken. I discreetly removed the label so that no one else would see that it was mine.

After we served ourselves, the classroom clamored with kids eating and chatting in little factions. I sat near Shelley's desk. Once everyone was busy eating, Ms. Manor discretely tapped me on my shoulder and led me to my desk. The kids all quieted down as they watched her lift my dessert dish from the table. She placed the tray on the floor beside my desk. In an effort to save me the embarrassment, she whispered softly in my ear, "It looks like your mom forgot to take off the foil. I don't want anyone to get sick so why don't you just take this back home." Throughout the feast, my tree sat on the floor beside my desk hidden under my sweater.

"Don't worry about it," Shelley said as she rapidly forked down mouthfuls of pasta. "There's too much food here anyway." She continued telling me about her mother's new boyfriend, who had stayed over for the first time the night before. But I heard little since my head ached from the humiliation. I rested my elbow on Shelley's desk with my hand covering the left side of my face and chewed on pasta without enthusiasm.

After school, I waited in the bathroom for the crowd of bus kids and walkers to die down. I contemplated throwing the *burfi* in the trash can, but feared that someone might somehow find it the next day and link it to me. After waiting thirty minutes, I began walking home carrying the sweater-covered tray of sweets. Luckily, when I entered the house my grandmother was in her room. Frantically, I emptied a box of Franken Berry cereal into plastic baggies and then filled the cereal box with the *burfi*. I grabbed fistfuls of *burfi* and furiously squashed each carefully etched and shaped leaf into the cereal box. Though it over-flowed, I forcefully rammed more into the box. I threw the heavy cereal box in the trash and then covered it with newspaper. After completing my duty, I went to watch my afternoon television programs.

A few minutes later my grandmother came down from her room. "My God, you are home. I didn't even hear you. I was fast asleep."

I just kept staring at the television as she stood next to me waiting for a response.

"Did you take the sweets for the smoke board?" she asked. "Did they like?"

"Smorgasbord," I corrected her. "And yeah. They liked it."

"They liked?" Her dentures unfastened, she was smiling so hard.

I gave a nearly invisible nod, fearful if I looked her in the eye she'd suspect the truth, and then I began changing the channels.

"Oh God," she suddenly blurted. "I woke up this morning to tell you, but you already left. You should tell them to eat the *burfi* after they eat the heavy snacks. The *varak*, the silver topping, is a digestive. It will settle their stomach nicely." She smiled at me and then at the television.

"Did you say to them, eat after the main dish?" she prodded.

I shook my head slightly, eager for the conversation to end.

"But they still enjoyed?" she asked, eager for any interaction. She began walking to the kitchen. "They enjoyed," she said to herself, tilting her head and smiling excitedly. Her eyes glazed over, as if she were imagining all the American kids' faces as they savored each mouthful of her *burfi*.

*

At my Pizza Hut party, nervous that my family couldn't hide their peculiarities, I made every effort to avoid mixing them with my friends. I became edgy, finishing their sentences and inserting nervous laughs, fearful that they might reveal some new abnormality.

Unlike my mother, who had adopted most American customs since she moved to the United States, my father and grandmother were firmly rooted in India. My mother had an ambassador's role, making sure we fit in enough with the American culture yet still pleasing my father by holding on to our heritage. She hand-made Christmas stockings for us and gave us gifts so we wouldn't feel left out when we returned to school from winter break and had to write a paper about "My Christmas Holidays." She called herself the "bad guy" since, despite her efforts, she could never please everyone. Negotiations got tougher as we got older, when she had to convince my father of more difficult things, like allowing us to go to senior prom with dates.

"Mom," I begged, "please don't let Dad or Grandma talk loudly in Gujarati in front of my friends at Pizza Hut."

"I'll try," she said without making any promises.

"I also have to invite Lance, and you know I can't have a boy if Dad comes."

"You know how your father feels. You are too young to have boys as friends. Only when you are an adult and married."

"Mooooomm!" I cried.

I asked if I could sit separately at a table with my friends, hoping to minimize the inevitable embarrassment. My mother compromised and said that the two groups could sit at separate tables but the tables must be joined together. "Your sisters never make these ridiculous demands," she stressed, not willing to let this request slide by unnoticed, but I didn't explain to her that this was part of the reason that neither of them would ever be on the track to popularity, as I was. Being popular came at the cost of conforming, but it temporarily filled my need to feel important.

We pulled two tables together and my father sat at the head of one table with the rest of my family, while I sat at the head of the other table surrounded by my friends. Much to my relief, for most of the afternoon there was very little interaction between the two connected tables. Everyone looked acceptable, including my father and grandmother, but only when they were silent.

"Don't you dare take ice," my father loudly reprimanded his mother in Gujarati. "You will catch a cough." I looked over at my mom in annoyance, reminding her of the language clause. She raised her hand calmly and said, "This is not the time, Zal." I quickly looked around at my friends to see if they had noticed and was relieved that they were caught up in a conversation about dance recital costumes.

My grandmother kept smiling from the far corner of the table, so pleased that my friends and I were having fun. Whenever one of them looked her way she would wave and say "Lovely to meet you" in a soft, self-conscious tone. She looked at them with a longing gaze, and I knew she imagined their home lives were like those of the stars in *Dynasty*.

"Nina, do you say, 'It is lovely to meet you' or 'Meeting you is lovely'?" she had asked earlier in the day when she stopped by my room for me to approve her Montgomery Ward skirt suit and matching Avon brooch and earrings.

My family's table ordered huge bowls of overgrown jalape-ños and made sure that they had three bottles of crushed red pepper: That way no one had to reach farther than arm's length for seconds and fifths. Following my dad's lead, my mom and grandmother covered their pizza in a quarter-inch bedspread of red pepper and began taking methodical bites. First, half a jalapeño, and then a small bite of pizza. The three of them were sweating profusely and my father began hiccupping.

"Please turn up the fan. My God!" my mother requested the waitress in her overdone Southern accent. "It is so hot!"

The waitress returned to inform them that it was already on high. The three of them spent the rest of the meal covered in their spicy sweat, despite their desperate efforts to fan themselves with the paper place mats.

It wasn't until I cut my cake that my father, who had been quiet for most of the evening, became talkative. As in any other Persian-Indian celebration, once the birthday girl cuts the cake, it is a family tradition to hug and kiss each person one by one. After I cut my cake, each one of my family members came to my side of the table and hugged and kissed me. My father was the last to wish me well, and after he did, he suddenly became animated, as if contact with me inspired him.

"You know," he said, looking at my friends, "they say when you get older, you get wiser."

I stared at my friends, desperately trying to gauge their reactions. I began breathing more heavily, overwhelmed at this rare interaction between my unpredictable father and my friends who only saw the American side of me.

"Did you know that, Shelley?" he asked confidently, as if he knew she would be on the same page.

"No, Mr. Godiwalla," she responded and then looked at me for advice, partly intrigued and partly unsure if it was a trick question.

"It's true," he said. "But Nina here may have a little trouble. You see this," he said, pulling my bangs off my forehead with a big smile.

"Dad," I shrieked and pushed his hand away. "Stop! You're messing up my hair!" My forehead was a small area, mostly covered in baby hairs. The top was covered in heavier hairs, which looked like a little fringe, making my already tiny forehead disappear. My forehead, just like my "sideburns" and "moustache," as my white friends called them, was a constant reminder of how hairy and nonwhite I was.

I looked at my mom, desperate for support. Unlike me, she had moved beyond anxiousness to acceptance of his unpredictable commentary.

"Zal," she hollered from the other side of the table, "let the girls have some time together."

But he was too caught up in his own amusement to hear her. "This," he said, pointing to my forehead with a big smile, "is a monkey forehead." He began laughing, and slowly his face reddened. His uncontrollable laughter could have been mistaken for gagging. My friends stared at him with their mouths slightly agape as if they were watching a late-night thriller. They looked to me for guidance, but I just looked down at my cake.

For a moment, he regained enough control to speak. "There is no room for a brain here."

"Daaaad, Mom is calling you," I said, pulling at my bangs to cover my hair-invading forehead. I stared at my mother, but she shrugged her shoulders, letting me know that I was on my own.

His laughter began to alternate between coughing and choking, causing his black, bulky, horn-rimmed glasses to slide down his oily nose. His nose, almost identical to mine, grew contorted as he laughed. A "fierce Godiwalla bull nose," my mother called it. When we smiled, the tips of our noses pointed downward, like those of Disney villains. At school I'd show off and challenge others to flare their nostrils higher.

I was proud that I was the only child who shared my dad's facial features. It felt like we had so little in common otherwise, but this proved that we were related. I had his big full face and his lips. Our top lip looked as if someone had punched it flat and our bottom lip remained full and round. Our eyelashes were straight and sharp, weapons that could pierce those standing too close. Our eyelids were bloated, as if too tired to fully open.

I stared at his contorted face, and for the first time realized that above my eyelashes, I had nothing in common with him. My eyebrows were thin streaks while his were bushy and out of control, and his vast forehead deceivingly made him look as if he'd already started balding.

After a long struggle to regain composure, he began speaking again. "See this," he said as he raised his hair. "Now, this is a real forehead."

"So, Kristy," he asked my friend, "do you think Nina will be wiser as she gets older?"

"Now, Nina," my mom said from across the table. "You know he's just teasing you."

"I think so," Kristy said looking at him and then quickly looking at me. "She is really smart already. She is in honors and that's really hard."

"Well," he said shrugging his shoulders, "I don't know, with this little monkey forehead. But we'll see."

Before he walked back to his table, he grabbed my neck playfully and shook it to remind me that he was just kidding.

Then he plopped a kiss on top of my head before he said, "Happy Birthday, Mickey Mouse."

But I didn't feel his kiss or hear any of his last words. I no longer looked at my friends. I just sat staring at my cake as I felt my friends staring at my forehead. Shelley was the first to break the silence. "I never noticed how you have those hairs all over your forehead."

"Ohhh yeah," said Kristy, lifting my bangs with her hairless forearms. "I don't think they're supposed to be there. You should shave them."

That night, while I was in the bathroom brushing my teeth, I caught sight of my shirt in the mirror. I put down my toothbrush and kicked the sink cabinets as I stared at it: *Smart? Cute? Adorable? Nobody thinks I'm any of these things.* Toothpaste dribbled out of my mouth onto the sink. "Mom doesn't even understand me," I said to the mirror.

I let the toothpaste drip out of my mouth onto my new shirt as I began haphazardly peeling random letters off *Smart*, and then off *Adorable*. After pulling off *b*, *A*, *S*, and placing these letters on the sink, I was reminded of a word that I had only heard once before, *bastard*.

One time Yasmin Aunty screamed the word to a man who passed by us in the grocery store in the Franken Berry cereal aisle when she came to babysit us for the weekend. I heard her explaining to my mom that he had tried to "brush by" my eldest sister, Shireen.

Farah and I ate Franken Berry every morning. We both hated milk and would only have it with this cereal since the marshmallows turned the milk a pink strawberry flavor. It was the only way they could force us to drink milk. Even though we already had a box at home, I convinced Yasmin Aunty to get another one because I wanted the album I saw advertised on television as the newest prize buried inside. Shireen and Farah were able to walk freely since they were not as likely to run off. My mother warned my aunt to maintain a tight grip on my arm at the grocery store. Yasmin Aunty dragged me along with her left hand as I clutched the cereal box in my right, trying to read the words on the box.

I was reciting the names of the songs on the record when I heard Yasmin Aunty scream it: "Bastard!" Her voice echoed viciously through the grocery store. I was so startled I dropped the cereal box. Abandoning our cart, she grabbed Shireen's arm with her right hand. Then, while I was still attached to Yasmin Aunty's left hand, she grabbed Farah's hand with it. Our heads crashed together, but she didn't notice. Tightly clenching all of three of us, she twirled us around 180 degrees, as if we were just beginning a merry-go-round ride.

The man ran away quickly, and there was no one else in the aisle. Other shoppers came up to the Franken Berry aisle just to stare at us. Even kids came. The three of us felt ashamed, but we didn't know why. Yasmin Aunty furiously pushed us through all the gawkers. Farah stood behind me and stepped on my shoe so many times that it fell off.

"My shoe!" I screamed. Until then, I hadn't realized my cereal was gone. "My cereal!" I screamed louder.

"Shut up, Nina!" Yasmin Aunty yelled. "Just shut up!"

We drove home in silence. My sisters and I were too scared to even talk to each other about the incident. None of us knew what had happened. The next day, unable to find a dictionary, I tried looking up *bastard* in the thesaurus, but only found words

I had never seen: *adulterated, baseborn,* and *counterfeit.* They were even more mysterious to me than the short word *bastard.*

I stood in front of the bathroom mirror feeling that I had shrunk even though I was supposed to be a year older. "Why can't he say something nice to me?" I mumbled to myself as I wondered if my friends would see me differently now that my dad had pointed out my flaws.

I finished peeling off more letters from *Smart* and *Adorable* to complete the word *bAStard.* "I am smart, but you don't even know it!" I said to no one. I had a sick feeling as I ruined the shirt that I loved, but there was something satisfying about pulling apart everything I wanted him to believe.

I laid the rainbow, metallic letters on the sink and stood staring at the word. Even though I wasn't clear what it meant, I knew I meant it.

CHAPTER 3

Busyness

Since we were lowly analysts, we had low desk partitions that gave us little privacy, as if everyone needed to keep an eye on us. Four people sat in each bullpen, which was a square almost completely surrounded by partitions. Each of the analysts faced one of the four corners, like a punished kindergartner. I shared my half of the square with a second-year analyst who had checked out and was doing the bare minimum to keep his job. Though he had no authority, at times he would pass on his work to us newbies. Soon after we joined, I got a voice mail from him. "Nina, I need you, Michael, or Luis to take care of the media prepaids by 3:00 P.M." I knew little about him other than the two things he bragged about: mastering sleeping at his desk with the help of his computer rearview mirror without anyone detecting it; and dry-cleaning his trousers only once every six months since he claimed that his legs didn't sweat. It was easy to keep watch on Luis and Michael, who sat in another square bullpen right across from me. Likewise, a pathway between our two bullpens provided easy access for officers to check on us frequently as they walked the floor.

Every morning I could smell the crisp mix of lemon and new-car spray aroma, that clung to our hallways. When I visited other banks they all had the same smell, as if the cleaning companies had the same "investment banking" air freshener. The dismal dark gray file cabinets and partitions gave off a powerful message: Blend in; don't stand out. The little bit of color in our office space was the blue carpet and the occasional Victorian emerald green banker's lamp on someone's desk, a relic of another era's decoration scheme. They were classic banker's lamps that had a dated elegance, reminding me of the Avon jewelry my grandmother stashed in her pink velvet jewelry box. The carpet was so worn that the ratty ends of each carpet tile were beginning to tatter.

Since the three of us—Luis, Michael, and I—were all a team, the work was divided between us. But both of them had learned the clever strategy of appearing overloaded. During our first few months, when we were supposed to be making a good impression, Steve, who was one of our managers, approached us one afternoon. He stood in between our bullpens and with a smile announced, "Hey, I've got a high-profile project. Nina and Michael, it's for one of you. It's going to be a big deal, but that means it's going to be a lot of hours. Even more than you have been pushing, Nina. We have a deal from one of our most prestigious clients. You've probably heard of him since his son is one of your workmates. They've even made a Wall Street movie about him."

Steve didn't need to say any more. Involuntarily, I clapped my hand over my mouth in shock, as if I'd won a car on *The Price Is Right*. Howard: "Wall Street's Mergers & Acquisitions King." Before I left for my JP Morgan internship in New York, my dad and I rented all the popular Wall Street movies and watched them with our mouths open in astonishment, hardly breathing during the intense scenes. My grandmother filled bowls with dry-roasted spicy chickpeas, but we didn't pause to eat. My dad's whole face lit up in admiration just like it would when he'd watch his two favorite heroes in action—Chuck Norris karate chopping an intruder and James Bond killing a gunman with his bare hands. Scenes like that made him clap his hands, double over, and laugh with childish excitement. "This doesn't look like a place for girls," my dad said. "You think you can handle these big tycoons, Mickey Mouse?" he asked after one of the movies, and I could see the look of vicarious thrill on his face at the idea that I'd be in skyscrapers next to such powerful people. I gave him one of my quick retorts: "This is just Hollywood, Dad. Not the real world." *I can be tough like that even though I'm just a girl, Dad.* This thrill of Wall Street was the first time I really felt bonded to him; I was finally doing something worthy enough for him to want to spend this much time with me.

Even though it seemed impossible to fit in more work, for a moment, I got scared that Michael would land the prestigious assignment since he didn't seem very busy.

Steve threw a penny between his hands and said, "It will be an honor to work with him. To be fair, I'm going to toss the coin to see who wins this big deal. Ladies first. Nina, what will it be—heads or tails?"

"No need," Michael said casually. "Actually, I'm too busy to handle it right now. I've got a bunch of stuff going on."

Steve and I looked at Michael, amazed. We both knew he wasn't working on much. *Are you crazy? Do you not know who Howard is?* Later I'd find out that Michael was already close friends with Howard's son, so he could meet Howard anytime.

"Oh," Luis interjected, trying to help Michael with his obvious exaggeration, "because of that stuff you're doing for Project Gamble and Project Bliss?"

"I'll do it," I said, not interested in listening to Michael's excuses. Should I shoot Dad a quick e-mail? Or was this deal confidential? It would be so hard not to tell him. Maybe I could hint. It'd be better on the phone. *I want to hear his voice.*

"Okay," Steve said with relief. His bosses depended on him to assign analysts to each project, and he depended on us to deliver. When we looked good, he looked good. That night, he handed me a stack of papers to read. "I'm leaving this in your capable hands," he said and smiled as he left for the evening.

Some of our officers were nice, but we hardly got to know them since they weren't the ones generating most of the "bullshit work." This was the kind of work Luis had to do earlier in the week, creating pro forma financial forecasts for eight companies as well as a detailed industry analysis. All this was prepared just so that Ken could make a "check-in" phone call to the CFO of Boeing: "Just calling to let you know we're keeping an eye on your business." The work would be FedExed the night before. We all knew it was unlikely the CFO would ever look at any of Luis's sixty hours of work, mostly done in the middle of the night. When Luis handed the documents over to Ken, Ken's response was, "Every number better be right," which led sleep-deprived Luis to spend another twelve hours frantically double-checking numbers. That was the beauty of hiring a bunch of kids from good schools who'd graduated at the top of their class. They tended to be hyperconscientious.

As Daniel predicted, our blue-chip group was one of the busiest since we had so many officers. However, the work was cyclical—ninety-five percent of the time we'd be extremely busy and five percent of the time there would be downtime. But even when analysts weren't busy, the workweek was still about fifty hours. Face time was imperative; otherwise, officers would think you weren't busy enough and give you more work. Busy times were over a hundred hours a week. Most importantly, as analysts in corporate finance, we never knew what to expect. It was understood that the company owned us.

8:23 P.M. Todd approached my desk and handed me a stack of papers. Todd was a senior officer who had been in investment banking for most of his career. He was old-school and didn't believe in wearing striped or colored shirts. He rarely made eye contact, letting you know you were wasting his time. After finding out his wife was an artist, I couldn't imagine what they talked about.

"We have a lot of work we need to get done on Project Drift," Todd said, leaning over my desk partition. "I need it finished by tomorrow. I hope you're not too busy. It's only eightish, and I'll need this by late morning. That should give you more than enough time," he said, fully aware that it wouldn't.

I had to think about how to respond. The last time he did this, I'd said, "That doesn't give me enough time," and he just dropped the papers off on my desk anyway, acting as if he hadn't heard. *Let's try this.* "I still have several more hours of work before I finish Project Empty," I informed him. *Why does he always lean so far forward? In my space!*

"I'm sure you can manage," he said. "You're quick. Listen," he handed me a projected income statement filled with numbers. "I'm going to need you to reforecast these numbers. The company has given us their anticipated profits, but we can't go to market with those. I've adjusted their profit numbers to be something more marketable. Realistic, one might say." He handed me the income statement with the company's projected net income over the next five years crossed out. His new numbers took the old and multiplied by one and a quarter. "Just use these profits to back into the revenue numbers."

"Do I just make it up?" I asked, confused. "I don't even know where you got these new numbers." I had just started to get comfortable with all the educated, back-of-the-envelope guesses we made daily. It was hard for others to challenge us since we were trained so well to defend our assumptions. But this was the first time I was getting forecasted profits directly from the company and then adjusting the numbers. I never had to do any of this projecting profits and revenues in capital markets. But this was basic stuff in corporate finance. It was our job to make "educated" assumptions about how well the company would do in the future. At times, it could be quite an arbitrary guess without much evidence to back it up other than officers' conversations with clients. But the most frustrating part was that the person who usually got to decide what that "guess" would be was the most senior officer on the team. Analysts could voice their opinions, but then were often not heard.

"It's called an educated guess. I spoke to their CFO. They're bringing a new product line to market and the projections they gave us don't account for that. Plus, our clients are good at writing down the sales and profits that they've made, but that's the past. They need our help to project their future," he corrected me. "You need to put some thought into it. Tomorrow you can explain to me how you got there. Also, try to think about how we can talk to the client and get them to those numbers."

"But doesn't the company have a better idea than I do?" I asked as I stood up. I pressed him even though I knew that asking questions for clarification irritated him—a sign of weakness. I was convinced it was a game of his to give so little information when I was sure he had more. "Did they provide you with any assumptions on the new product line?"

"Think strategically," he said, throwing some papers on my desk, already beginning to walk away. "I'm leaving this in your capable hands."

Half an hour later Todd walked through the passageway that divided my bullpen from Luis and Michael's. With his Morgan Stanley coffee mug in his hand and his Morgan Stanley banker tote bag on his shoulder, he leaned over my low partition. "How's it going?" he asked.

"Great," I said with a smile, trying to keep up the good attitude that a star analyst would have. "There's just one thing. I didn't see any new product line assumptions in the papers you left me. Am I missing something?"

"Do you think you can handle it?" he asked.

I feel like I'm dealing with a politician who can't answer the question. Maybe he didn't hear me. Impossible. Is he avoiding me?

"Of course," I said defensively. *Now will he answer me?*

"I know you won't let me down," he told me. "Isn't it a little dark here for you? Why don't you have your light on?"

I let out a sigh since it was now clear that I wasn't getting any further information. I clenched my jaw, and I could feel my irritation building since I had to base my work on Todd's judgment call.

"I can't stand the green tint," I said. "It distorts everything."

"Only a few of you even have them and every banker wants one of these antique banker's lamps," he said, leaning over and turning on the solid brass lamp with an emerald green rectangular glass shade. "You'll get used to it."

"Good night," he said.

"Good night."

As soon as he left I turned it off. Four minutes later I turned it back on and muttered, "Get used to it."

9:35 P.M. Someone with a 713 area code was on my caller ID. Houston, my hometown.

"Hey, Nina. It's Freany Aunty. I called you at home, but you weren't there. What are you doing at work so late?" Without pausing she went on excitedly, "You won't believe this, but we're going to be in New York this weekend! Where do you live again? We'll be in Manhattan. Isn't that where you live? We'd love to see you."

"Wow, I had no idea you were coming. I'm really sorry, but we have a client meeting next week so I'm going to be stuck in the office all weekend, Freany Aunty," I said, feeling as I always did that I was constantly disappointing my family and friends. I shook my head as I remembered that Farah had called a couple of weeks ago, and I still hadn't called her back. Or was it a dream? Everything seemed to blur. I had to prep for a client meeting, which meant I'd be in the office all weekend crunching numbers into spreadsheets, putting together pitch books until the middle of the night, and waiting in the office for faxes to come through without a page missing. Freany Aunty was from our Parsi community, but because my family wasn't very close to her, I don't think she realized that I wasn't working a nine-to-five job. "I really don't know if I'll be able to get away from work."

I stopped speaking as I saw Ken walking by and started typing numbers into my spreadsheet. It seemed like whenever I was on a personal call, he'd feel compelled to interrupt and talk to me while I was on the phone. Was that a control thing?

"Are you there? Nina?"

"Yeah, sorry," I said and then paused, wondering whether I was typing the right row of numbers into my spreadsheet. "I just don't know if I can." I used my thumb and middle finger to pinch and stroke my eyebrow hairs in a rhythmic, anxious motion. *Maybe I could get out for thirty minutes. But what if Steve is here all weekend helping me with the pitch books? When he's here on the weekends, he keeps his eye on us like a hawk so we're not wasting his time.*

"Sweetie, we are going to be there for the whole weekend. You don't think you will have a chance at all?" she said in a tone that sounded as if she thought I was just confused. "We would love to take you out for dinner."

I realized I had copied and pasted my capital growth rates on to the wrong Excel spreadsheet, deleting pertinent information, and I couldn't get the Undo function to work. I eyed the clock and wondered whether I would get home tonight. I hadn't even started my new project. *Why is Ken still hovering around my desk? I hardly ever have personal calls. I really am busy. Please don't give me more work.*

"I know it sounds ridiculous, Freany Aunty, but things are so busy here. I just can't plan ahead of time even though it's only a couple of days away, since clients are coming in." *I'm not sure she even knows what investment banking is. She's going to think I'm lying.* "I'm really not exaggerating. I don't know if I'll even make it home tonight. I'm so sorry, but I really don't think ..." I said, covering the side of my face at the thought of once again failing people. "How about we just talk on Sunday? Either that or I could try and make plans with you now, but then I may have to cancel them at the last minute." *I knew both of these options sounded absurd to her.* "Does that sound too crazy?"

"Okay, let's talk on Sunday," she said in a perplexed tone.

"Can't I just see you at Christmas?" I blurted out, anxious for a solution while making a mental note to tell my mom to explain to her that I didn't work regular hours.

"Uh, yeah. It's quite a while away but— "

"Okay, great," I said and let out a deep sigh after we hung up. She had always loved the Broadway shows that would travel to Houston. I was disappointed that I wouldn't be able to show her around New York's theater district. That would have been fun. She would've loved it. I would have, too. If only I had the time.

12:45 A.M. I ran upstairs to our internal graphics center to pick up work I had submitted.

"I have a job that was due at 12:00 A.M. for Nina," I said.

"We left you a voice mail about that. It won't be ready until closer to 2:30 A.M."

"But it was marked urgent."

"We saw that. Get a cup of coffee and join the others," she said, pointing to a row of analysts waiting for work. Two were sitting upright fast asleep with their arms in midair holding their beepers close to their ears.

2:40 A.M. Graphics finished the map, and I looked through it for mistakes.

"Aren't these dots on this map supposed to be stars?" I asked the graphics coordinator, whose eyelids hung low. I guessed he was a musician, given his long, noncorporate bangs. Many of the graphics coordinators were actors or other artists trying to make ends meet with overnight shifts after long days of auditioning.

"You can't do stars. If you want stars it takes much longer. It's a horribly tedious process. You've gotta wait for the computer to import each star and there's at least a hundred on that map. No way we could do this for tomorrow."

I rested my elbow on the counter as I considered what to do, but then stopped myself, realizing that I had limited options.

"Well, I need this for tomorrow. I'll just keep the dots."

5:14 A.M. The black town cars waited for us in a queue outside the lobby of our office. They reminded me of a funeral procession.

I got into one of the cars. "Hey, Nina! I haven't seen you in a while. How have you been?" This was routine. Most of the drivers knew the analysts.

"Busy, I never went home last night," I said. I looked down at my suit, which I had worn for two days straight. My head was an unwieldy sphere I could no longer balance on my neck. I threw it against the headrest and undid the uneven Avon gray-and-cream flowered silk scarf that my grandmother had sent me. I thought of Farah and me running up to my parents with our pent-up complaints as they came in through the back door after a long day at work.

"Nina kept changing the channels while I was watching," Farah would complain.

"Play nice," my dad would say with an exhausted smile, placing his briefcase along with his engineering designs, which he rolled up like posters, next to the sofa.

My mom would eagerly flip her heels off into the laundry

room and my dad would loosen his Indian silk tie. With them they carried in an aroma of cologne, which was reserved for workdays. By their fourth step, their sweet smells were overpowered by the potent dinner aromas of my grandmother's cumin and fried masala. But in my New York apartment, I had no one eagerly awaiting my arrival. The air was stale. It was a lonely feeling.

I wore things to work that looked particularly conservative. Anything that would remind me of my grandmother would be a fine addition to my wardrobe. Better plain than attractive. My hair was always tied back tight in a low ponytail so as not to give anyone the impression that I was flirting. I learned from how they talked about my female counterparts that you would quickly get permanently compartmentalized. You were either brutish because you were there to succeed or flirty because you were looking to hook up. Once you got into the flirty category it seemed impossible to dig yourself out. My colleague Pam was told during her review that her good work would be taken more seriously if she toned down her provocative clothes and overly friendly personality. My long, permed hair and made-up face on my Texas driver's license looked nothing like the mascara-free face my coworkers saw daily. I kept it hidden in my wallet like a dirty secret. Once an officer from another group saw it while we were at the security check in the airport. "Is that really you?" he asked, looking back and forth between me and my license.

I looked down at the wild yellow stains my sweat mapped onto my white shirt. My head wobbled as I used my tongue to excavate yesterday's afternoon cookie buildup from the grooves of my front teeth. I opened the window after noting the musty scent of yesterday's sweat that clung to me. I couldn't tell whether it was my right armpit, which sweated twice as much as my left, or my saturated pantyhosed feet.

"And you're here till 5:00 A.M. tonight?" the driver asked. "Everyone has got to make time for dreaming. If you don't, you'll get run-down."

I tried to remember my last dream, but I couldn't think of a time I slept deep enough to dream since I started working. My life was so focused on the basics: finding time to eat, shower, go to the bathroom, and sleep. I was so desperately focused on meeting my basic needs that I had little capacity for those of other people. I tapped my foot as I remembered my aunt's call about her visit. *This job is taking over my life.*

"If I had time to dream, I'm not sure I'd still be working here," I said.

"What do you mean? That you'd realize you don't want to work here or that they'd fire you?"

I closed my eyes and smiled at the question. Since I never had time to slow down and reflect, I almost felt incapable of thinking. After a pause I said, "I'm not sure—maybe a little of both," and then dozed off.

That night, like most nights, my Excel spreadsheet churned through my head like a digital whirlpool, and I mentally combed through every number I had entered. Each cell was a vortex. At 6:23 A.M., I shot up in bed after realizing that I had double-counted the interest expense in cells W17–AF17 and W102–AF102 of my cash flow forecasts. I desperately grabbed for my Palm Pilot, which I kept on my nightstand for these vital emergencies. I set my beeper, which we were encouraged to carry at all times, to go off in thirty minutes. I tried to fall back to sleep, but my breaths got shorter and shorter at the thought of disappointing

Todd, which made me get dressed and leave for work.

Just as bankers were very clear on the entry and exit strategies for an investment, we had our own strategy to sneak in and out of work. Coming in, to make sure everyone noted I was five minutes early, typically, I would first come to my desk, turn everything on, and then go to the cafeteria downstairs to buy coffee. In the evenings, if I left before other people, I would wait until they were on a phone call, run for the elevator, and wait in a panic, hoping no one would walk by the glass doors and catch my betrayal.

Luis was the most imaginative since he worked hard to create the image of occupation. He rarely shut off his computer. Instead, he had the technology staff set up his computer so that his screen saver would stay on anytime he was away. It would also constantly change images to give the impression that he had visited his computer between now and the last time you saw his screen saver. In order to come in unusually late, yet look as if he had been working all morning, he would go to the floor below us, take off his jacket, and leave it in that closet. Then he would climb up to our floor with papers in his hand so that it looked as if he had just come out of a meeting. His stair strategy was foolproof. It also helped him set up his exit strategy, where no random passerby or bathroom visitor could see him through the glass door waiting for the elevator in the evening.

When he was getting ready to leave early, Luis would ask whoever was around, "So, what time are you leaving?" Since it was difficult to gauge, I just used to reply, "In a couple of hours." Luis would say, "Well, I'm running up to word processing to take care of some stuff. Do you want me to drop any work off for you?" He would then leave the office and go out to eat and drink with friends. Most of the time he didn't return, though on occasion he would come back several hours later, always with papers in his hands. At times when he arrived, I would still be there. "Wow," he'd say. "I am bushed. You wouldn't believe how stupid they are in word processing. It has taken me hours to sit there and explain all that shit to them." His slippery ways were so obvious that I ignored his comments, knowing that he had never been there, since I had stopped by the department twice in the last few hours. Master networker Michael would never attempt any of this nonsense. Why would he need to? He would just walk in and out of the office when he liked. His attitude was, "I have a beeper, and they can use it if they like."

This morning Michael walked in at 9:30 A.M.

"Michael," I said, "Ken was looking for you this morning, and he seemed pretty upset. He said you were supposed to have some comparables on the auto industry ready for him."

"Oh, I'm not finished with them," Michael said calmly.

Daniel, one of our colleagues from training who sat on the other side of the our floor, came over in a panic with his undershirt showing and his shirt partially untucked, as if he'd been here since last night.

"Does anyone have a pair of conference call headphones?" Daniel motioned as if he were making a halo on his head: "Those things traders wear."

"You mean like this," Michael said, making the shape of a headband, ear to ear.

"Yeah, whatever," Daniel said impatiently. "I'm late for a conference call, and I've got to get a mini-merger done too."

"Those are impossible to get," Luis said. "You should ask an associate."

"Here you go," Michael said, pulling out a brand-new headset still in its box from a locked drawer. "Don't forget to give them back to me."

"You're awesome!" Daniel said as he greedily grabbed them and scurried away.

"Michael, you have everything!" Luis said. "How about hooking us up?"

"Headsets are treasures. Not easy to get," Michael said. He then gave Luis the "call me" hand signal that I always thought looked like UT's longhorn hand gesture turned sideways.

Whenever they had "secret" business, they would talk into their phone receivers, even though they sat about nine feet away from each other. Michael did this because he mistakenly thought no one could hear him, but Luis did it because it made him look busy in case someone was to walk by.

"I just spoke to Tim in the media group," Michael said. "He's the one that got us those U.S. Open tickets that time we went with Nina. He said this year he's going to have tickets for a downtown Oscar party, too."

"Sweet," Luis sang.

"Tonight, Casey from the thirty-fourth floor—you know, the daughter of the gazillionaire—is having a party. Penthouse of the Trump Tower. She's good friends with Gwyneth Paltrow, and Tim said Gwyneth will definitely be there. And Roger from the trading floor is bringing his girlfriend, who's the redhead from *Melrose Place*."

Luis was so excited he turned his head around to face Michael, and instinctively Michael faced him. They stared at each other, with their mouths open wide like cartoon characters frozen midway through a laugh.

"Shit! I think I'm going to be stuck working here tonight," Luis said.

"Just come out with us for a while and then come back at night and get started. I'll give you all the details later," Michael said.

I could hear Luis panting. It wasn't completely clear to me why they got so excited by parties and clubs that were difficult to get into. They would wait hours to get into the "hottest" clubs that were next door to clubs they could walk into. I figured they would meet people tonight and start hanging out with them for a while until they found a new crowd that was even harder to break into.

"See, I always hook you up," Michael reminded Luis. "One more thing I meant to pass on. Yesterday I went to the nurse's office and slept there for an hour. It's so easy. You just go to the eighth floor and tell them you don't feel well and that you want to lie down. The nurse gives you a room of your own. Set your alarm beeper and—voilà!"

"No way!" Luis said, so excited he turned around to face Michael again.

"For real," Michael said, facing Luis. "If someone comes around looking for you, I'll beep you. You're in the building and everything. It's so money." He paused and nervously looked around: "I'll tell you more later." He glanced at his caller ID and pointed to his phone and said, "It's one of my college buddies on the other line."

Michael switched lines. "Dude, how are you? I am *so* psyched you're going to interview here. This place is amazing. Yesterday we took clients out to the '21' Club and had the most amazing power lunch—steak, calamari, and bananas Foster. All the booze you want," he said with a lingering laugh that would normally follow an inside joke. Leaning back in his chair as if it were a recliner he went on, "Next month I'm going on a road show, which is basically just a trip around the world with the CEO and CFO. I-banking is seriously the only way to go. Just say the word, and I'll do my best to hook you up."

I shifted my head over to look at him with eyes that said "talk softer," but he was too excited to notice me. It was just me staring at his nameplate, 32-143NE. Unlike officers, we did not merit engraved nameplates. Instead, there were labels posted on the side of our desks: I was 32-142SE and Luis was 32-143NW.

Michael suddenly sat up and leaned slightly forward. "But I've got to tell you, the work here is a challenge. I have never worked so hard in my life. Everyone here is so brilliant. For real."

He hardly let his friend speak before he went on. "Well, I don't know anyone in derivatives. They're with the traders." He started to finger through his stack of business cards even though he wasn't reading them. "Did you try Andy? He was a year ahead of me in Skull and Bones."

Unable to focus because of his loud talking, I began typing louder, hoping he'd remember that he had officemates.

"Of course. I know quite a bit about derivatives," Michael exaggerated. He stood up and began speaking loudly, as if he were a lecturer in a classroom. "Since I've had the opportunity to work on a variety of projects. Derivatives are your basic equity and debt hybrid. You get a coupon payment, maybe one a month or semiannually, while you maintain a stake in a company."

My head shot up as he provided the interviewee with the definition of preferreds instead of derivatives. I looked over at Michael and Luis. However, Luis was engrossed in an e-mail and Michael was still deep in conversation. I stared desperately at Michael, but he was too distracted to feel my gaze. He went on. "It's really basic stuff we're talking about. Anyway, it's hectic here, and I'm about to run into a meeting. But, hey, just call me later if you need more help. Good luck, dude."

After he hung up he looked at Luis and me and asked, "Does anyone want to go to Tasti D-Lite for fro-yo?"

We both said we were too busy, so Michael called another friend from the technology group to join him. I wanted to blurt out that he had misinformed his friend, but it was clear from the smile on his face that this was irrelevant to him. Along with most of our analyst class, I envied his ability to just get by at work. I stared at him as he waited for his friend and realized something we shared in common: While I was trying to prove myself at work, he was trying to prove himself to his friends. With an involuntary smile, he played with a dump truck deal toy—basically a fancy tchotchke used to commemorate a financial transaction—that he'd gotten from Project Scoop, a deal closed by Goldman Sachs. Since Morgan Stanley was only a cobanker, Michael's contribution to the six-month deal was only a handful of hours, but he made sure he received the toys he earned. He spent two weeks following up with the lead underwriting analyst. "Are the deal toys in yet?" "Don't forget to send mine." "I still haven't got it." "Did you specify the thirty-second floor when you mailed it?"

Michael corrected anyone who called it a truck or a tractor—"Skidder," he would interrupt.

"Morgan Stanley," I said, picking up a call with a 713 area code, keeping my professional tone so that it might sound like I was on a work call, since there was no privacy. "It's Lena," she said; then, without a pause, "I know you don't have time, but I drew your name, so tell me quickly what you want for

Christmas."

Before I could respond, Todd leaned his head forward, hovering over my desk. Just like Ken. How did these officers time their visits to be just when I'd get my rare personal calls? I turned around so my back was to him and whispered, "I don't need anything." Before she could respond I said, "Uh-huh," to Lena in a thoughtful tone, hoping to make it look like I was on a work call. Todd was the worst of the officers. If he saw you not working, he'd assume you weren't busy and give you more work. I opened my stapler nervously as if I were fixing something that was broken, trying hard to look productive.

Too impatient to wait until I finished my call, Todd started giving me directions on how to change some financial model he needed.

Soon after, Steve came by and leaned over my three-foot cubicle wall. It was just low enough that I always had to look busy.

"Hey, do you have a minute?" he said and started walking toward his office before I could look up.

"Sure," I said. I knew right away to follow.

When I entered, I spotted on his desk the map I had completed the night before and my stomach involuntarily churned.

He handed me the map. "What do you think of the job you've done?"

"If it's about the stars—"

"I'm not asking about anything specific," he said calmly. "I want to know what you think about it. Do you think you gave it your best?"

I clutched it stiffly and stared at the map until it all blurred into a graying cloud of nothing. *Why do they ask these esoteric questions? We both know there's a right answer. Why not just say*

I screwed up?

"I think so," I said, unconvinced. I couldn't bring my eyes to meet his. He sat in front of his desk and I just looked past him to his desk. *Don't look down—that looks so weak.* Hundreds of company information booklets were lined up with the binding no more than two millimeters out of place. He kept only the necessities on his desk—paper clips, a calendar, pens, and an HP-12C calculator etched with his name. During training they had advised us to do so since calculator theft in panicky moments was common. His calendar offered daily quotes. Today's was: "He that cannot obey, cannot command." Steve was one of the few professionals who had a picture of any sort of family on his desk. He was also one of the few who seemed to have a healthy marriage. In a silver frame, he and his wife posed at a Wharton formal, where they had met. They looked like overgrown teens in a homecoming picture. Though it had been three years ago, and we all knew bankers aged faster, he looked precisely the same. I could imagine the *New York Times* wedding announcement they must have had, at least a quarter of a page. Even though she had grown up in North Carolina and he was from Boston, they'd been in the appropriate New York City circles for the last few years, which granted them a *New York Times* announcement on the Weddings and Celebrations page. "Mr. Crane, 33, is an associate at Morgan Stanley. He graduated from Duke University and received his MBA from Wharton. His mother, who retired as the executive director of communications at MIT, is a communications consultant in Boston. His father is the executive vice president and CFO of Fidelity Investments. . . ."

Steve paused, embarrassed, "You're one of our best, Nina. That means you have a standard to maintain."

He looked around the office as if something on the wall

could begin to explain this calamity. "First, look at the title, does it look like it's…?" He raised an eyebrow, letting me know he was waiting for a response.

He's shifting to the "fill in the blank" game. My associate over the summer seemed to like this game too. Easy enough. "In the middle?" I asked.

"No," he said. "Centered at the midpoint. Does it look centered to you?"

I looked at it, and it looked very much centered. "Yeah."

Steve took out his ruler and put a little mark in the middle of the page followed by two more on each side. He looked up to meet my eyes. "It's an entire quarter inch off. How did you miss that?"

His officemate turned around to see my obvious error. When she swiveled back to her computer screen, I saw her shaking her head at my sloppiness. I had already established a reputation for being unemotional and tough, which was critical for my success as a woman. Luis, on the other hand, felt no shame sharing his frazzled nature, which was probably why Ken screamed at him across the floor yesterday. This conversation with Steve was mild in comparison. I reminded myself of this, hoping it would make me less edgy.

"And what are these dots?" he asked.

"That's what I was trying—"

"No," he said. "These dots represent . . ."

"Where we can sell the client's stock in the United States," I said, clasping my hands behind my back to hide their uncontrollable trembling. *No matter what's happening inside, you have to stay in control.*

"No," he said. "The dots on the map signify . . ."

"The location," I suggested. *This question game didn't last so long when I played it in capital markets.*

"That's it? The location? Nothing more?" Though he spoke calmly, his lip quivered in frustration. "Is that what we want the client to think? There is a reason I wanted stars," he said, with his spit falling on Des Moines, Iowa. "We want them to believe that their stock can be a star. They can be stars. By using us, they can be stars!" His voice was growing louder with panic. He caught himself and, in a moment, found his usual composed, supportive teacher's voice and asked, "Do you get it?"

"Yeah," I said as I looked out the window behind him at all the people walking in Times Square. I could hear Todd's voice from earlier in the week at a company event. "The world is full of incompetent fucks. We aren't here because we're lucky. It's because we're the best and the brightest. You don't want to end up like one of them," he had said, pointing around the bar at all the other people milling around as we waited for our drinks. "It's not a pretty life."

From thirty-two floors above, the *Beauty and the Beast* marquee looked like a glowing deal toy. Most people would never have the prestigious opportunity to be here, I reminded myself. I took the map from Steve and felt nothing but disdain for the innocent sheet of paper. "I'll fix it." I didn't want to be Steve's failed investment.

"Small mistakes can become big ones," he reminded me. As I was walking out he said, "Oh yeah, I forgot to mention: We have a meeting in thirty minutes at the Starbucks in Bryant Park. I know that doesn't give you a lot of time to fix it, but I'm sure you'll figure it out. Also, can you drop this by Ken's office, please?" He handed me a binder. It was his way of giving me an extra opportunity to interact with an officer. As I grasped the binder, Steve offered me a small smile, which reminded me of what I overheard him say to one of his MBA classmates in the cafeteria earlier in the week after introducing me. "Don't you just love it when the public school kid is the one that shines." Remembering his words gave me an instantaneous jolt of excitement. But only seconds later I was struck with an intense pressure to not screw up.

On my way out of Steve's office, I passed by the secretary Steve and I shared. She was skimming an L.L. Bean catalog, and I almost made the mistake of asking her to send out a fax that needed to get out before noon. It would have been a blunder indeed. Analysts' secretaries were in name only. Secretaries only helped the highest people they were in charge of. We were so lowly that we couldn't ask them to take a phone message. Once I had asked her to do my expenses; she had returned them to me with a hot pink sticky note that gave me instructions.

"Ken," I said, standing at the door of his office, too hesitant to walk in since only his eyes moved to glance at my reflection in the window before he chose to not acknowledge me. "Steve asked me to give you this binder." He continued to type as if he hadn't heard me. I turned around, looking at my secretary, who sat right next to his office, and wished I could give it to her to give to him. *Is this what people meant when they said corporate finance is hierarchical? I'd rather he shouted at me than treat me as if I'm invisible.* "Ken," I repeated, "Steve wanted me to drop this off."

"What is it?" he mumbled, still not looking up.

I started to walk in since my presence had been acknowledged. "Steve didn't say, so I assumed you'd know." *Should I just drop it on the floor and walk off? That would be funny.*

"Well, I assumed *you'd* know since you're dropping it off," he said with a smile to himself while steadily typing.

"I'll just leave it here on the chair," I said, placing it on one of the two chairs that faced him. He sat in a European imported chair that looked incredibly comfortable. I could imagine napping in it. It was nothing like the analyst chairs, which had the back support of a folding chair. The two chairs that sat across from him looked uncomfortable and stubby, ensuring guests wouldn't stay too long.

Staring at his shelf, I admired his deal toys, especially the Gillette toy, which was in the shape of a razor with foam sudsing out. He had five shelves of toys, maybe twenty-five toys total. I calculated that I'd need to close at least four deals a year to match him. Ken displayed them behind his chair so that it would be impossible for visitors to miss them during a meeting. The standard toys looked like clear slabs of glass the size of a greeting card with all the imperative details—number of shares and amount of money issued—of a stock or bond offering displayed on them. Ken's collection included these standards, plus many of the coveted trendy deal toys like cars, frogs, and planes.

I stared out his window and remembered the story that Luis said Ken had told him. That's how I learned that windows should be evaluated by inches. While Steve was out of town on a business trip, Ken told Luis that he would love to hire a personal contractor to knock down their shared wall. That way he could expand his office by a few inches just to get part of his inferior's window. Luis and I laughed as we imagined it: When Steve returned, Ken would say, "Hope you don't mind. My lighting was terrible." And maybe even add a friendly slap on the shoulder.

While walking back to my desk, I thought about Steve's

picture on his desk. I wondered where Steve came from and what his family was like. All I knew was that he had an older sister who worked at Goldman Sachs, and I assumed he had heard enough stories about her experience to make a concerted effort to keep an eye out for me as the only female on the team. We rarely spoke about family or our past other than basics.

Just as Steve and I were strangers when it came to family life conversation, my father rarely spoke about his early life. Even though I grew up with him, I hardly knew anything about him, and he knew just as little about me. He'd recite the names of cities where he lived and the boarding schools he'd attended, but if you asked, "Did you have a lot of friends?" his response was limited to yes or no. He wasn't one to reflect on the past or evaluate experiences as good or bad. They just were. I got the sense that, unlike me, he didn't spend too much time wondering.

When I was in junior high, for extra credit, I gave both my parents a confidential survey to fill out separately that asked questions about how they grew up. When my dad read the questions, he handed it back to me and said, "Tell your teacher this is not academic."

"Dad, it'll give me twenty extra points toward my spelling grade," I begged. "I'm not going to read it. I'll staple it right after you finish it."

The next morning on our drive to school my mom asked, "Let me see your dad's survey."

"No, Mom, I don't know if—"

"Give it to me!" she demanded. "Stop being dramatic. He's my husband."

When we reached the school parking lot, she lifted my foot and grabbed the sheet. "So many years and he has so little to say about the past. He was in so many boarding schools even his Mother can't keep them straight." It was odd to hear my mother speak so candidly about my father.

She ripped open my dad's secrets only to find "N/A" written after every question, along with this message: "Note to teacher: I don't have an opinion on these questions. Make sure you give my daughter credit."

Before heading over to Starbucks for my meeting with Steve and Todd, I walked briskly to the bathroom, taking deep breaths even though they were not enough to calm me. I had no idea how else to rid myself of the sting in my gut that often turned my bowels into liquid. There was a rumor that a few years ago they fired a woman from India who used to stick her feet on the toilet seat and squat since she was used to the Indian squat-style toilets. When I heard it, I thought it sounded ridiculous, but people would circulate the story with profound confidence as if they were there when it happened. I was careful to spend less than five minutes in the bathroom, which was more challenging on pantyhose days. Even though there were no cameras within sight, urban legends like these tended to work on our subconscious fears.

Within fifteen minutes, I left the building and was on my way. I forgot my watch at my desk so I turned around to see the time posted on our flashy building. Its sleek forty-two-story tower looked starkly different at the pedestrian level, where you could only see stock quotes and financial news: "Texas Instruments rated outperform" scrolled by, reminding me that this crazy lifestyle would be worth it when I got to see my parents' proud faces as they saw me walk out of this iconic Wall Street firm's building. Having to swipe my ID card at least twice just to go from my desk to the front door automatically made me feel important. But I didn't want to bring them into work since it would be obvious to them that I didn't fit into this corporate finance scene. I could hear my mom asking her typical questions: *"Did you take Steve downtown to the Parsi restaurant to try Persian food?" "Do you want me to make shrimp curry and invite your work team over?" "Do you think I should bring some delicious Texas barbecue sauces for all your managers?"* I wasn't sure how to explain to my parents that bringing in your family seemed completely inappropriate considering that no one at work seemed to care about you outside of your ability to meet deadlines and not make mistakes. And in the back of my mind, I could hear my dad reminding me, *"If you aren't proud of your heritage, you're nobody."*

Our building was sandwiched between Times Square and the red-light district, which had buildings with blacked-out windows and bright neon signs that read PEEP SHOW, LIVE NUDE, and XXX. While I was standing in Times Square, I stared at our flashy skyscraper listening to three different languages buzzing around me. *Why are people inside this tall glass tower so uncomfortable with anything different from them?* Everyone blended in on these streets. It was at moments like this that I realized how confined I'd been in Texas. It was such a relief to fit in because in New York everyone belonged. There were so many people with dark hair that even the white people kept their dark brown hair—not like bleached-blond Texans. In fact, I, as a full-breed minority on the streets of New York, would be considered boring compared to these multiracial crowds of one-quarter Caribbean, one-quarter Ecuadorian, one-quarter Japanese, and one-quarter Lebanese blood.

I elbowed my way through the crowds of people in Times Square, cringing at the loud screaming of the Twelve Tribes of the Nation of Israel speaker dressed in purple robes in front of a Star of David made out of faucet pipes. "Aren't you jealous of a black man?" he yelled at anyone who would listen. No sooner had I pushed through this crowd than I had to fight my way past the usual MTV mob. I walked past four teenage boys from Idaho who had come to see 'N Sync live at the MTV studios, videotaping their friend as he wrapped a massive yellow and white boa constrictor around his body. Their rapt faces reminded me of my first summer in New York. Scared of the subways, I had only taken buses for my first month until what I came to think of as my traumatic incident. As I rode to work one morning, a man's body smashed against our bus and fell to the ground. One of the passengers screamed, "You hit him!" but the bus driver drove off without flinching and said, "He ran into the bus. Those damn fools will do anything for money." The rest of the bus ride I held my hand over my gaping mouth, unable to forget the image of the man in blue cargo pants and yellow flip-flops lying on the ground. I went into work distraught and asked my coworkers if I should report the incident to the police. They laughed at my innocence: "It's not your problem."

On my walk to Starbucks I thought about how I had become just as indifferent. I was so caught up in my life drama that I didn't have the capacity to care much about anyone else. I breathed in Times Square's odd aroma, a mix of sickly sweet honey-covered nuts and a weird burning smell, mumbling to myself, "Don't fuck up!" I felt like a magician carrying a mysterious black box full of presentations as I pushed my way through the dense swarm of tourists in Times Square. In a panic to get there on time, I ran past tourists standing in front of me who would not walk on a DON'T WALK sign. It was the responsibility of the analysts to carry the presentations to meetings. We also had to cover any expenses such as food or transportation and the company would reimburse us. I was carrying two hundred dollars.

I winced as I passed by Morton's Steakhouse, where, just a month ago, we'd had a group dinner. This was one of my few opportunities to be with our group's head officers. Steve made sure I got to sit next to Larry, one of our senior officers. Larry had a gruff attitude that belied his loneliness. He was in his midforties and divorced a couple times. He seemed to see this as a big advantage, since he could spend his evenings dining with clients, while other officers were held back by their families. As Steve had trained me, I had gone online to study the menu. Since I was the only female at our eight-person table, all my officers insisted, "Ladies first." I confidently ordered my Tanqueray Ten dirty martini and a rare—even though I preferred it well done— filet mignon with béarnaise sauce.

"Pittsburgh," the waiter said after I ordered.

I opened the menu as if deep in thought, but only wondering whether it was a question or a statement. Did it even have to do with my order? I sat for a moment too long, frozen by the sixteen eyes on me.

"Steak edges," Steve leaned over and said softly, guiding me with a small nod.

"Sure," I said to the waiter, hoping that was an appropriate response.

"Guess you don't get out much," Larry said with a friendly chuckle.

"Guess not," I laughed. "Ladies first" always felt like a dirty trick, especially when you were caught in the back of the elevator and an older man near the front would say it. Smushed in the back corner, as the only woman, I'd grudgingly try and squeeze my way out.

Larry turned his back to me as he and Todd recalled a rowing event at Camp Pasquaney, where they had gone every summer growing up.

After a few moments, he politely attempted to integrate me into the conversation again. "What was your camp?"

Until I got to New York, I had never heard of the concept of going away in the summer. I'd only spent a couple of days at a Girl Scout camp. By now I had learned that most of my colleagues spent their summers at elite New England camps, so I didn't feel like sharing my summers of eating boxes of Pop-Tarts and watching soap operas and game shows with my grandmother.

"My summers were spent mostly with friends in the neighborhood," I said, smoothing the napkin in my lap.

"Did you all spend a lot of time at the club? Any golf or tennis?" Larry asked, trying to make small talk.

"My family isn't too sporty," I replied with a smile. "The closest thing to a sport I did growing up was dance."

"Dance? That's some kind of childhood," he said to me with a smile of confusion.

Those were close to the last words he said to me before turning his back to me for the rest of the meal. He and Todd bonded over Scores, a strip club close by the office that many of the guys frequented. Steve stayed out of those conversations and unsuccessfully tried to change the subject several times. After a few different Scores stories, several officers started swapping Scores Money, the club's exclusive cash. To be polite, Todd turned to me and asked, "Nina, you don't mind, do you?"

"No," Ken intervened. "Nina's cool." He winked in my direction and gave me an approving laugh.

I sat smiling, silently.

*

As soon as I entered Starbucks, I looked on empty coffee tables for reading material out of fear that I might fall asleep if I didn't have something to distract me. I walked up to a table with a magazine and rested my hand on it. The loud talking of the customers and the baristas shouting, "Tall skim double-shot vanilla latte with whip," carried through the shop. Though it was noisy, my exhaustion made the commotion sound distant, as if I had a slight buzz. I hoped I didn't have to speak much, since I wasn't sure if I could respond to impromptu questions coherently. On the table were a *New York Post* and a *People* magazine, neither of which I had any interest in. But I needed something. I reached for the *Post* and shrank back after I saw the front-page headline: "Upper East Side Rapist Strikes his 23rd Victim." I read the first couple lines of the story: "Once again, he trapped a 23-year-old woman in her apartment complex's vestibule as she returned home. . . ." I took a deep breath and shook my head. The Upper East Side wasn't that far from my Upper West Side apartment. I quickly opted for *People* magazine. At this point I was starting to wonder about the pitch I had initially bought into—the exciting pace, intellectual challenge, unparalleled exposure to top executives. I hadn't quite realized that they'd be at the cost of dignity and sleep. I tried to convince myself of other reasons I was lucky. Working all the time kept me safe, I told myself.

I sat at a coffee table waiting for my coworkers as I flipped through *People. Did I remember to footnote the earnings before interest and taxes on the summary statistics?* Then my thoughts got wrapped up in preparing myself to deal with Todd. He and most of the other officers in my group had a level of superiority that I hadn't dealt with before. I was both in awe of their power and disgusted with their callousness. During my internships, I'd dealt with supervisors more like Steve, who had some obnoxious banker traits mixed in with considerate traits. My fingers tapped on the table as I drank my triple shot of espresso. I hadn't felt the effect of any of it.

As soon as they arrived Todd asked me, "You didn't happen to catch the Knicks game, did you?"

"Knicks 79–71," I said quickly, knowing it was less for his information and more of a test. I was pretty good about getting the sports scores off the Bloomberg machine each morning.

"That doesn't sound right," Todd started.

"Thomas came off the bench to score twenty-one points, including ten straight in the fourth quarter," I said, quoting an article and not caring what straight scoring meant.

"All right!" Todd said, high-fiving Steve.

Steve gave me the smile of a proud parent.

"Did you catch last week's game?" Todd asked Steve.

"Oh, it was amazing!" Steve said. "Weren't you there?"

"Hell yeah," Todd said. "I'll tell you about it later. I can't talk about it in mixed company," he said.

Utterly confused by his comment, I looked up to see if someone else had walked up to our table, and then I glanced at Steve for guidance. Though I could sense Steve's discomfort, he joined Todd's laugh, which abruptly stopped as they looked my way, informing me what "mixed company" looked like.

"Nina, let's see the presentation," Todd said, clutching a *New York Times* folded into fours. I sat there still dumbfounded by his "mixed company" comment. *He must see that I'm only a few feet away and that I can hear him. Right?*

I handed him a copy, and he immediately flipped to the

financial projections. "What do you think of the profit projections, Nina?"

"Well, they look better," I said, laughing uneasily, "but I just used the profit numbers you gave me." I was expecting we'd all look at each other and laugh together, while saying, "We know these are just assumptions—who knows what will *really* happen. But instead, I could tell Todd was annoyed at my lack of confidence.

"These numbers are more realistic," Todd said definitively with a penetrating glare that would have made my heart race had I not been so tired. He looked toward Steve to make sure he was on board too. "I'm sure Steve explained it to you. Is there something you don't understand?"

"No, I do under—" I started.

"Well, you don't seem convinced of it, and as a team member, we need you to believe in these financial projections."

"Well, there're a lot of unknowns so I had to make a bunch of assumptions," I said, starting to feel helpless and annoyed that Steve supposedly had already bought in. *Am I missing something?*

"Steve—" I began again, expecting that he'd clarify my confusion.

"The company doesn't understand their own fucking numbers," Todd interrupted. "They have no idea what this new product line can do for their business. The CFO doesn't know what the hell he's doing. He's just married to the right person, which keeps him employed," Todd said to me, and then looked at Steve and began laughing. "Remember, Nina, they rely on us to guide them."

It wasn't long before Steve joined in, and I noticed that his laugh was almost identical to Todd's, just like his tie clip and leather binder. *Is he exaggerating, or does the CFO of a huge, successful corporation really have no idea what he's doing? Didn't we all sit in the same meeting and listen to Todd tell the CFO what a wonderful job he was doing? Even I was moved by Todd's "we can make you even better" speech.* He was the first major CFO I'd met, and now Todd had wiped away all the glee I felt about meeting someone so important. I felt so silly as I remembered how I ran back to my desk, ecstatic after our confidential meeting, and since I couldn't share the news with anyone, I just kept typing, "I met a VIP CFO," and then erased it over and over.

"I don't know anything about this new product line either," I tried to explain, looking at Steve to see if he was supposed to explain something to me that he'd forgotten. But from both their faces I could see that they had given me all the information they planned to, which was virtually nothing. All the assumptions we were making were based on a conversation Todd had with our client, which he couldn't be bothered to take the time to explain to me, yet he expected me to rally behind him. *Was Steve in on this conversation? I can't tell, and these people make an art out of avoiding questions. This is so frustrating!*

"You know, Nina," Todd said, "when I was an analyst years ago we used paper. We had these huge sheets of graph paper and with every small change we would have to go back and change every single little cell. But you all have it so much better. Now you have the time to get comfortable with the numbers. We know you're stretched to the limit, but we expect you'll take the extra time. It really makes all the difference."

Todd was suddenly distracted. "Teem!" he blurted out randomly as if he'd forgotten. *Is he talking to us?* "Four letters for the clue 'pouring cats and dogs,'" Todd said, raising the *New York Times* crossword to his face and quickly scribbling his answer.

"Great! What's the next clue?" Steve asked eagerly.

Suddenly they'd forgotten all about the immensely important meeting and my presence. Would I ever get used to this erratic behavior?

Fearful that I would fall asleep, I flipped through my magazine, utterly uninterested but compelled to look busy.

"Steve," Todd said. "Four-letter word for 'false god.'"

"Zeus. No . . . no," Steve said.

"Just a second," Todd said as he stepped away, crossword in hand, to get some coffee.

I looked up in his direction. A woman at a table across from us sat with her screaming baby in a high chair and her toddler, who was kicking the table because he didn't get a chocolate graham cracker. I wondered if she felt trapped—like my mom was with four kids. After watching my grandmother and mother be financially dependent on my dad, my worst fear was to be dependent on anyone and not be able to set my own rules. I looked at her overstuffed diaper bag, grateful that it wasn't my life.

The baby's high chair blocked Todd's way, so instead of taking another route, he lifted the baby's chair and moved it out of his path. The mother glared at him with annoyance and yelled, "Excuse me!" but he paid no attention and kept on his way.

It reminded me of the time he and I had stopped by a small family-owned electronics store next to our office building so he could buy a Discman to listen to on a train we were about to catch. Todd asked the salesclerk where the Discmen were and was pointed in the right direction. Since we were in a hurry, he just quickly grabbed one. He began opening the packaging while we were still exiting the store and then realized that there was no radio, just a CD player.

He walked back to the sales counter and said, "You gave

me the wrong one. I need one with a radio."

The clerk, a Middle Eastern–looking man with a carefully groomed mustache, replied, "You can't return it because you've already opened it, and I won't be able to resell it."

We were carrying our banker bags, bags that New Yorkers recognized. All investment bankers sported the same blue-and-green tote bags, which were differentiated by the embroidered investment bank's name. Todd hoisted his bag forward onto the counter, as if to remind the man that we should be treated with respect.

"Give me a new radio!" Todd shouted.

The salesclerk, though nervous, continued to be polite since he knew we were important.

"Please don't yell in the store, sir," he said, joining his hands as if to pray. "I am very sorry but because you have opened the package, I cannot take it back."

Todd tossed the Discman across the counter and yelled, "That's why you work here! You don't know a goddamn thing about business." He stormed out of the store. The moment was so surreal that I stood there frozen. Before this, I'd assumed that he said rude things about others just to sound tough, but this incident made it clear that he actually believed he was superior to other people. He really got away with acting like this outside our building? In capital markets, there was no after-hours work with officers—dinners, travel, client meetings—so I'd hardly seen an officer outside of work. Once I realized Todd had left the store, I gave the salesman a small, apologetic wave and trailed down the street behind Todd.

"The world is full of incompetent, lazy fucks!" he instructed me. "You've got to remind them of that so they keep on task."

At Starbucks, as I flipped through my magazine and

desperately tried to keep awake, I could feel Steve's stare on me.

"What's wrong?" he asked me.

"Nothing," I said, raising my eyebrows in confusion.

"Well, a senior officer is sitting here and you're reading *People*? You could be using this as an opportunity to show off your knowledge," Steve rattled off in one breath. He smoothed out his tie, and I could tell he was impressed as he said, "Just so you know how dedicated he is to his job, his wife is going into labor very soon. But he's still here."

Todd returned and asked, "Have either of you tried their new pumpkin spice latte?"

"I have," Steve pretended.

"I don't like flavored coffee," I said without looking up.

"You should try it," Todd said, as he poured a fourth of his brown pumpkin slush into my espresso. "You can go up there and get a stirrer to mix it," he suggested with a smile, still standing over me.

He poured so quickly that I didn't even have a chance to stop him. *This guy just can't be bothered to listen.* "Thanks," I said, sickened at the thought of pumpkin in my coffee. I glared up at him curious to know if he was doing this to annoy me or if he was really that oblivious. *I'm getting the feeling people do whatever he says—all the time!* "Can you believe that the guy at the counter didn't know what Swiss water process was?" Todd asked us.

"How crazy," I said, trying to dredge up some energy. Slowly, I was realizing what Steve had pointed out. I had so little in common with these people that I needed to use every opportunity I had to make an impression. "You would think they would know the basic decaffeination methods," I said, grateful that my uncle, who owns a coffee shop, had often bored me with the details.

Todd nodded his head to show me that he was both surprised and impressed, which was a relief, because the last time we'd spent time together, he'd brought up topics like scuba diving and pipe coiling, both of which I knew nothing about.

"Now, Nina," Todd said. "You do realize that the Swiss water process is the only cost-effective chemical-free method to date."

"Yes," I agreed. "And it's one of the few that removes almost all the caffeine."

"Well, that's not quite right," he said. "It actually removes ninety-eight percent."

I was catching on to his habit of bringing up random facts to impress others. Many officers did this. I was fascinated with how much it impressed clients. It was most effective with clients who were blinded by Todd's exceptional credentials. They figured he must be brilliant since he appeared to know everything. The most powerful knowledge was in-your-head math, because you could argue something so quickly that everyone else was too scared to admit that they couldn't calculate as fast and would defer to you. Todd was a master at all of these strategies so I watched him diligently. One day I'd be the one driving the conversations.

"I'll be back," I said. "I'm going to get a stirrer." I had walked just a few yards toward the condiments station when I heard Todd say to Steve, "You think she'll make it?"

"Why wouldn't she? I think she'll be one of our strongest analysts."

I left quickly, not wanting to overhear any more.

"Nina, have you ever thought about being a doctor?" Todd suggested when I returned.

Steve looked over at me with eyes that said, *"It's just a*

middle-aged man comment. He doesn't know any better. Just go along with it."

I laughed and played with a button on my jacket. "Never. I've never had an interest in biology," I said. "Why?"

"Oh, nothing, just a thought." Todd looked at Steve and said, "You know Christy, Jim's daughter, is just starting medical school." He looked back at me. "Ultimately, you could make your own hours, so it's a great career for a lot of women."

"Interesting," I said. "I've never thought about it." *Nor will I. Does he really think doctors have flexible hours?*

"So, Nina," Todd changed the subject yet again, "Steve tells me you had to cancel a family vacation earlier this month."

I appreciated Steve sharing this with Todd to show my dedication. Showing that you were willing to sacrifice your personal life was strongly rewarded. Steve had always looked out for my career. "Yes. My family traveled to visit some relatives in North Carolina."

"Golfing?" Todd asked.

"No, just my aunt's home," I said, amused at the idea of my family on a golf course but too tired to even smile at the image I had of my mom in tennis shoes with knee-high socks and my uncoordinated family running around shouting at one another, "Why can't you hit the ball!?"

"Where are you from again?" Todd asked, confused as to how to place me.

"From Texas," I said, at once regretting the inevitable reaction.

"Texas!" Todd screamed. "Now I didn't know that! You don't seem like a cowgirl." He shook his head and said with a put-on accent, "Well, you must have seen a lot of horses down there in *Tejas.*"

"A few," I said. "But I'm from Houston. It's not like I grew up on a ranch," I added sarcastically.

Todd gave me an "I'll make the jokes" stare and turned to Steve: "Didn't you say one of our new analysts was a Skull and Bones member?"

"That's Michael," Steve said.

"I'd like to have lunch with him. Can you set that up for next week?"

"Sure," Steve said, making a quick note. He looked up at my perplexed face and said softly, "It's a secret society." He smiled at Todd and said, "She had me fooled, too," in a tone eager to raise my status. "You'd never know she was from Texas."

"I guess you lost your drawl pretty quick, Nina," Todd said. "Smart girl." Nodding his head, he looked at Steve and then at me. "So I bet now that you're in New York you'll never go back. Am I right?"

"That's right," I said. Telling him exactly what New York-ers want to hear. "I definitely wouldn't go back. New York is so much better." My face didn't quite match my words, since every move seemed to exhaust so much energy. Interacting with Todd and Steve was like being in a play, except I had to make up the script on the fly.

"Smile," Todd commanded, startling me as he reached his hand out toward me and then smacked it down on the table. "She doesn't smile enough. Does she?" he said to Steve.

"Yeah, Nina," Steve said. "I don't see you smiling very often."

I tried on a smile and said, "I smile all the time."

"You should smile more often," Todd said with a model's smile. "Life's not so bad.

"Well," Todd went on about my vacation even though we were well beyond the subject, "it's too bad that you weren't going somewhere fun for vacation, like St. John Island or even Fiji.

We pay you enough," he said, laughing.

"That's true," Steve said with a smile.

"What would a client say if you told them you were vacationing in North Carolina without playing golf?" Todd added with a hearty laugh.

"Well, this was just a onetime thing with my family," I said. "Otherwise, I go other places." I looked at both of them and desperately tried to gauge how much this would affect my potential for upward mobility. "I'm planning a trip to Nantucket and the Cape," I offered, remembering two places that I'd heard Michael mention.

"Back to our clients," Todd went on to educate me. "You do realize that they want to be us. They are infatuated with us, and we live out their dreams. That's why they keep coming back," he said. "Don't forget that this is as good as it gets. That's why you came here. Isn't it? We're not reporting in to some head of marketing or crap like that. Instead, we're telling their CEOs and CFOs what to do. They look up to us. People coming out of the top business schools would kill to be where you are, and only a small number of them will get that opportunity. Don't forget that you're with the best of the best."

"That's right," Steve parroted. In my peripheral vision I could see Steve's obedient head bobbing up and down.

"Maybe it's not such a bad thing that you missed your vacation," Todd said. "I'm sure Steve will set you up with some IPO projects that you might have missed out on otherwise."

I gazed down at my pumpkined coffee and nodded my head in agreement.

Todd looked down at his crossword. Within a second, once again, his diversion became our focus. "Steve," Todd remembered, "I forgot to ask if you assigned someone to Project Night?

You said Nina couldn't do it. How about someone from a different team, like Andy?" Todd asked.

My eyes shot over to Steve to see his reaction. Andy sat on the other side of our floor. Rumor was, he was a cocaine user. It was a mystery to me whether officers thought so too. He often seemed out of it and edgy, but I wondered if it was really from cocaine or just sleep deprivation. After clubbing for two nights straight, Andy would come in with bloodshot eyes and brag that he could be completely alert after being awake for more than fifty hours straight.

"There's no need to reach out to a different team," Steve replied. "I was thinking more of Luis."

"What?" Todd said. "He couldn't figure out how to back into pretax earnings from after-tax on my last deal." Todd quickly looked to Steve. "Remember that analyst from the consumer products group who messed up the whole valuation because he used the wrong discount rate? What an idiot!" Todd laughed and looked at me to join in.

Embarrassed, I looked across the table and acted as if I were trying to read the crossword clues from upside down and afar.

"He covered the BQG deal just fine," Steve said, defending Luis.

"I can't have him working on such a big deal," Todd said.

"I'm sure it was just a mistake," I offered. I thought Steve and I were both defending Luis until Steve changed his mind abruptly.

"Small mistakes can quickly become big," Steve reminded me. He paused, realizing that Todd wasn't going to back down. "He wasn't my hire. I'll have to check schedules and find someone else."

My stomach burned as I thought about Luis. All of us had

heard the harsh chatter once you made a mistake. Even if it was a rare occurrence, you'd need to be prepared to be treated like you were incompetent. Ignoring the chitchat wasn't an option. Once your reputation was affected at the company, people would look at you with judgmental eyes. You could already hear your colleagues and friends discussing how weak, unintelligent, and pathetic you had always been. It felt like we were quickly boxed into roles—Luis was watched more carefully since he'd made one small mistake early on. Michael got the celebrity title (he was one of the rare analysts in our class who wasn't a billionaire's child who could get away with avoiding work), and I had become the reliable one.

I put my hand on my stomach, unsure how to weaken the sting. *You have to be more competitive to succeed here. Never mind*, I tried to convince myself. *If Luis looks bad, I look good.*

"What about Project Globe?" Steve asked Todd. "When does that need to be staffed?"

"It's not happening." Todd said flatly. "Too many cultural differences with the management team. I told you, they're Chinese."

"But they all grew up in America. It's not like they don't speak English," Steve said. "Their team tripled revenues in only a few years."

My ears perked up. I'd seen the deal; all of us were impressed with the powerhouse they'd created. Todd closed me out of the conversation by shifting his body to face Steve and talking more softly, as if I wouldn't be able to hear from just two feet away.

"Steve," Todd said, moving closer to him, "it's not just the CEO and CFO. Both heads of the departments are Chinese too," he said, raising his eyebrows as if now Steve should understand.

"We need a more sophisticated management team than that. Lehman's team has done work with these kinds of people before, so we're letting them take it."

They were so used to being around people just like them that anything different felt too foreign. With the lack of sun, my skin was much lighter than usual, but it was still darker than his. *Does he realize I'm a minority, or does he just not care what I think?*

"Todd," I said, interrupting, "I don't understand the big cultural difference if they grew up in America. They're probably pretty similar to any of our other clients. Shouldn't we at least meet them? We were all blown away by their business."

They both looked up at me for an instant as if I were a mere interruption, like someone breaking a plate, and then went back to talking to each other. I looked away since I could sense it was one of those moments I was expected to be invisible. It was precisely what Michael would have done from the beginning—either that or play on his Palm, ignoring them. *Hopefully, I won't have to work with Todd too often. We have so many officers. Maybe I'll be shuffled around so much it won't matter.*

Uninterested in listening to Steve any longer, Todd picked up his crossword and spoke over him. "Steve, five letters," Todd demanded. "A symbol of Pharaoh's power,"

Steve was suddenly nervous, as if realizing that not knowing this answer would not be good for his biannual performance review.

"Snake," I said, eager to use this easy opportunity to impress. "No! Cobra! Cobra." I looked at Steve, whose nervousness had now become contagious. "Does it fit?" I said eagerly.

"Well, it is a five-letter word," Todd said. "There is a blank, then an *O*, then a blank, then an *R*, and then another blank. You tell me."

"Yeah," I said faster than I was able to visualize the answer with confidence.

"I guess you've decided to join in," Todd said, looking up at me with squinted eyes that were unsure how to categorize me. But I was too busy looking at Steve for a head nod or an approving smile, and Steve was gazing down at the crossword trying to get a head start on the next clue.

I took a big gulp of my contaminated coffee. "I really like crosswords," I said, shaping a smile that could pass as real.

CHAPTER 4 Rules

"Too much coffee and not enough hydrating liquids," my father would advise. "A minimum of eight glasses a day is necessary."

Ms. Danes, my seventh-grade honors math teacher, had her face so close to mine that I couldn't focus on her annoyance. Instead, I concentrated on her painted face. Her already emaciated lips were pushed together so tightly that they looked like dried cranberries. She tried to ripen them by using a mauve lip pencil, but by 8:00 A.M., after her fourth cup of coffee, only an outline of lip liner remained. I assumed she was severely dehydrated, given the slice of dried-up skin that hung loose and the thin bloody cuts on the sides of her mouth.

Ms. Danes had just announced, "You belong in Siberia!" as she clutched the two sides of my desk in an attempt to move me into the corner across the room. She squatted and swiftly swayed back and forth as if preparing herself for her opponent's hard first serve, down the line. Her lavender shoe heels unsteadily rocked with her. Despite all her struggling, my heavy desk didn't budge.

Taking a breather, she looked up at me and said, "We have honors students here who, unlike you, want to learn. What do you think I should do about that?" The school tested us annually through standardized exams, which placed me in honors courses. Each honors teacher knew who I was because they were warned by my prior teachers.

By junior high I had become a disruptive student, constantly eager for attention. I felt hopeless trying to compete academically with my older sisters, Shireen and Farah. It seemed impossible to stand out. When Shireen was the first (and presumably the last) in the history of her middle school to get all As the entire time she was there, the school created a new award for her and invited all the parents and students to attend the ceremony. "Nice job, Mickey Mouse," my dad said to her before he turned on the world news. *That's it! "Nice job" for three years of work!* Just as his parents had expected academic perfection, he expected nothing less from us.

But I needed more than that. It was easier to get attention from him when things went wrong. That was when the trouble-shooting engineer got involved, since trouble meant that he was losing his American-bred kid to a culture unfamiliar to him. I was exhilarated by all the attention I received when I disrupted the class. Everyone was focused on me. The morning after Ms. Danes moved me to Siberia, she announced, "Nina, you will sit here permanently."

I had no intellectual interest in math, but it came easily to me, which intrigued Ms. Danes. Plus, facing my dad with a B in English was easy compared to getting a B in math. My first week of class, I kept talking while Ms. Danes showed us how to solve second-degree algebra equations on the overhead projector. She used her typical disciplining tactic of asking the disrupter to answer the question. "So, Nina, you obviously understand the question. Why don't you come up here and solve this for us?" "Sure," I said, with a smile. Without going up to the overhead, I looked at the problem for a few seconds, and did the trial-and-error method, one that many students struggled with, in my head: "$(x - 3) = 0$ and $(x + 2) = 0$, so $x = 3$ and $x = -2$." Confident that my answer was correct, I turned around to continue my one-sided conversation with Deanna. "So do you think Jacob is definitely going to go on Friday?" I asked. Deanna just smiled uncomfortably, torn between the teacher's and my need for attention. Ms. Danes was caught off guard by my quick answer. She took some time to solve it before she could comment on its correctness. Deanna silently nodded her head to answer my question. "Well," I continued my conversation loudly, "if he goes I want to make sure that we're there, so I'm going to find out whether Jennie's mom or my dad will take us." After finishing, Ms. Danes announced the answer. "Well, class, $x = 3$ and $x = -2$." She nodded her head and raised her eyebrow as she said to the back of my head, "You're very versatile." A word I later looked up.

After she moved me to Siberia and I was quiet for a few days, Ms. Danes took me out into the hall. "It looks like math comes quite easily to you, but it's clear you have no real interest in it. So tell me, what is it that you are interested in?"

"I don't know," I said. No one had ever asked me that question before.

"What do you want to be when you grow up?" she asked.

"I don't know," I said. I'd never given much thought to it. "My older sisters are probably going to be a doctor and an engineer, which is what my dad thinks we should be."

"I remember your sisters. Such bright girls," she said looking away from me in admiring thought. "It seems to me that you have a lot of restless energy and you just need to channel it, so I suggest you find something you enjoy. You have a very curious mind, but it's not focused on school right now. You'll be good at many things in life, Nina, but your toughest job will be choosing that one thing to focus on."

I stared at her long and hard, finding it unusual that someone believed I would be something more than a disruption. At home I only got the sense that they expected something from me, but not this heartfelt belief that I could actually *do* something.

"I don't know what I'm going to do, but I want everyone to wish they were me," I said softly, as if confiding in her.

"I'm sure they will," she said with a smile as her cold hand touched my cheek. I was touched that despite my disruptions, she had a soft spot for me. Did she really see something in me?

After our talk, I felt bad disrupting her class. Some days I would try to concentrate on things that kept me busy in Siberia, like writing an urgent note to a friend: "Hey, I can't believe that Joey said that. He is so wrong. I'm going to call Steve and let him know. Otherwise Jennie will end up going with Steve, and that would suck for us." If I were decorating the note with doodles and Depeche Mode lyrics, then I would become completely engrossed in carefully filling the note with colorful details as I frequently clicked different colors of my four-color retractable Bic pen.

Since I found it hard to sit there quietly day after day, and I no longer wanted to disrupt Mrs. Danes's class, I began coming in really late or skipping her first-period class. Every morning I woke up early to go to my friend's house to play Super Mario Brothers. I was jealous of Jennie since no one was at home to see if she went to school, unlike in my house, where my grandmother made sure we had finished our porridge and went on time. Each morning, we would set a goal to advance to a new level in Super Mario Brothers.

"Nina, we're already fourteen minutes late," Jennie warned.

"Just one more second. Let me kill one more Spiny, and then I'll be ready.

"If we hurry we can beg them to just make us tardy."

I took another bite of a Pillsbury orange-iced cinnamon roll, our morning treat. "I dreamt about the castle full of lava pits and Bowser last night. I already killed the maximum number of Koopa Troopas and Goombas."

Whenever we arrived at school late, we had to sign in at the office and write the reason we were late. Everyone's answers looked so similar—"alarm" or "sick." Mine said "playing Super Mario Brothers." When we walked into the office together to sign in late, Jennie would always try to act as if she didn't know me. She begged me to allow her to sign in first so that she could run out of the office before being associated with my excuses. She would wait for me around the corner of the office, eager to hear what I wrote. "Oh my God!" she'd shriek and cover her mouth. It gave her a vicarious thrill.

It was quite a while before my parents learned of my truancy. One evening, after returning from work, my dad walked up to the television, where Farah and I sat, and turned off *The Brady Bunch*. "What do you mean, not attending your classes!" he shouted. "The vice principal called to say you won't get credit if you miss one more class. We moved to this neighborhood so you'd get the best education, and you're skipping your classes?"

The room suddenly felt very small. He had caught me off guard. Since I still had all As in the class, I didn't expect the school to call. *How do I get out of this one?*

Even his eyebrows shuddered as he spoke, and I knew where his added anger came from. He thought he had it all figured out last week when we negotiated a deal. He would now start paying us for good grades. I even had him agree to pay double for my honors classes.

"Double!" he exclaimed. "It's not twice as hard."

"I'll drop them," I threatened, knowing it was the only power I had over him.

"That's totally unfair," Farah screeched.

"She's saying that because she's only in one honors class, Dad," I said with my hand stickered to her face so I could get his buy-in quickly without her interruptions.

Farah screamed, through my hand, "Daaaad!" But her screams were futile. He nodded in agreement.

I stared at my reflection in the television as I tried to construct an excuse. "Dad, it's my first class and you know I have to jump the fence to get to school. I'm just a girl," I said, hoping to appeal to his delicate notion of women. My knack for quick retorts was a huge asset with him. Even if I were scared, I could snap back within seconds. Sometimes even if he were mad, I'd say something so funny we'd both start laughing together, but I could sense this wasn't going to happen today.

"Don't jump the damn fence!" he screamed. "Leave early and walk around. What bullshit you talk about jumping the fence."

"But if I walk around, then I'll be late."

"You already are!" he screamed louder.

"Oh," I said. "I never thought about that."

Confused and unsure what to say next, he walked off mumbling.

Within four seconds, he came back, his face fiery red. "I better not hear you missed another class." He raised a disciplining finger at me and said in desperation, "Or I'll give you a tight slap."

Unlike my mother, who would slap us on rare occasions, he would just threaten us out of desperation, uncertain what to do with American kids who didn't respect a parent's orders. One of his greatest fears was that we'd marry outside our religion and lose our culture's traditional values. Only a month earlier at the Jack in the Box drive-through he had seen a teenage couple walking by—an Asian boy and a white girl.

"Dad, I want a chocolate milk shake, too," Farah hollered from the backseat.

He turned around to his thirteen- and fourteen-year-olds and said, "If you dare marry an American I will disown you. Do you hear me?"

"Sir," the woman speaking from the Jack in the Box board said. "Sir?"

"Do you hear me!" he yelled at us.

We both nodded our heads. "Empty threats," my mom explained to us. "That is just his way of scaring you into doing what he thinks is right." Our religion's existence depends on marriage within the community since people can't convert in. My father's life mission was to keep the community alive.

He expected obedience from us, just as his dad had expected it of him. Whenever I asked my father why he studied engineering, he paused for a moment and looked away, embarrassed by my absurdity. Then he would look straight at me, trying to make sense of my foolishness—inferior forehead, crooked ears, narrow eyes. Only after reminding himself of these physical deficiencies could he process the question. He slid his fingers through the front part of his hair, massaging his forehead. "My father wanted me to," he responded. "My father worked at Tata Steel for forty-three years and died of emphysema from the hot furnaces in the steel mills. He had a very successful career. He was dedicated, disciplined, and loyal," he said. "He did what his father told him to." Every time I heard him say this I saw it as a confession that he had no idea how to discipline his disrespectful kids.

He walked a few yards—3.56 yards, the engineer would argue—from the television, then turned back again, still unsatisfied. He approached me again and raised his finger—this time it shook involuntarily—and opened his mouth slightly. But he couldn't speak. For the last time, he turned around and left.

Later that night my mom took my sisters to buy science fair supplies. My grandmother and I stayed home to watch *Dallas*. My father was in his bedroom reading the *India Abroad* newspaper, which my mother said confused him, often making him think he was still in India. I suspected he was reading the matrimonial ads, planning our futures. It was the season finale of *Dallas*, so my grandmother made twelve pints of pistachio *kulfi* to celebrate.

I was playing a game with my ice cream–like scoops of *kulfi*. So far it had lasted twenty minutes and although the second scoop was soft, it still hadn't melted. I sat lounged all the way back in our maroon recliner, facing the television, and tried to see how long one spoon of *kulfi* could last if I only took minuscule bites. I slid a spoonful into my mouth and removed it, almost untouched. The most one spoon had lasted was thirty-four slides. My goal was to make each a bite last for fifty slides.

After half an hour of holding in her pee, my grandmother rushed to the bathroom during the long commercial break. I shook my head, knowing that the article in *Soap Opera Digest* about Holden and Lilly from *As the World Turns* would keep her in the bathroom a long time. I shouldn't have left it open to that page, tempting her. Now I would have to catch her up on the *Dallas* she would miss.

"Grandma, it's starting!" I screamed.

A couple of minutes later my dad came out of his bedroom in his worn pajamas and walked in front of the television to get to the kitchen. He did his usual nightly routine of taking specific vitamins to prevent a variety of diseases, and then washed them down with Ovaltine before he went to bed.

"Grandma, it already started!" I screamed as I watched a "Calgon, take me away!" commercial. I completed my thirty-first spoon slide, confident I would make it to fifty, when I felt his hand grasp and twist my ear as swiftly as he would a gum-ball machine. It was a common Indian disciplining tactic my dad saved for his most desperate moments. After twisting, he yanked my head down and back with his firm clutch, and said loud enough for only me to hear, "Who the hell do you think you are!"

My mouth involuntarily clenched shut, trapping my spoon. My head was pulled back far enough that the tiny mound of ice cream on my spoon slid down my throat. My bowl slipped out of my hand and the green milk dripped all over my legs. "I make the rules here," he said. "Do you understand?"

With those words it was clear to me that he was still angry about my skipping class and this was just unfinished business from our earlier argument. I couldn't see him. I could only feel his clutch. I was afraid the spoon would choke me if I opened my mouth. Even a slight nod might detach my ear. I remained the only way I could—silent and immobile.

Satisfied, he walked peacefully across the living room.

As soon as I heard his door slam shut, I ran upstairs, one hand grasping my ear and the other muffling my gasps. There was no physical pain. It was his disgust with me that bruised me. I sat in front of my unlockable bedroom door in a split, blocking intruders with my legs. One leg against the door and the other stabilized against the base of my bed. Anyone who forced the door open would have to crack both my legs.

I heard my grandmother scream from downstairs every few minutes, "Come, Nina! It is almost over. Quickly come!" Tired of screaming, she knocked on my door during a commercial break. "Nina, what are you doing?" She heard my gasps and began shouting, "Let me in at once!"

I released my split stance and let her in.

She opened the door and found me on the floor, panting. There were no tears of pain, just frightened inhalations.

"My God!" she said. "My God!" Without needing any explanation, she always had one solution. Immediately she began moving her lips in silent rhythms of prayer, which she said had vibrations powerful enough to wake God. She picked me up off the floor, holding me against her black and magenta *kaftan*, which smelled like a mix of mothballs and saffron. In the house, she always wore a *kaftan*, a bright-colored gown that was the equivalent of wearing a bed sheet with a hole cut out in the middle for one's head. After placing me on my bed, she reached onto my dresser and grabbed the eau de cologne bottle, which she insisted we use to heal any type of scar. She rubbed it on my forehead and arms to calm me, and for the first time this sandalwood oil concoction, which I thought smelled like worn banknotes, actually helped.

Lying next to my grandmother, I felt the same comfort I felt when she had looked up at me one day across the breakfast table and arbitrarily announced, "I'm proud of you." "For what?" I asked over and over, eager to know what exactly I had to do to hear her repeat it. "Just like that," she said. I wondered if I'd ever hear that from my father. After an hour of lying next to me, she tilted her head sideways to suggest that she would leave, but I clutched her arm, wanting the comfort to last as long as possible. She immediately lay back down and we both slept on my twin bed, her protective right arm outstretched across my body.

As we lay there together, I knew I had to escape from this house. The older I got, the more I understood why my mother would get so frantic after an argument with my dad. One event was almost theatrical. She had rounded up her four girls, rousing us out of bed in our pajamas, taken us into our bathroom, and asked, "Who will you go with — me or him?" But she already knew we would choose her. We too were ill at ease with my father's unpredictable, stern nature. "You, Mom," we all agreed in the bathroom. She then took us to him. "Tell him! Tell him who you chose!" But we all stood mute in front of him.

"We are leaving!" my mother screamed to him and my grandmother. As we left I whispered to my grandmother, "We'll be back," but my reassurance didn't make the sight of her at the top of the stairs like a forlorn prisoner any easier. We drove around the neighborhood as my mom cried while brainstorming, "How can I care for four of you on my secretary's salary? Farah and Nina, will you quit dance?" We kept driving until it became clear to her that even after all our sacrifices, she rationalized, we could never make it on our own. After McDonald's chicken nugget Happy Meals to cheer us up, we returned home.

Like my mother that day, I felt trapped. My dad's expectations of silent obedience would never work. I was determined to make my own rules. But he couldn't understand my need for independence. He'd listened to authority most of his life without regrets. I'd never heard him talk about all the things he'd wished for and how he didn't get them. It never crossed his mind.

Lying next to my grandmother, I thought of jobs I could get. I had learned from listening to my mom that if she had more money, she might have had more independence. Soon after, even though I was younger than the legal age, I got a job at the mall, and I relied on my parents less and less. Money bought me the ability to make more of my own choices. In high school when my parents said I couldn't join the dance team, I saved my own money and joined anyway. I purposely chose to work at a store in the mall that sold trendy clothes so that my friends would come by and visit often. Going to work was quite social, and this outweighed the monotony of folding clothes and ringing up customers. Even my dad was pleased that I got a job since he hoped it would teach me the value of money and discipline. Either he or my mom dropped me off and picked me up each night, even during the holidays when I wouldn't get off until after 11:00 P.M. On one late-night ride home, I was complaining that my company didn't give me time and a half for Christmas Eve, and my dad explained to me, "You have a good job. No need to make a fuss over something so small." He went on to share his attitude about his work experience: "When you are a foreigner, you take what you can get and hope that your kids have it much better."

I became fixated on the idea that money would not only allow me to live by my own rules but also, down the road, win the love of my father, who was still in awe of the American dream—wealth and prestige. Wall Street was the epitome of this dream. His expectations of us to become doctors or engineers were attainable goals for immigrants who worked hard, but Wall Street was a whole other level of success considered unattainable for people like us.

My grandmother always took her grandchildren's side, even though my father's threats were handed down to him from his parents. After my periodic blowups with my father, she never asked questions about why I was upset. Most things went unspoken.

Even so, the morning after my father's ear-twisting tirade in front of the television, for the first time in thirteen years, as punishment, my grandmother didn't make his daily porridge with a dollop of raspberry jam and Darjeeling tea.

CHAPTER 5

Gold Star

Nine months into our first year, Scott called me one afternoon in a desperate state. We hadn't seen each other in months. Both of us felt like we'd get along really well, but we hadn't had time to get to know each other. We'd gone out a few times in large corporate finance groups, but the last long conversation I remembered with him was at Au Bar during training. "Can I come to your floor and talk to you?" he asked. "It will just take a minute."

"Well, I am just in the middle—"

"Please," he begged.

"Okay," I said, even though I was slightly surprised. Since we hadn't talked for months, it was odd for him to need to speak so urgently.

I had developed a steely resolve, desperately working to turn my sensitivity to ambivalence. My family rarely called, and any friend I once had was now an acquaintance. The more I had to give up for work, the more frantically I clung to my job, which felt like the only thing I had left. I was so sleep-deprived that anytime I spent more than five minutes doing something non-work-related I panicked.

Within forty-five seconds Scott had come down six flights of stairs, and now he stood at my desk. "Hey!" he said, out of breath.

The more I felt controlled by this place, the more obsessed I became with controlling others. My eyes zeroed in on Scott's crooked tie. "Just a minute," I said, without looking up. After I was done with my e-mail, I looked at my online calendar. "Scott," I said, still not looking up, "I can't talk for longer than fifteen minutes." I had learned this habit from Steve: "When you have control, articulate your exit plan. Don't wait for others to dictate it." At first I found the tips he offered unsettling, but I started to realize that following them made it easier to survive this culture.

Michael walked over to my desk, massaging one hand against his chest in small circular motions. "Hey, Scott! How's it going, pal?" he said, putting his other arm on Scott's shoulder. They had gone to college together, but Michael hung out with his secret society buddies, while Scott was saving the environment. Neither cared for the other's passions.

"Nina," Michael said without waiting for Scott's answer, "did you see that I hooked us up with cookies again?"

"Yes, I ate three earlier," I said, aware that whatever he was about to say was for Scott's benefit since the cookies were brought in hours ago.

"The receptionist adores me," he explained to Scott. "I just have to say we need them here, and they're here."

"It's true," I said. "Every day Michael brings us cookies. He knows exactly when each meeting is going to end so that he gets them while they're still soft." It was impressive that he went up against VPs making several millions of dollars, who were also fiercely scavenging for the free leftovers.

"No," Michael corrected. "Now, Sandy calls me as soon as the meetings are over. That's how I got those almond brownies last week."

Too distressed to think about food, Scott continued to stare at me.

"Steve said you could show me how to do the debt paydown," Michael said to me.

"At 7:00 P.M. tonight I can help you, Michael," I said, feeling no obligation to rearrange my schedule to get him out of here by his normal 6:30 P.M. departure time.

"Great!" he said and then began calling friends to go to an early dinner.

I looked up at Scott and saw he was in bad shape. For the first time, Michael, even though his cheeks had fattened and begun to hide his cheekbones, looked far more appealing. Scott's nose hairs stuck out like overgrown weeds and his typically carefully styled hair was disheveled and oily. I looked back and forth between the two to confirm the results. It was clear. Scott's intense blue eyes were dull and muted. I wondered whether something had happened to his family.

"Do you have a moment? Is there a place we could talk alone?" Scott asked me timidly.

I noticed Michael staring at Scott's lips. The dried skin was peeling as if it were about to bleed. "You have something right here," I said as I pointed to my lip.

He wiped the back of his hand across his lips harshly.

As we walked around the floor looking for a conference room, I continued gawking at him sideways. His once smooth skin was now covered in tiny craters, like a golf ball.

"Here's one," he suggested.

"Windows," I said, pointing to windows that allowed people on the floor to see who was inside the room. This was common protocol for an analyst to note. You wouldn't want others to see you idle, because talk would get around that you needed more work or that you were a slacker. I looked at him again, trying to gauge the severity of his situation. He normally was more conscientious than me. "Let's go on the other side of the floor since conference room 32E doesn't have any windows."

"Oh, what a relief it is to see you. We haven't talked in ages," he said as we sat down in a cramped, sterile conference room that housed two sofas decorated with blue and gold stripes that looked more appropriate for Father's Day wrapping paper. "Oh, Nina, I don't know about you, but this is too much. I'm so miserable! I actually broke down crying the other night. I just want out of here. I haven't slept in weeks." He collapsed into his seat, slouching over, and spoke with animated hand gestures.

As he spoke, I vacillated between strong and weak. I had been operating in a fog for the last month, shutting off all feelings. I considered using his pause to tell him that I completely understood, but my defensive body, with one arm across my chest and the other hand covering my mouth, stopped me. Would I too fall apart if I let down my guard?

"Even when I do go home," he continued, shifting his eyes around the room quickly, "I'm too stressed to sleep. I've hardly even seen my roommates since we started working. And I have four of them!" he said, raising his hands and shaking them. "I even called a psychiatrist because I'm really starting to scare myself. I had to tell my associate. But this place sucks, because even though I told him, they don't always let me out to go to my appointments."

As he spoke, I anxiously began biting chunks of skin from around my fingernails. *Stop! That's how you get hangnails,*" I could hear my mom reprimanding. I had spent the last month convincing myself that all the feelings I had, like Scott's, were not real. Fearful he would take me down with him, I nodded my head, trying to hear but not feel his words. All of which I understood too intimately.

"I feel so trapped!" he screamed as tears welled up in his eyes. "They're putting me on antidepressants," he informed me. His hands were clasped in his lap with his right thumb, rhythmically etching circles on his left palm. "I can't wait! I won't make it otherwise. I even suggested leaving this place, but my associate keeps reminding me to be careful since it could ruin my career."

This was my moment to say something to make him feel better. I ran my index finger up and down the bridge of my nose, looking for strength. Listening to him gave me a sense of relief to know that I wasn't alone, but it also made me feel helpless. Weren't we both looking for the same answers? How could I help him?

"Nina," he said leaning forward with wide, bloodshot eyes. He reached out and grabbed the arm of my sofa. "I was interviewing a prospective analyst last week. She was so chirpy and eager. She said, 'I just can't wait to be in such a dynamic and challenging environment and work with so many brilliant people. What is it like? Are you just thoroughly stimulated every day?'" He stopped and let out a loud deep breath.

I couldn't help but think back to when I first heard those same words during interviews and corporate events: brilliant, ambitious, fast-paced, challenging—they set off a spark of intrigue. And I'd felt that thrill during my summers and even during my first few months in corporate finance. In the beginning, it felt great to pull an all-nighter and then hand off perfect presentations to Steve to share with our clients the next morning.

But now the fast pace seemed never ending and the thrill had long faded. I didn't know how much longer I could keep up my reserve.

"Of course," Scott went on, "I said yes to everything and I told her how brilliant it all was, but what scared me is that I believed my lies. I almost convinced myself!" He put his hands over his face and rocked back and forth as he stared at the ground.

As he spoke my suppressed feelings began rushing through me like waves. My heart knocked at my chest as if it were determined to escape. I got up and walked to the door, wanting to run out, but sat back down. Instead I pressed my crossed arms over my chest as if that would slow down the pumping mass. But Scott was too engrossed in his thoughts to even notice.

"But what I didn't tell the recruit is that the night before I was here until four in the morning fucking page-checking 522 pages!" he said as tears started to cloud his eyes. "552 pages of looking for typos! Page by page," he said. "Looking for typos and graphics errors. What a fucking joke! That is my challenge—to find where EBITDA may be written EBIT or where a bar may be in the wrong column!"

I sat in front of him looking just past his head, staring at the blank white wall, and saw that his nose was starting to run and drip onto his chapped lips. Eager for a distraction, I looked around for a box of Kleenex but only saw a stack of leftover Haru Sushi paper napkins.

"On top of that," Scott went on, "my family keeps telling me how proud they are of me, and I can't seem to tell them that I'm about to go on antidepressants just so I can make it through the day. How is it that everyone is so impressed with this job?" he asked. "All my friends are so envious that I have the Yale economics dream job."

Scott's frame shook as I wordlessly handed him the napkin. I remembered during training our colleague Bryan had this utterly calm demeanor. "Even when I thought my internship at Merrill was miserable, I just pushed through," I remembered Bryan saying to Scott. How could I help Scott if I got just as emotional, too? *Pull yourself together!* Bryan had a rational reason for everything. He was so grounded and, unlike me, his confidence was no façade. *Be Bryan,* I kept repeating in my head. It was a game I played with myself in high school when I worked as a checker at our local grocery store. The repetitive, mundane work made it hard for me to smile and be friendly with each new person, like Missy, the cheerful checker in front of me who had no trouble with the constant stream of unpredictable customers. The "be Missy" game made it much easier to create the big smile even though I didn't feel like carrying on with frivolous "how are you today?" conversations.

"Scott," I offered in a calm voice that couldn't mask my shaking hands. I repeated everything I thought Bryan would say. "You are just letting them control you. They want you to get to this point. They're waiting for you to quit so they can look at you and say they knew you would never make it." He bit his bottom lip as he listened. "Keep pushing through." I repeated and repeated this mantra.

After the relief of sharing, self-consciousness set in and Scott stood for a second to straighten his pants, as if this would help him regain control. He plopped back down in his chair harshly. "I heard your roommate was having a tough time recently. Didn't she work for fifty-six hours straight? I forget what group she's in."

"It's been pretty bad the last two weeks. She woke up crying a couple of mornings," I said. I shivered faintly, thinking of the second morning, when I didn't stop to reassure her. Instead,

I walked past her room, terrified that if I tried to pacify her, I wouldn't be able to go into work myself.

"I heard you work a lot too," he said.

"Most of the time," I said. "Corporate finance is a lot different from the groups I interned in. My group now makes capital markets look like a tea party. It's more of a hazing culture here. I think if I knew I could go home at night and still have time for family and friends, it would be easier to remind myself that this is just a job, but somewhere along the way it has taken over my life." I cupped my hands together and I could feel myself slowly becoming less anxious and more relaxed.

Scott kept staring at me. I couldn't tell if he was thinking about something else, so I continued, hoping that what I said might help. "Two nights ago, I had a convertible model to create. I had no clue where to start. Everyone else was home." I could feel myself wanting to vent, but then realized my story was not unlike other analysts' tales. "You know how it goes."

"Well, aren't you jealous of that?" he asked, lighting up. "Don't you wish you could be like Michael?" Scott asked. "I mean, doesn't he have it figured out?"

"What do you mean?" I asked, raising my eyebrows so high that thick ridges covered my forehead. "Michael is going to regret it when review time comes. Plus, my deal experience is vast compared to other analysts, and it's going to show on my résumé. Every time an important deal comes in, they call me in to work on it. I get first dibs." As I spoke, I realized how all these things that sounded great were part of what was digging me deeper into a hole. I'd reached that point where I'd proven both to my officers and myself that I could handle this job. My label of public school kid from Texas was long gone. "Anyway, seems like some officers don't really care for Michael. And Luis keeps a low profile, so even though he may be working a decent amount, I don't think he's covering that many deals."

"Forget Luis!" Scott announced loudly. "He cares what they think. He's no better than most other analysts here." Scott began gently kicking the underneath of the dark wood coffee-table top. "You do realize your group has very unusual dynamics—most of the groups have two or three analysts working around the clock. That's what makes Michael such a rarity. He doesn't care what they think of him, and he's having a great time. He's the only analyst in our class that isn't a billionaire's kid who is blowing this place off. After we leave Morgan Stanley, we'll all be in the same place."

"No way!" I almost shouted, fearful that it might be true. "You can't get into the best business schools or great companies if you don't really work hard here."

"All you need, once you leave here, is one person," Scott said, holding up his index finger. "One person," he repeated. "One person to be a reference for any job. One person to write you a strong recommendation for any business school you choose. One Morgan Stanley person as a reference and your career is golden."

"I don't think you get it, Scott," I said. "He only gets away with blowing them off because he's so connected, mostly to people more powerful than our officers. One of my associates told me that some officers have requested to *not* work with Michael."

"Think about it, Nina," Scott went on. "He only needs one officer in your group to like him. He's not going to have a problem between all his secret society pals and the officers he buddies up with. It doesn't matter whether he does a good job." He looked toward the door, and I could tell he was debating whether to share something. "I don't know if you know this, but Michael went in and had a long conversation with Larry. Isn't he one of the highest officers in your group?" Scott asked.

"Yes," I said. "So? Maybe they're working on a deal together."

Scott looked away as he went on. "I heard he was telling Larry about how two women approached him to have sex at the hotel next door to Le Bar Bat after the corporate finance division's dinner."

"So what?" I said, clenching the arm of my chair as I thought about how I arrived late to the party since Larry insisted that I was the only one he trusted to finish a sales force presentation for the next day. Larry's round, hairy belly hanging out of his tight T-shirt one weekend when he thought no one else would be around flashed through my head. He was one of the few overweight officers. I was sure he hadn't joined the firm in such shape, since I hadn't seen overweight people make it past the first round of interviews. I assumed it was an unspoken "good fit" criterion.

"So!" Scott said looking at me as if I were dense. "Now Larry loves Michael! He and Michael are in there shooting the shit pretty often, if you haven't noticed. I know because Larry hangs out on my floor with my VP, and even though they close the door, they get excited and start to talk really loud. I'm pretty sure Michael goes drinking with them—they're probably all buddies. Don't think for a second that Larry won't hook Michael up with whatever he wants after he leaves."

"Look," I said, realizing we were getting worked up about something hypothetical. "Maybe Michael has got it all figured out. I don't know. We can debate about it all we want and get nowhere. But what's important is that the rest of us, who aren't Michael or a celebrity, don't have the option to just blow officers off or we wouldn't last long here."

"Maybe that's it," he said in a defeated tone. "There's something about feeling like we have so few options here that is killing me." Scott's eyes focused on me while my eyes involuntarily closed, taking a luxuriously long blink. "At this point the costs have outweighed the benefits for me."

"I can understand that," I said, nodding. "It's funny... when I first started working in banking, I just assumed that people pulling in millions of dollars had to be brilliant. But now I feel like I'm working with a bunch of people just trying to prove something, which isn't nearly as glamorous."

We both sat in silence. I could smell the lemony air freshener that they sprayed every day.

"I don't care about being good anymore; I just want to survive," Scott said, leaning back calmly and crossing his arms.

My cupped hands cradled my cheeks. "You know, we have a lot in common—this awareness of things," I said, starting to kick my foot against the coffee table. I looked down at the ground, not confident in the advice I was about to give. "The only way I've been able to deal with it is to stop feeling."

Scott looked my way and then down at the ground, joining me in kicking the table. We both sat in silence, deeply distracted by our thoughts as our feet tapped a rhythmic melody.

There was something about this professional circle we hung out in that could rationalize anything. Since I didn't have much of a university network in New York, my only nonbanker friends were my coworkers' college friends, who were mostly bankers, lawyers, and consultants. They also worked odd hours and would tolerate our flaky way of rarely planning anything until twenty minutes prior and then canceling four minutes before. I'd been out with one of Bryan's college classmates, who was at McKinsey and was having trouble with her boyfriend since she was only in town about seven days a month. "But you know," she said to Bryan and me matter-of-factly, "my frequent-flyer status has skyrocketed, and if I get platinum, it stays with me for life."

I had learned that rationalizations could strangle unwanted emotions, at least temporarily. When I was down, I would remind myself how lucky I was to be there: After talking to Scott, I went online and read all the impressive Morgan Stanley profiles that got me there in the first place:

"Once inside Morgan Stanley's numerous but well-guarded portals of entry, employees feel as if they are among the chosen few—those good enough to make it into the club. The firm breeds incredible people... Lots of other Wall Street firms lay claim to overused, overblown adjectives such as *bulge-bracket*, *premier*, and *global*. Morgan Stanley is all of these. Clients choose MS for its prestige, muscle, and ability to deliver."

We are the chosen few, I would remind myself. I spent my years before college acting up and looking for attention, and now here I was: I had a place where I could shine and be the best. Suddenly, I was being recognized for an accomplishment rather than singled out for being disruptive. My grandmother never had such an opportunity. I opened my desk drawer where I kept her sticky note that was stuck to my folder my first day at JP Morgan:

FAST, EASY, HEALTHY.
FAGOR PRESSURE COOKERS THE SINGLE MOST IMPORTANT PIECE OF COOKWARE YOU'LL EVER OWN.

FOR A STORE NEAREST YOU CALL 1-800-207-0806.

BEST POT EVER!

Every time I read her note, I imagined her in the building. The image of her pashmina covering her hunched-over posture and her white waves of hair seemed out of place in this sleek glass tower. She'd think I was particularly important since I had to use my ID at least twice to get to my desk. She would want to sit in my chair to see if it was comfortable, and she'd raise her eyebrows while shaking her head in a sideways back-and-forth motion, giving her approval of the cushiony seat and never noticing it was inferior to all the officers'. But she'd be most impressed by the unfamiliar supplies on my desk that she'd feel compelled to touch: the three-hole punch, the fax machine, and the HP-12C calculator with my name etched on it.

Before we were eighteen years old, my parents and my grandparents in India had jointly saved enough money to send my sisters and me to India. My father would methodically save, missing his brother's wedding and not visiting his family for fifteen years, until he could send all his children. My first trip to India was when I was nine. It felt foreign and startling. I was shocked to see toilets that were holes in the ground. The sight of them made my urge to pee instantly disappear. I found it impossible to imagine my parents, who were now accustomed to their two-story, carpeted house and spacious cars, at home in India. I was a stranger in the country I told people in the United States I was from. Some of my Parsi friends would say, "My parents are from India," when Americans asked where they were from, but it sounded like they were unnecessarily distancing themselves from what Americans would consider them anyway: Indian.

In India one of my uncles once leaned over and said to his wife in Gujarati about Farah and me, "These kids are as American as apple pie." He smiled at us when he said it, incorrectly assuming we couldn't understand. "There is nothing Indian about them," he continued as he looked at us in fascination as if we were Disney characters. My biggest surprise was the unmistakable, unconditional love that the numerous unknown relatives felt for us. Instead of closets, many of them had armoires that they called cupboards, which looked like huge lockers. When Piroj Aunty opened her cupboard door I saw a row of pictures on the inside of the door. Wallet-size pictures of my sisters and me since kindergarten were posted, with the dates and names written on the back in my mother's neatest cursive. I saw pictures of Shireen without teeth, something I'd never seen before.

"How did you get those?" I asked, covering my mouth in shock while adjusting my paisley Indian scarf that kept slipping. Our aunts spoiled us with clothes, dressing us like twin dolls with matching *salwar kameez* outfits and taking pictures as all our aunties in bright flowered frocks squealed, "How sweet they look!" One aunty even introduced us to pumice stones, which she rubbed in circles on our forearms to remove our hair until our arms were "nice and clean."

Piroj Aunty smiled, forgetting the pictures were even there, and she put her soft hand against my cheek. "Since you were born your mother sends every wonderful thing about you girls. Rupy and Putli Aunty all have your pictures too. Look what else she sends us," she said, opening an accordion folder.

"This is a Halloween poem when you got an A plus."

"That's from first grade," I said, holding it with protective hands. "I don't even remember writing it."

"This is your award for perfect attendance." My mom had even made a color copy so the document would retain its official feel, the large gold burst with blue ribbons under it that made it look more impressive.

Piroj Aunty handed me a plastic sandwich bag that protected a picture of Farah and me holding a dance trophy.

"Why would she send you these?" I asked, confused.

She laughed, amused by my shock. "All Parsis are successful," she informed me. "You girls will be extra successful in the States." Parsis were known as the Jews of India, living in small, tight communities that actively helped members prosper.

"What if you aren't a successful Parsi?" I asked fearfully, thinking of the B that I might get in English. "Do you get kicked out?"

She laughed, straightening her pink-and-white polka-dot nightgown. Cradling both my cheeks in her warm hands, she said, "You will be successful. Your parents have given up their lives here to make a wonderful life for you."

I had a whole community rooting for me. It weighed on me like both a compliment and burden. More and more I saw that my father's life wasn't about him; it was about the choices he made for his family. Graduating at the top of my class in college was checking a box in my family. It was working on Wall Street that, for the first time, got me something I craved most: a gold star from my father.

*

At 7:23 P.M., Michael returned to the office after enjoying *moules marinières* and rabbit *au* Riesling along with a bottle of Château de Sales. He and a few college buddies had gone to Artisanal. Immediately after arriving, he sat down and unpaused a video game.

I was just checking through the paydown Excel spreadsheet that would do all the work to calculate future financial projections on Michael's project. Steve had helped me build this work of art. I didn't have the energy to explain to Michael how to create it from scratch. The worksheet I made months ago would attach to his income statement easily. I went over to his desk and waited impatiently behind him.

"Just one second," Michael said, as he frantically pressed the arrow keys. "Dude," he screamed as his 3D Tetris score went up. "Ninety thousand!" he shouted and threw his arms up in a heroic V. "Look, I'm freestyling," he said dancing in his seat.

"Michael," I said deflated and not amused, "I've still got prepaids to finish tonight."

"All right. All right," he said, as disappointed as a three-year-old denied Jelly Bellies. "You should go out with us sometime. Chris had the most *divine* pig cheeks sauce *gribiche*. The best I've ever had!" He got up so I could sit in his chair as he stood behind me.

For a moment, I wondered if he had really said "pig cheeks," but I didn't want to think about it. "Can we move some of this stuff?" I said, pushing away the items on his desk near the mouse. "What is this, anyway?" I asked, surrounded by all these unnecessary gadgets.

"This is a business card holder. Look, I got my name engraved on it. And I differentiated my business card," he said, showing me the extra logo he'd printed on the back.

"I also got these hanging desk accessories," he said. "It's a cherry finish."

"Ohhhh," I said excitedly, more interested in the packet of strawberry Bubblicious gum near his stapler. "I haven't had fat pieces of bubble gum in so long."

"Take whatever you want. I also have sour apple and cotton candy," he said, opening his desk drawer and showcasing his neat stash of gum, along with pumpkin granola bars, chocolate-covered pretzels, Cool Ranch Doritos, and Teddy Grahams.

"Thanks," I said, taking a piece of strawberry and a piece of cotton candy. Even though we'd correct her, my grandmother would still say, "I'll have a gum." Maybe it was for the same translation reason she'd say, "Where's the scissor?" I carefully put the gum in my pocket, excited over the small pleasure of having a treat for later. I looked on Michael's computer screen for the file. "Is it this one?" I asked sarcastically, pointing to a file that said, "Eat shit."

"No, that's a file that Ken asked me to open and print," Michael said, laughing uncontrollably. "Open it!"

Out of curiosity, I had to. I clicked on the file, which opened up to cover the whole screen and was only a foot away from my face. I saw a profile of a woman's head leaning back to welcome a man's hairy anus, which squeezed out a hearty piece of shit that was just ripe enough to fall into her mouth. The image was so close up that I could smell it. I closed it and tried to hold back the involuntary gag I felt building. *Should I say that's disgusting? But isn't that exactly what they're expecting me to do so they can keep leaving me out and distancing me as "mixed company"?*

"Great," I said, donning an "I'm calm" expression. "That

would be quite a thirty-six by twenty-five," I added in a cold, sarcastic tone.

"You are so awesome!" Michael said, grabbing my neck to squeeze my shoulders. "You are totally one of the guys."

"Clearly that's not the right file. So where is the paydown file?" I asked, trying to keep my hands moving.

"Look, Michael, these are the debt paydowns," I said, pointing to the tiny rows of cells in the Excel spreadsheet. I looked at him to gauge how much I needed to explain. "I'm linking the worksheet to your interest expense lines." I had created my four hundred cells of numbers so that the spreadsheet would attach to his file as easily as I had affixed my grandmother's diamonds to her ears for a fancy function. Within seconds, the entire worksheet calculated the next five years of projections in four different interest rate scenarios. I was done.

I started to explain to him the if-then logic of the formulas in each cell, but when I looked over to see if he understood, he was busy fondling his business cards. "Do you get the basic idea?" I asked prematurely, since he didn't look like he was listening. I let out a deep breath as I wondered if I could slack off just a little bit more without tarnishing my reputation.

"Definitely," he said. "It's just a paydown," he said, shrugging his shoulders and repeating the title that I'd written at the top of the worksheet.

"Right," I said as I stood up. "After you walk through it let me know what questions you have." Though the image on Ken's screen never left me, the gag that I had carefully controlled let loose as soon as I walked into the bathroom. I washed my face with the generic pink liquid soap, rigorously scouring my lips in circular motions, the way my grandmother taught me to wash after eating so that ants don't bite your lips at night. After three minutes I walked out. Michael was already gone.

Only a few hours earlier I'd been told to finish six more prepaids. I opened my file that we were given during training with all the menus of the restaurants in the area. I picked up the phone to order *sag paneer* and *dhunsak* from Jewel of India, and then changed my mind and ordered sushi instead. My e-mail inbox was full, so I glanced through it to so see if there was anything urgent. My family rarely e-mailed my work account, so it was odd to see an e-mail from my dad. Ever since I started working full-time, even though he didn't really have hobbies, he made finance his new pursuit—he watched *Nightly Business Report* and diligently read every *Investor's Business Daily*, *Fortune*, and *Forbes*. The risk-averse man even tried trading derivatives. He was living the Wall Street life alongside me.

> Read this article I've attached on Howard—cover page of *Forbes*. He's a master. Also, call me because I have another derivative question, and I need my financial expert's opinion.

My dad wasn't even taking this much interest in his daughter who had become an engineer. Once a month when I'd get an e-mail like this from him, it gave me a thrill to be reminded that he was finally interested in me. This one helped me forget most of the craziness of the day.

While waiting for my dinner to arrive, I could take a quick break with Daniel, who sat on the other side of my floor. He worked more than I did. He only had one other colleague to compete with for the star analyst title: Jason. The third analyst in his group was the son of one of Morgan Stanley's largest clients and hardly needed this job. Every officer was dying to take him out to lunch *and* dinner. Unlike the members of my team, Daniel and Jason were both incredibly competitive. Each would use tactics to try to bring down the other.

"Hey," I said, standing over Daniel's desk and staring at his Pop-Tarts and Twix wrappers. "Break?"

"Sure." he replied. "I'll meet you in 32G in a minute."

Daniel and I hadn't spent much time together in analyst training, but since we sat on the same floor, we hung out more than we would have otherwise. Just as New Yorkers put a mental divide between the East Side and the West Side, we tended to draw barriers between floors. Unless it was for a specific work task, having to go to another floor was often accompanied by a sigh of annoyance that someone was asking you to go out of your way. A year would pass by before I'd even see some of my colleagues from training who sat only a floor below me.

Two months earlier, late on a Friday night after having to cancel plans with friends, Daniel and I had started this exercise of playfully punching each other, which took the edge off our daily frustrations. I was stuck waiting for a fax from a client that I had to have couriered to Greenwich, so my VP could review it, and Daniel was waiting for his associate to send him feedback on a presentation. That was the same night Daniel confided in me that his real name was Hansel because his parents knew the Hansel and Gretel story and thought that it was a popular American name.

"When did they get brown sugar cinnamon with frosting?" I asked, touching his Pop-Tart wrapper to see if there was any left. "That vending machine only had blueberry without frosting forever." Even though we all ate junk food—we often didn't get a chance to make it downstairs to the cafeteria before it closed at 2:00 P.M.—I was surprised to see Daniel eating Pop-Tarts. Just before coming to Morgan Stanley he had tried out for the Olympics but hadn't made it. He knew if he took this job as a banker he would essentially be foregoing his dream of diving in the Olympics. After his first tryout failure, his parents, both Korean immigrants, insisted he do something more stable than diving. Just as Morgan Stanley expected, he put all his competitive energy into being the best analyst, but this made him very bitter.

"D4 switched to brown sugar a few days ago. I love the frosted ones, too." He looked up and leaned closer to share this secret with me. "When I have time, I peel off the frosting and eat it first." He peered at me with intense pleasure through his thick, black-rimmed glasses, reminding me how surprised I was to find out that he was a diver when we first met. Daniel graduated from Stanford on a full scholarship. When I heard we had a U.S. chess champion in our class, as soon as I set eyes on Daniel, I mistakenly thought it was him. Daniel revealed his secret in an awkward way that reminded me I worked with many who were academic overachievers but still craved to hang out with the popular kids. The banking experience was one of the first times they were able to win over women and everyone else they otherwise weren't able to get attention from before. For me, it was a relief to not have the added burden of needing to prove myself socially. That's what I did in high school.

Daniel picked up his phone. "Ross, I'm so sorry, man, but I'm not going to make it tonight. I hate to keep canceling but that's how things are here." He went on, "No problem. Give me a call next month." He hung up and with a smile said, "Ross is this college friend who's such a tool. I'm going to miss the beauty of using this job as an excuse to ignore folks whenever I feel like it."

I began walking off and he called me back. "Hey," he said. "Did you hear that Scott was crying?"

"Yeah," I said. "He told me."

Daniel opened his mouth and started twisting his fists over his eyes, like a crying child. He then slapped his fists on his keyboard and started laughing uncontrollably.

"Don't be an asshole," I said, shaking my head. He started to laugh even harder as his competitive counterpart, Jason, walked by. "Laugh now, because one day it'll be you," I said as I walked off.

Daniel was just one of many colleagues who would permanently label Scott as weak. When I first joined the group, one of my associates told me, "We had a girl on this team before. I remember seeing her crying once." *She worked with you for two years and that's all you can remember?* Their views of women were so limited that it made me even more determined to prove them wrong. They'd have to rip off my arm to make me cry within these walls.

The day was so busy that it was hard to even remember that earlier in the afternoon Scott and I had talked. It felt like a week ago. I dialed extension 4432.

"Hey," I said. "It's Nina. How are you?"

"Fine. Fine," he said in a controlled voice. I could hear him punching his keys in a rhythm that sounded like he was changing a bar chart, maybe a league table. "Thanks for listening this afternoon. I'm so glad I stopped by. No surprise, but I'm already working on something new, so I may be here late." He laughed and said sarcastically, "We get to keep pushing through. Isn't this fun?"

As I waited for Daniel in the conference room, I closed my eyes and imagined putting two dabs of my grandmother's eau de cologne on Scott's temples.

He was temporarily back to normal. In this environment, we learned to move through emotions so quickly. There didn't seem to be much time to be upset, because there was too much work to get done. Forgetting was also a skill most of us seemed to master. A year from now, Scott and I would find out that the majority of our colleagues had gone through this same kind of meltdown around the same time, but most kept it to themselves so that they wouldn't get labeled "weak."

Daniel entered and hit me lightly on my shoulder. "Wake up!" he said with his obnoxious laugh that would make me wonder what woman would ever be interested in him. He took off his glasses and rubbed his eyes with two fists like a tired baby. It had become a routine before he would punch me in the arm. Growing up close to Houston, I was more familiar with Asians from China and Vietnam. It was in investment banking that I met so many Koreans, including Daniel, who introduced me to one of my favorite foods, *bulgogi*. Out of the minorities in banking, the largest group was Asians: among them, Koreans were high in numbers. Because I enjoyed learning about new cultures, it became a game for me when I met an Asian to try to determine where they were from before I heard their last name. Daniel had a very distinct square jaw that I'd only seen on Koreans; Yuji, a Japanese analyst on the trading floor, had a much narrower face.

I punched Daniel back harder. As usual, we didn't say much, just passed punches and let out groans at the really good, hard ones. On an exceptional one we would laugh uncontrollably. There was an understanding—the punches were limited to the shoulders. We always knew what to expect. But this afternoon, Daniel broke our trust.

"How's your group?" I asked.

"We've had two client meetings recently and it's been crazy."

"I know how that is. Where were you the last couple of days?" I asked as I put my hand up, signaling him to stop as I took a sip of water.

"We had some clients here, so we were out a lot. We did so many things I've never done before," he said with his giggle, which I assumed had something to do with strip clubs.

"Ouch," he said. "That one's a bruiser."

I could see from the look on his face that he was distracted. "You wouldn't believe what our client asked me. Stupid fucker," he said, shaking his head and punching me harder.

"Hey," I shouted. "Not so hard." I assumed divers had shapely bodies, but it was hard to tell with his small frame. The top of his head reached my nose. The rumor was that investment banks had a higher number of short guys hoping to overcome their Napoleon complexes. It was only from Daniel's harsher punches that I could tell he had solid muscles.

"What did he ask?" I said as we continued to exchange lighter punches.

He was lost in his own thoughts recollecting the incident. "My stupid vice president didn't even have the balls to say anything. Instead, he looked at me with these pathetic eyes as if I was supposed to come up with an answer."

"What did he ask?" I repeated, annoyed at his carrying on without context.

"He asked if Asian women had slits 'down there' like their eyes." Right after he said it, I could see his face space into another zone, and he put all his energy into a solid punch right in my stomach. I howled and folded in half, grabbing my gut.

"Sorry, dude," he said shaking his head and giggling

uncontrollably. "I just had a bad fucking week!"

"You idiot!" I shouted once I caught my breath. "What the hell is wrong with you?" Sitting down on a chair, I held my stomach and watched him in disdain as he continued to say sorry over and over with his delirious giggle. "If you're so sorry, you shouldn't have done it."

While formatting a spreadsheet at my desk, periodically I'd massage my sore ribs. There wouldn't be time to go to the doctor, I reminded myself. Daniel had already stopped by a couple of times to make peace, but I just ignored him. He knew our shoulder-punching breaks were now over for good.

"Morgan Stanley," I said, picking up my phone.

"Godiwalla!" Bryan said with great excitement. "You're still here. What are you doing?" I could tell it was Bryan from his distinct voice, but I was surprised to hear from him since we had only met a few times for lunch since training.

"Why are you calling from the lobby extension? I thought you were my sushi."

"Forget about your sushi. We're all leaving for a dance performance—something like Allen Alley. They'll have a VIP reception with food and drinks. I'm sure you'll get to meet the dancers."

"Alvin Ailey!" I shrieked. "That's the most amazing dance company." I had only seen them once in college, when I volunteered as an usher at Bass Concert Hall so I could see all the dance performances for free.

"During training you said you loved dance. You're probably the only one here who does, so it wasn't hard to remember. We're in the lobby and leaving in five minutes. Come down.

We're already late."

"I can't," I said, feeling my frustration build. "I'm supposed to get these prepaids done for Steve by tomorrow."

"Is it a live deal?" he asked.

"No, just a pitch."

"Perfect, then come downstairs," he said. "My VP, Bradley, will call Steve for you. He's trying to win a client who is sponsoring the event. We need bodies in the seats." He paused, understanding that wouldn't be enough to satisfy my fear of not getting the work done. "Our VPs are tight, so I promise he'll override Steve on this one. He'll call Steve on the drive over. Come downstairs now. You have nothing to worry about!"

At 8:24 P.M. I stood at the elevators, ready to leave. I kicked the wall excitedly as I glanced at the familiar posted signs, which I read for the first time:

WE ARE BUILDING A CULTURE OF EXCELLENCE.

IT EXTENDS FROM THE WAY WE THINK TO THE WAY WE BEHAVE, TO THE WAY WE OPERATE, TO THE WAY WE DEVELOP PROFESSIONALS AND MEASURE PERFORMANCE.

OUR CULTURE OF EXCELLENCE INFORMS OUR ACHIEVEMENTS AND THE ACHIEVEMENTS OF THOSE WE SERVE.

That's so vague: A "culture of excellence." Is that deliberate? It was all written in an unrecognizable sixteen-point type. "Idiots," I mumbled as I shook my head. We weren't even supposed to use a sixteen-point font. Over the last few months, I'd watched myself begin to criticize people more often and somehow hope that it would make me feel better.

When the elevator door opened, two guys stood in front of me. By their stacks of papers and their Chinatown imposter suits, I knew they were from the copy center. On our way down, the elevator stopped on the twenty-fifth floor, where the back-office staff worked. While the door was opening, I repeatedly hit the door-close button since I didn't see anyone right in front of the elevator door. Even though I hit it frantically, fearful Bryan's team would leave without me, the door still remained open. I shouted from the door, "Did anyone call the elevator?" I again banged the button and announced, "This elevator better not be stuck!" Just as I reached for the red emergency button, the mirrored doors began to close.

One of the copy center guys in the elevator nudged the other one, and they began snickering at my frantic one-woman show.

"I can see you in the mirrors," I said, squinting my eyes in annoyance. Fearful that I would complain to someone about them, they both stared at their shoes for the rest of the ten-second ride. Even though I held my head up high like an officer would, keeping my eyes fixed on the bright blue display that showed which floor we passed, I felt ashamed, disgusted by the sick sense of satisfaction I got from having control over someone in this building.

I handed the sushi guy thirty dollars for my food and immediately gave it to the Morgan Stanley car dispatcher.

"It's sushi," I said. "I didn't have time to eat it. There's eel avocado, yellowtail, and spicy salmon." I saw his face shriveling like a prune as I spoke. "You can eat it or throw it away." My grandmother would be disgusted at how wasteful I had become. She had several plastic spatulas on hand to get every last drop of curry out of the pot. In college, less than a year ago, thirty dollars was my monthly budget for social activities. If I shared an entrée or only ordered an appetizer, I could spread it out over three dinners and one night at a bar, ordering a twelve-ounce locally brewed Shiner Bock.

"I can't believe you all really eat that raw fish stuff," the car dispatcher said. "Nobody I know can stomach that crap," he said with a heavy New York accent that I rarely heard inside this building as he dumped it in the trash.

When we arrived at the theater, we were greeted by an usher assigned solely to us, who escorted us to a large section with RESERVED written in gold. Bradley's and his wife's names were written prominently in the program. Since he was playing with his Palm Pilot most of the time, I assumed he knew little about dance or had little interest. I knew funding it served the dual purpose of impressing his potential client and following his accountant's advice of sheltering his millions through donations.

The ten of us sat like outcasts in a large section of thirty or more empty seats. Several analysts slept through the performance, only waking for the quivering of a beeper. During the dance "Revelations," Bryan's officer took a break from snoozing to lean over to educate Bryan and me: "It is so important to support the arts." Since he wasn't my officer, I didn't feel the need to be as attentive. But when I didn't take my eyes off the dancing to listen to him, he tapped my knee. I glared at him as he spoke, hoping he could see my annoyance even though it was dark. He went on: "Modern dance has a specific nonformulaic art to it that is hard to find in other classical types. Alvin Ailey plays a social role, bringing to life the African-American heritage."

I nodded my head and made sure I didn't flip to page twelve of our playbill since I was quite confident that he had paraphrased the director's thoughts from that page. During intermission, I went to the ladies' room and confirmed my suspicion. I was relieved, because otherwise I wouldn't have known how to make sense of him being such good friends with my VP, who had once leaned over and whispered to me in the middle of a Broadway play, "Not everyone can get paid for brainless horseplay."

Bryan's VP used intermission to find his potential client and mingle, and when we returned he waited until the show started to begin his commentary. "I take real pleasure in supporting these nonprofit events. That's the beauty of being who we are. It is an honor," he said, holding a fist toward his heart as if this were rehearsed. "Last year I gave a full-year scholarship to a college student, and when I met him at the reception he just said thank you. Nothing else. This boy had no sense of gratitude." He paused and I promised myself that if he spoke again I wouldn't look away from the performance. Even if he touched my knee. I had already decided I'd say, "I really want to see this," and then I'd put up a finger, letting him know he could wait. I didn't look at him as he continued to educate us. "You get what you deserve in life. Luck is for those who need to make up an excuse for their failures. Be careful what you feel entitled to," he warned us. I was glad I wasn't looking at him because I couldn't hide my annoyance. I glanced at Bryan, who looked at me with a small smile and elbowed me, which I knew meant, *Don't let him get to you.*

The first half of the show was interrupted by commentary from an analyst behind us, who kept saying, "They're so naked!

This is soft-core porn," whenever a chiseled guy came on stage with his shirt off. Soon after intermission most were dozing, including Bryan. It was a relief to finally watch the performance without distractions. In this rare reflective moment the honesty of the dancers' moves put me in a peaceful trance. My hand covered my face, blocking anyone from seeing the tears that welled.

When I got home, even though it was already midnight in Texas, I called Farah.

"Is everything okay?" she asked.

"Just calling to say hello," I said as if it were normal.

"That's unlike you."

"I got out earlier tonight and we went to see Alvin Ailey," I said abruptly, not wanting to be reminded of what a poor family member I had been.

"Wow! I didn't take your colleagues as dance buffs. Did you like it?"

"Loved it! Are you still dancing?" I asked.

"I've almost finished my minor in dance so I can teach after work. Thought it would be a good balance with engineering."

"That's great," I replied, impressed with her determination to finish her minor, even if it meant staying in college longer. "Since you may be the only family member I speak to for the next month, give me a two-second update on everyone."

"Mom and Dad still spend every weekend driving over an hour to go to some Parsi function and then come back and talk about whether the food was good or bad."

"Sounds like nothing is new," I said.

"Lena had a scare that she may have to have some shoulder

surgery, but you missed the whole thing. Now she's fine, but you should call her."

"Yikes, I will call her," I said as I wrote her name on the palm of my hand.

"Grandma is lonely with none of us in the house. She still tapes *As the World Turns* and *Guiding Light* for Dad. Now they watch it together when he gets home from work. I can imagine all the new things he'll have to say about dating Americans. 'Not only will it lead to cheating and divorce, but American husbands may try to exchange your child with someone else's or even kidnap it,'" she said, laughing.

"What about Shireen?"

"Morocco's still hard for her since the culture is so different, and the Peace Corps is much more bureaucratic than she thought. It's funny because she did the program thinking it would look great for medical school, but she's having a change of heart and is considering public health at Johns Hopkins instead. She thinks she can have a bigger impact on people's lives that way. It goes unsaid, but don't tell Mom and Dad until she's sure."

"It can't be easy in an isolated village without a phone," I said. "The last time I spoke to her, we had so little to talk about. I told her about what I did that night, and she almost hung up on me. She said that the amount of money we wasted in one night could have fed her whole village for six months." I shrugged my shoulders. "Sad but true."

"It's hard to talk to her," Farah agreed. "She's going through this phase where all she talks about is how obnoxious and wasteful Americans are, i.e., us."

"What have you been up to?" I asked.

"I'm going to a lot of high school friends' weddings. I don't get it. So many of them have never even left the Houston sub-urbs, not even for college, and they're getting married and stay-ing in the burbs."

"Soon they'll be popping out four kids. Who's the guy you're dating?"

"This guy I met co-oping at DuPont. It's pretty casual," she said unenthusiastically. "You would laugh so hard. We got into an argument because he came over with Chick-fil-A nuggets and started eating them at my place without even offering me any."

"Ohhh. I hate it when people do that."

"I totally lost it. I was so angry," she said.

"That guy I dated from Jester dorm used to do that too," I said. "There are a lot of people who don't think it's rude. I'm pretty sure it's only because Grandma has ingrained in us that food is love. Remember when we'd start to eat something and if we didn't offer everyone, she'd immediately say, 'Give us half,' as punish-ment. She used to always get me with the last fruit roll-up."

"She's still the same," Farah said. "So, what do you worka-holics do for fun?"

"We go to dinners that cost as much as a monthly mortgage for a Texas family and convince ourselves that these perks are worth it by spending more of the company's money to get back at them," I said. "Remember when we used to be nervous about ordering an iced tea with our meal, and we considered Red Lob-ster fancy because our meals came with a salad and six salad dressing options? Yeah, those days are over."

"We haven't talked much, but from what you've told me in our few conversations, it sounds like you work with some unhappy people."

"Well, they're successful, but it's not like they have time to enjoy it. There's something missing in their lives. I guess I should say *our* lives."

"This is *so* you. Totally drawn to the miserable people searching for something. They look great on the outside and feel empty on the inside. Just like you and your little homecoming queen friends in high school."

My gut stung as I realized there was some truth to her harsh statement. "I guess I'm drawn to people who are trying to be somebody or prove something. But it's not like you took some rebellious path. You ended up being an engineer just like Dad encouraged you to be."

"Funny, I was just talking about that last week, since everyone is surprised when I say I'm an engineering major and a dance minor. I think I did engineering partly because I felt limited to a few options and partly because I enjoyed it. Would I have chosen it if I didn't grow up in our family? Probably not. I chose dance because I love it. I consider my major and minor choices a calculated risk." She waited for me to comment and then decided to add, "You always do what gets you the most attention. Wall Street gets you this celebrity status you crave. It's the American dream times ten, and you love the way people light up and want to talk to you. Shireen and I found things we liked within the limited molds we felt resigned to—medicine and engineering—and made them work for us. We already got the stamp of approval. No need to torture ourselves to get that gold star."

"I never thought of it that way," I said.

"So you're not happy; but at least you're not stressing over every dollar you spend anymore," she said, trying to make sure I was grateful for no longer having that burden.

"It's all bittersweet. I need my first bonus to pay off a huge chunk of my student loans. I have no idea how Mom and Dad paid for four kids. Mind you, my lifestyle here is wasteful, but I'm so grateful I'm not responsible for anyone else."

"Do you think you'll leave New York?" she asked.

"Not yet. Even though I haven't seen much outside of hotels and restaurants, I still like the energy here. There are a million different kinds of people to meet and cultural things to do. Plus, everyone is striving to be someone, and I'm still trying to figure out what I want to be. I didn't get that buzz growing up."

"Maybe it was our limiting suburban life," she said. She paused before she went on. "Listen, I'm scared to get off the phone because I'm not sure when I'll speak to you again, but I've got an exam tomorrow I still need to study for."

"Okay, I'll let you study," I said. "I may come home to visit in a few months."

"Everyone will be happy to see you, but I'm warning you, don't come here looking for any big answers. I'm not sure this is the best place for you to turn."

I sat silently on the floor in our living room, Indian-style, for a few minutes after we hung up. I put my hands on the front of my pelvic bones and winced at the stinging pain, wondering if hips could fall asleep. My frequent backaches lingered from sitting all day. My fingers rubbed in circular motions against my ribs, still feeling the tenderness from Daniel's unexpected punch.

I looked at the front door, wondering when my roommate would get home. She was probably out at a bar, trying to forget work. I wouldn't see her for hours. Long, inviting hardwood floors stretched from our living room area to the door. I'd never seen the potential in this before, but I also couldn't remember the last time I'd sat still for so long without fixating purely on work. Before the beeper or the phone killed the moment, I moved our rug, chained our front door, and put in a pirated *Dance NYC* CD I had bought in Times Square from a woman nervously looking for cops, squatting with twenty CDs spread out on a tie-dyed blanket.

A techno song blared so loud that I could feel the vibrations below my feet as I did split leaps across the long stretch of hardwood floor. Linking eyes with the glare of the television screen, I spotted sharp turns. My legs stood powerfully and my feet ground firmly into the wood floor. The lyrics of *Fame* whirled through my head as I remembered my mom saying to me and my sisters, *"The best gift we'll ever give you is each other."*

CHAPTER 6

Good Night

I thought you said you were working on your senior-year English project," my dad said with his hands in the air as he walked into the living room. "How is it that you are sitting here with your two best friends?" he asked, giving a broad grin to Jennie and Summer. He then looked over at the guy sitting next to Summer and quickly shifted his eyes.

"Hi, Mr. Godiwalla," Jennie said, smiling and laughing at the same time while running her fingers through her fine, light brown hair. My friends thought my dad was so funny. Usually when he entered it meant that he and I would trade one-liners back and forth like playful punches. Jennie and Summer were often our audience. But outside of teasing and discussing engineering, my dad and I didn't always have that much to talk about. We struggled to find a subject that we were both interested in.

"Dad, we *are* working on our English project. Mr. Thompson let us choose teams." His hands jingled a few quarters in his pocket as he eyed us. "This is Kyle," I said, motioning my hand toward him. My dad looked his way and quickly looked away as if Kyle were only a mirage. This was his unique way of barely acknowledging the boys that we introduced him to. Purposely, I sat across from Kyle, knowing if I sat on the couch next to him my dad would come out more often to check on us.

"She kicked everyone out of the house," my dad explained to my friends, "saying she needed the living room quiet for this study group." My mom had agreed to take Lena and my grandmother out to Luby's Cafeteria and then Marshalls to buy Lena a dress. "Boy, you are really something," he said, looking at me and laughing. "Only Nina can make a school project a party. We don't even see her carry home books. She thinks a backpack looks 'dorky.' I wonder if she's even a student sometimes. What, is she your class mascot?" he asked, putting his hands on the tops of my shoulders and squeezing.

My friends laughed as they watched him throw out his arms like a kindly grizzly bear.

"Yeah, Dad, I'm the Bearkat you always wanted," I said, playing with my large flower earrings and laughing. My family's differences from others didn't bother me as much in high school as they had when I was in middle and elementary school: I had many close friends, and our suburb had become more diverse, so we were now a minority rather than an anomaly. Plus, as we got older, our childhood friends tended to be more interested in our background, which my parents loved. Once, when Summer stayed over for dinner, my mom explained to her, "Summer, this is the way we eat curry and rice with a spoon and fork." My mom used her fork to mold a nice heaping spoonful and then gave Summer her silverware, eager to see her try it. My dad interrupted my mom midway: "Summer, this is turmeric. Many Persian dishes use this bright yellow spice to color rice. It is so powerful that it can also help fight cancer and arthritis." They went back and forth like this until Lena and I looked at each other and in unison said, "Here they go again with the PBS special—We Are the Parsis."

"Mr. Godiwalla, did Nina tell you about Homecoming Court?" Jennie asked.

"What court?" my dad asked.

"I didn't explain it to him yet, Jennie." My squinted eyes and long pause showed that I wasn't sure how to explain this. It would have been easier if I could have related it back to a soap opera. "Dad, all three of us are nominated for homecoming queen and Kyle for homecoming king. Your class votes for you if they like you. It means you have a lot of friends. So we're all walking down the football field together during the homecoming game. You and Mom are supposed to escort me down the field."

"There is an award for socializing?" he asked. "Only in America." He folded his arms in front of him across his shirt's green Izod logo, and I could tell he was trying to control his amusement. "Just put the date on the kitchen calendar so your mom and I remember. So, do you have to represent your class?" he asked, still unsure what this was all about.

"Something like that, but I don't have to do any work."

"How does she always get away without doing any work?" he said, looking at my friends in wonderment. "How many people are in your class?" he asked me.

"About eight hundred," Kyle said.

"Oh boy! You better not screw up," he said as he cupped the back of my head with his hand and shook it endearingly. As I had taught him, he was careful to not touch the front of my head and mess up my bangs that I had practically freeze-dried in place daily with my All-Set aerosol hair spray. My thick, dark hair was further puffed up by a perm and thirty minutes of artistic work with a hair pick. I even went along with the Texas trend of using the Mane 'n Tail horse shampoo that my girlfriends used, hoping to make their hair fuller. I was one of three girls with the biggest hair in school, which was a huge status symbol in Texas.

"Dad, I'll have to choose your outfit," I announced.

"Why can't I wear those Docks you chose for my birthday?" he asked.

"Dockers," I corrected him. "No, too casual, and no polyester pants either. I'll leave something on your bed the night before."

"I live in a girls' dormitory," my dad announced to my friends. "They dress you, and you don't get to speak much because you're outvoted by six other ladies." Even though Jennie and Summer had heard his famous line many times, they still giggled along with Kyle.

"Okay," my dad announced, clapping his hands as if the fun was over and serious business was about to go down. "I stayed home only so I could make you hard workers some Darjeeling tea with mint and lemongrass. How many cups?" he asked.

Actually, he'd stayed home when my mom had mentioned a boy would be part of the team project. Having a guy over was a rare occurrence in my house. It was preferable they didn't come over, but if they had to, they were expected to stay within the confines of the living room or kitchen.

Jennie explained to Kyle, who was visiting my house for the first time, "He makes the best tea. With milk and sugar," she said, holding her hands out in a cup shape as if she were enjoying the warmth of the tea. "I've never tasted such good tea."

"I went to school in Darjeeling," my dad announced proudly as he linked eyes with Kyle for the first time. "Best tea in the world." He got a faraway look in his eyes, and I was sure he couldn't help but be imagining the Himalayan Mountains.

"I've never had hot tea," Kyle said. "Only iced tea with sugar."

"Neither had I," Summer said nodding. "You'll love his tea."

"Okay," my dad said, excited to have a new student. "This tea is straight from the Himalayan Mountains. This is Darjeeling tea," he said, enunciating the *jee* and putting on a heavier British-Indian accent. "It comes from two thousand and fifty meters above sea level. But America is one of the few countries that doesn't use the metric system. It translates to about 6,710 feet."

He particularly enjoyed mentioning the meters-versus-feet part because it was a reminder to his kids that not everything we learned in the United States was the right way. He started making these comparisons after I informed him, "No one I've met has even heard of a Zoroastrian." With a shocked face he looked at me and said, "Our people dominated the Persian Empire. Are you trying to tell me your friends don't know who Cyrus the Great is?" But it was hard to explain to him that all this seemed so irrelevant in the twentieth century when I was pretty sure I was one of few non-Christians in this small suburb.

"Mr. Godiwalla," Kyle said, "You've sold me on the Darjeeling tea."

My dad walked off to the kitchen with his hands behind his back, looking down at the ground and smiling. Now he was less concerned that there was a green-eyed boy in the house and more excited that someone new was about try his trademark tea.

"Her dad is a riot!" Jennie said. She leaned over to Kyle and whispered, "He's going to bring out two cups for each of us, and if you say, 'I only want one,' he'll say, 'That's okay,' and still give you two."

"Welcome to my world," I said. "He does the same thing

with all of us daily. Kyle, don't try and reason with him. It's a losing battle."

"Something about him reminds me of you," Kyle said. "Maybe it's his humor?"

"Yeah, there is nothing subtle about either of us," I said. It was such an odd thing to hear. My dad and I thought of ourselves as opposites, always butting heads with each other. Toward the end of junior high, when arguing was getting old and we realized the other person wasn't going to budge, we decided to settle for poking fun at our differences. Most things I did, he'd just laughed off. When he saw I'd unknowingly clogged our kitchen sink drain by pouring a half gallon of melted candle wax down it, he covered his mouth and snickered, "Your mom is going to be really mad." His disciplining tactics had become rare and were reserved for dating and academics.

"Did you visit UT yet?" Kyle asked me.

At our high school, if you did well, you went to the University of Texas or A&M. For the majority of my classmates, there was no question of leaving Texas. Almost all my friends were going to UT and had already lined up their sororities and fraternities. But my status was still up in the air since I was too nervous to bring up the subject with my dad, who kept reminding me, "Young girls who don't listen shouldn't live away from their parents." My friends and I were all eager to see where I'd end up.

"I went to campus last weekend," I said, talking softly so that my dad wouldn't overhear from the kitchen. "Farah took me to the career office and then we went to visit the chemistry lab where Shireen is studying premed, the engineering school where Farah is, and then the business school." Farah had walked me around the different departments on campus, cleverly skipping liberal arts and any others that would not be acceptable majors to take home. Given the way my dad grew up in India, there was a clear hierarchy. Those who scored the highest became doctors or engineers. The mediocre kids studied business, and those with the lowest scores studied liberal arts. Lena was the least affected by this hierarchy. Later on, after I graduated from college, she came home and announced that she was majoring in advertising, a field unfamiliar to my parents, who thought it sounded like a hobby rather than a career. A family meeting was called to discuss whether advertising was a financially sound option. The verdict: She could study advertising, but she should minor in business, "just in case."

"I thought Farah was taking you for a career test?" Jennie asked.

"Oh yeah, I took it, but it didn't work. That's why Farah decided to walk me to the different schools. The test said I should be a minister or a psychologist."

"A minister!" Summer shouted as we all cackled. "You don't even go to church on Sundays," she announced, while using her hand to scrunch her hair for a fuller effect.

She shouldn't have said that. Sore subject. When Summer's mother found out in junior high that my family not only didn't go to their church, which resembled a football stadium with a marquee out front, but didn't attend *any* Christian church, she sat me down after dinner and explained how she could "save" my whole family from hell. These were the kinds of things my sisters and I didn't explain to my parents, since it would just create a further divide between them and our American friends.

"So what'd you decide?" Jennie asked excitedly.

"Well," I said, remembering the day vividly, "I was a little freaked out by the biochemistry lab full of people with bright yellow goggles who didn't lift their heads to greet me. Then we went to meet Farah's engineering classmates, who all spoke in this weird language of acronyms that I didn't quite understand. I just didn't click with the people, since they all seemed like loners. They didn't even *want* to socialize."

"That would kill you and your big mouth," Summer said shaking her head, half joking but mostly serious.

"Exactly," I said. "But the business school seemed much better. They were all confident and polished. The boys wore khakis instead of cutoff jean shorts, and they carried messenger bags instead of backpacks. And it was nice to be in the bright building rather than the dingy basement labs. Everyone ran around the business school in a frenzy as if they were going somewhere. Plus, one guy we talked to said he was studying abroad in Italy, and I want to travel all over. It just felt like the right vibe for me."

"That sounds so cool," Jennie said. "That's sounds like something I'd like. I'll probably do business too. My older brother always says that the people in the business school are the ones who didn't know what else to do. Business is so general, you know." She paused, looking around for our reactions before it clicked: "We could study at the UT business school together, Nina."

Summer was the first one to jump out of her chair and grab my shoulders and started shaking them vigorously, while she chanted, "You have to go to UT! You have to go to UT!" Soon Kyle and Jennie joined her. My body vibrated fiercely, as if I were a shock therapy patient. I would have stopped them, fearful that my dad would hear, but none of us could stop laughing. Plus, I knew my dad was still outside, carefully cutting fresh lemongrass leaves for our Darjeeling tea.

The next day we had a lunch celebration at our Parsi temple. Even though I had already tried to get out of it, dreading aunties and uncles asking me about my college plans, my dad insisted. Not long after we walked in, Zia Aunty spotted me in the appetizer line.

"So, Nina, what are you planning on majoring in?" Zia Aunty asked as she sank her teeth into a tandoori chicken wing.

"Well, I don't know yet. I do well in math because it comes easy to me, but . . ." I paused.

"That is wonderful!" she chimed in before I could voice my uncertainty. "With good math skills you could be an engineer or go into accounting. Even lawyers and doctors use math."

"I don't know if I want to have any of those jobs. I can't think of anything I'd enjoy doing for forty hours a week."

"Don't be foolish," she warned. "Those who look for too much love in their work will flounder. Be a smart girl: Choose a stable job and husband. Only then you will be happy."

My dad kept a close eye on my bright green sweater for most of the party. Why hadn't I worn something more muted? About every twenty minutes, he grabbed my arm to introduce me to someone new. Typically, he had an agenda. I'd watch his eyes dart around the room, trying to see who he could introduce me to next as he nervously flipped his tongue back and forth. Since I'd mentioned I wanted to study business, he was introducing me to aunties and uncles in finance and accounting.

After talking to Jal Uncle, who insisted that finance and

accounting were the only two business majors I should consider, since they were the best paying, I eagerly moved over to the drink line. I stood behind Mehroo Aunty and Darius Uncle, catching them in the middle of a conversation about their respective kids, who were only a few years older than me.

"Zeenia has again graduated with high honors," her mother said. "In high school she graduated number four." She nodded, reminding Darius Uncle.

"Wonderful," Darius Uncle responded. "Cyrus is now doing a double degree, BBA and master's in accounting," he said, looking around the room for his son with pride. It was clear he hoped to bring him into the conversation.

"We are hoping Zeenia goes the neurosurgeon route. Just like her father," Mehroo Aunty continued while crossing her fingers. "Even just neurology would be fine." She saw me standing quietly behind them and put her arm around me while Uncle spoke.

"Really," Darius Uncle offered, pausing for a moment and nodding. "Cyrus says only five years for both a master's and bachelor's. Can't beat that," he said, giving the Indian head nod of approval, a side-to-side tilt.

"What about you, Ms. Nina?" Mehroo Aunty asked as she gave me a tight, loving squeeze with her arm wrapped around me.

"I haven't gotten that far," I said, laughing uncomfortably and wanting all the comparisons to end quickly. "For now, I'm just trying to decide whether I want Dr. Pepper or Sprite."

We all laughed and then Mehroo Aunty whispered "lawyer" in my ear as she nodded her head in thought. "You'll be a lawyer since you always have a quick retort."

Toward the end of the function, all the college talk made

my dad even more anxious. He could tell I wasn't attentive to all the advice I was receiving, which he found unsettling. I assume the idea of marrying me to a nice Parsi boy seemed more comforting, because minutes before we were about to leave, he approached me. "Nina, remember when you were visiting India and you and Farah were doing cartwheels on the lawn in Dadar Colony?"

"What's that?" I asked.

"How can you not remember?" he said, almost frantically. It's the biggest Parsi colony in the world. Remember in Bombay the Parsis lived in gated communities? With beautiful gardens in the middle?"

"Dad, I was eight or nine," I said. "I'm eighteen now. I hardly remember that trip. That's weird though—why do Parsis live separately?"

"That's not weird," he said. "It's called loyalty. They're preserving our culture."

"Daaadddd," I yelped as he grasped my arm firmly and escorted me across the room, all the while politely smiling at guests. Sensing his own desperation, he tried a lighter tone. "Neville says he remembers how nicely you pointed your toes with every cartwheel while you were in that beautiful park. He wants to meet you. He is a nice boy, and he is five years older. You need someone more mature," he said right before he placed me face-to-face with Neville, who was as confused as I was. "This is my lovely daughter," he announced right before he walked off.

I closed my eyes and rested my head against the car window the whole ride home from the Parsi function. Anything to avoid my dad asking me what I planned to study after the long party of informational interviews. The real elephant in the room was where I would go to college, and my dad and I had avoided it for the last couple of days after having an argument earlier in the week. The next conversation would no doubt be an eruption.

The tension between my dad and me was at its height by evening time. Our biggest commonality was our stubbornness. Even though both my older sisters were at UT, he insisted that I needed to live at home, under his careful supervision. The idea of his third daughter, who had a mind of her own, out of his supervision for even one night terrified him.

My bank account balance was not as high as I'd have liked. I worked long hours at the local grocery, taking advantage of the time-and-a-half pay for working the Christian holidays. Most of my money went toward trendier clothes and travel expenses for my high school dance team. Had I known that my dad and I would come to a standstill negotiation on college, I would have saved more.

"Nina!" my dad called out from the kitchen. Even out of eyeshot, the image of his protruding Adam's apple and square face zipped through my head. I kept my eyes fixed on the *Glamour* magazine article "Six Steps to Financial Freedom."

"What, Dad?" I responded. I imagined him in the red-and-white striped pajamas that he always bragged were over twenty years old. Countless washes had blended the once distinct red and white stripes into a pale rose color. It was only because he referred to them as his "striped pajamas" that we knew of their formerly crisp color boundaries. His ability to see the value in things that I couldn't was the crux of our head butting. But our different opinion on pajama quality was going to be the least of my problems tonight.

"Do you want water with your vitamin?"

"No, thanks," I said.

Peering just past the article's first step at the top of the page, "Arm yourself with cash," I stared at the maroon recliner. It was my father's chair of choice when he was waiting for us to come home. If any of his girls was out late, he simply couldn't sleep. He would silently read *India Abroad* in this recliner and flip through television channels for breaking news or accidents, anxious until we returned home. Sleep-deprived, he would be in a complete daze the next day. My mom would plead, "Come to bed, Zal. The girls are old enough now." Even though he sat up anxiously for hours while we were gone, he wouldn't dare show it when we arrived. As soon as he heard the key rattling, he'd thrust down the recliner footrest with relief and walk up to us in complete calmness. "Good night, Mickey Mouse," he'd say with a kiss on top of our heads. "Don't forget to say your prayers and brush your teeth."

Lying on the couch, I listened to his familiar nightly sounds of microwave beeps, spoon jingles, and vitamin bottle jostles. I could hear his rhythmic flip-flop slippers exiting the kitchen. I kept my eyes on the page as he came my way, so I wasn't prepared for one of his favorite ninjalike tricks.

"Aaaahhh," I yelped loudly as I felt his fingers lightly tickle my feet. Involuntarily, I tucked into a tight ball just the way we were taught to do in Mrs. Brown's third-grade class in case a hurricane came our way. "Make yourself the smallest target possible," she instructed.

He laughed hard but was determined to spit out the words even though they came out over a long period of time in stutters: "Pay . . . pay . . . pay . . . attention," he said. "Mickey . . . Mo . . . Mo . . . Mouse."

"You got me, Dad!" I said, laughing and slapping his

shoulder. His amusement continued way too long and only slowed once I warned, "Shhh. You're going to wake everyone else."

"In the Indian ROTC we were taught to always be alert," he said, still standing over me.

"I'm in the living room, Dad, not at war," I shot back quickly, which made him laugh even harder.

"Okay. Here you go," he said, still snickering, but now making major attempts to fight his laugh. He would visualize how silly I looked when I balled up and laugh about it all week. Finally, he handed me a purple Wilma Flintstone vitamin, still our vitamins of choice, and went back to the kitchen.

For the last fifteen years, he had handed each of us our vitamins every day, never missing a day. Farah would eat hers in sections, never changing the order—Dino's neck, then his butt, and last, his legs. As usual, after he had handed me the vitamin and walked away, I threw mine across the room to fall behind one of many pieces of furniture. This evening, purple Wilma flew behind the television. As the vitamins decayed, they turned black. By the time my father found them, they looked like shrunken turds. My parents were convinced they were mouse droppings. That was why we had mousetraps behind the television and refrigerator.

I sat waiting anxiously for his transition from the kitchen to the bedroom. Perfect time to ask him about UT. But he was only on the first phase of his routine—vitamins. He took Co Q10, B2, lycopene, and an Essential Man vitamin. Then he moved on to his imported Indian ayurvedic vitamins from the Himalaya Drug Company—amla berry and Indian gooseberry gallnuts mixed with cardamom. I imagined he felt immediate results, since he'd take stronger, surer strides toward the refrigerator. In his second phase, he ate three raw garlic cloves and one-fourth of a raw onion as excitedly as if they were Hershey's kisses. Phase three was Ovaltine in a mug filled with eight ounces of skim milk. Next I listened to the clickety-clack of the spoon hitting the mug, usually somewhere between thirty-two and forty rotations to ensure each Ovaltine granule was dissolved. After placing the mug in the sink, he would place his hands on his hips. An involuntary smirk would form on his face, so pleased was he with his nightly disease-combat routine.

"It's bedtime," he said as he walked across the living room toward his bedroom. "Your health is your wealth. Never forget that!" he reminded me. He started to turn the knob to his bedroom door. But instead of entering the room, he stood there playing with the safety pin that he used as a substitute button.

I didn't look up from my page, knowing that his exit was always in several stages. Closing my eyes, I just blurted out what I'd been dying to say all evening. "I'm still thinking about going to the University of Texas."

"What about our deal?" he asked, referring to our conversation a few days earlier.

That evening he'd approached me in a favorable mood. "Nina, I will make you a deal you can't refuse," he said confidently as he put an arm on my shoulder. "If you go to the University of Houston and live at home, I will pay for all your expenses and buy you a car."

"Dad, that deal is totally unfair," I replied. "You know I want to go to the University of Texas. It's only two hours away. Farah and Shireen have agreed to watch my every move."

"Forget that school. The University of Houston is a great school."

"Dad, I'm probably studying business and UT has the best business school in Texas," I said, hoping to appeal to his dislike for academic mediocrity. "What's the rest of the deal?" I asked. Normally, every choice my father made revolved around making sure it would support his children's success. Even at his expense. He chose the most stable job, moved to the neighborhood with the best schools, and introduced us to the most connected people he knew. He knew UT was better, but this would be one of the few times in my life that he would forgo prestige. Nothing was more important to him than protecting me.

"That's it. That's the deal," he said, smoothly gliding his hands through his hair. "Take it or leave it."

"Why can't you pay for half if I go two hours away? Or a quarter?" I desperately negotiated.

"If you stay here, you can come with us to Parsi functions on the weekends."

"Dad, what if I swear to come home every weekend? I swear!" Fury and helplessness pumped through my body as I clenched my magazine and glared at him. I wanted so badly to scream, "*I don't need your deal or your money!*" But we both knew I only had $437.65 in my account and made only $4.25 an hour. My mom had already bowed out of being the bad guy in this negotiation. "It's between you two," she said to us.

"Take it or leave it," he repeated.

He cleared his throat and then debated whether to enter his bedroom or continue his cameo. After a long pause he added, "Notice that you are the only one up. Now, shut off the lights and go to bed." He walked into his dark room and closed the door. From behind the closed door, I heard a faint "good night."

"Good night," I halfheartedly mumbled, and slouched into a more comfortable position on the couch, picking up on the sentence where I had left off before his entrance.

CHAPTER 7

Merchants

Monday morning at 5:00 A.M. I called the office to explain that I would be a little later than usual because I had been throwing up all night and had a severe fever. I hadn't slept at all because when I was not gagging, I was trying to compose a voice message for Steve. I had already tried fourteen different messages:

"Steve, I feel so sick I can't . . . ShIT!

"Hey, I feel so bad. I know you all need me to . . . shiT!

"Hey, Steve. I may not sound bad, but I feel . . . FUck!

"I have been throwing up and burning . . . Fuck!

"Hey, I wanted to call earlier but I've been too . . . DAmn IT!"

After deleting all of them, I decided to speak to him directly in the morning. He was as supportive as expected and said, "It shouldn't be a problem. We'll just put an extra trash can right next to your desk. Let me know if you think you can't handle it."

"Of course I can," I said, annoyed but not willing to sound weak. "I'm only calling to say I'm running late." *Why do I always fall for that trick, when they use my fears against me?*

"By the way," Steve said, "if you don't press star-three after composing messages, they get sent automatically. I've left you voice mail instructions on your desk. Be sure to refresh yourself when you get in."

Did he mean he just heard all my pathetic voice mails? Maybe my fever is so high I'm just misunderstanding. As I lay pressed up against the headrest of my bed, the truth registered, and I felt a bottomless sense of humiliation. I bowed my head in embarrassment. For about a minute, I sat there cradling my face in one hand and the phone receiver in the other, dredging up energy to start the day.

On my way to work in the town car, I looked at my Palm to calculate the weeks since Scott's breakdown in conference room 32E. Ever since then, I'd felt erratic. My actions seemed out of my control. Some days, like today, I'd try to differentiate myself from those who would not succeed — determined to be the best; some days I was completely indifferent; and other days I would fall into a depression I couldn't seem to shake. My finger traced the rain as it trickled down the windows.

Sitting diligently at my desk, occasionally I'd start to gag and run to the bathroom, groping for the trash can in case I didn't make it in time. Each time, either Michael or Luis would look up with sympathetic eyes and ask, "You okay?" But coming in sick was expected of all of us, so there was no big sympathy party necessary. "Uh-huh," I'd reply. On one return trip to my desk I heard them talking about some team dinner, during which an officer was rumored to have bitten his analyst's ear in an angry fit. The image almost sent me running back to the bathroom.

Midway through the day I took a thirty-minute power nap in the nurse's office, and by the evening I felt much better. At 8:00 P.M. I sat at my desk, playing Tetris and scrolling through my phone trying to think of who would go out with me. I limited my choices to bankers since they were the only ones who wouldn't ask why I never returned phone calls. I called the media group analysts, but they were all working late that night. The mergers and acquisitions analysts—all busy or out of town. I even called Michael's cell phone, knowing that he would probably be out. I closed my eyes and started grinding my teeth, trying to think of someone to at least talk to on the phone.

What happened to the person who needed to sit at different high school cafeteria tables every couple weeks just to keep up with all her friends? If I didn't find friends soon, I'd be like my officer, Ken. Once, at two in the morning, while I was finishing up a presentation, I found him reading the *Wall Street Journal.* "What are you doing?" I asked, surprised. "I'm just catching up on a couple of articles," he said with a comfortable smile as if this were normal. I was embarrassed for him that he didn't recognize how pathetic he sounded. "My wife's still at work. She's at Skadden closing a huge deal this week. She said she won't be home before 3:00 A.M., so there's no need for me to rush home."

Before I could find someone to go out with, Larry called with a small project that kept me there until midnight. By the time the town car brought me to my neighborhood, a production crew was taping a film a block away from my apartment. The directors had changed all the street signs: Eighty-fourth became Oak Moss and Eighty-third became Peach Tree. Since my street was closed off, my driver dropped me off a block away from home with an apology.

"Where are we?" I asked, alarmed at the unfamiliar apartment buildings.

"This is your neighborhood," the driver replied. "You're a block away from home."

I got out of the car and approached a guy my age carrying a

microphone on a stick. "I can't find my building because you've covered up the street signs. Which one is Eighty-fourth?" I asked, pulling at his sleeve.

"Don't you live here?" the production assistant asked.

"I don't live here. I live on Eighty-fourth," I explained. "Which one is it?"

He shrugged his shoulders. "Can't you just use landmarks?"

"Take off the signs so I can see," I insisted as I pulled again at his sleeve anxiously, genuinely unfamiliar with my neighborhood.

That night, I made a note in my Palm Pilot: "U R btwn Ollie's and Poe Café."

Standing over the trash can in my kitchen, I opened my mail to read a letter from Citibank that said that it had to withdraw a thousand dollars from my bank account because of an error they'd made months ago. *What!* There was no neat stack of bank statements I could sift through to figure out whether it was true or not. Most of my mail went straight into the trash, probably along with the phone bill that had been overdue for the last couple months. "How am I supposed to know?" I mumbled hopelessly, throwing it away, knowing that without the paper trail or time during working hours to talk to a Citibank representative, nothing could be challenged.

Lying down on the sofa, my hands covering my face, I tried to hide from feeling empty. A few weeks ago when I came home late to my deserted apartment—my roommate and I left each other notes; we hardly saw each other anymore—and felt I couldn't be alone, I rode up and down the number 2 subway line just to be around others. A warm chill ran down my spine when I exchanged a smile with a waitress at French Roast, who was holding two heavy sacks of potatoes.

As a woman, I found it difficult to balance a life with intimacy and remain the model banker. A couple of times my roommate and I got phone bills with 1-900-hot-dude numbers charged to it. We both asked each other, "Was this you?" Then, we both looked at each other pensively as if trying to remember if we had called in the middle of a drunken or sleep-deprived night. Eventually, we shrugged our shoulders and just paid the bills.

It would be an enormous mistake to hook up with someone at work, even though these were practically the only men I might see for weeks. I couldn't let them see me as anything less than a banker. I started to understand why my male colleagues spent so much time at strip clubs. Besides the need to control and humiliate someone—after so many others had controlled and humiliated you all day—loneliness takes over. Who had time or energy to nurture a relationship? Picking someone up at a bar and trying to bring him home is difficult when you only have an hour or two. Plus, you're tired and all you can talk about is work.

At times like these, hookups felt like my only viable solution. Nothing else could make my loneliness evaporate. I called a guy whom a friend of mine said was good looking. I hadn't seen him before, but tonight any guy was appealing. When I called him, he suggested we meet another day when it wasn't so late. "I work crazy hours," I coaxed. "It's the only time I can hang out."

I shaved my legs since my hair was now almost curly. I had stopped wearing skirts after the first two months, which made it easy to forget about these things. Absolut Kurant shots warmed my throat and restrained my anxiety.

When I opened the door, I was surprised to find that he

was Indian. *Is that why she thought I would find him attractive?* I'd never dated an Indian guy before. I'd only dated American guys, carefully concealing any evidence from my father that I'd strayed from our community. I'm sure my friend didn't realize that going out with an Indian who wasn't my religion was considered just as bad as dating a non-Indian.

"Nice to meet you, Nina," Shyam said with a friendly smile, offering me a damp, limp handshake that would have made any career services representative cringe. Within twenty-eight seconds I knew that Shyam was a nice guy but not my type. But that didn't stop me from using the next fifteen minutes to grill him, making sure we didn't have any mutual friends other than my one friend who introduced us. After I was satisfied, I turned on a Dave Matthews song and poured him a second vodka tonic.

I treated the rest of the evening like a doctor's visit, a procedure that was necessary yet needed to end quickly. I leaned over and kissed him abruptly, making him feel as uncomfortable as I was. He kissed in harsh, abrupt woodpecker motions and he self-consciously groped my back and face. *This is so awkward! What if I just rush it? Get it over with?*

Well aware that this whole episode was painfully uncomfortable, but more fearful of being alone again, I blurted, "I'm going to get a condom."

"A condom?" he asked, opening his palms to the sky as if checking for rain. "I feel like I hardly know you," he said, touching my hand and angling his head sideways in a pleading motion. "I want to get to know you first." It was obvious from his confused expression that I'd made him uneasy. Something about Shyam's surprised eyes made me suddenly aware of my cold, detached approach. *What the hell am I doing?* There seemed to be a part of me that was growing out of my control. I could feel it, but I wasn't sure how to stop it.

"I'm sorry it got late so quickly," I said, jumping up, suddenly more uncomfortable than he was. "Let's get together another time." I walked him to the door. *I hope he erases my number before he leaves the building.* We exchanged a stiff hug and he was gone. I walked back to the kitchen for a glass of wine.

"Godiwalla, get up!" Bryan shouted as he squeezed my arm. "Get up!" I saw the panic on his face, but I couldn't move. My eyes kept closing as if I'd taken sleeping pills, but really I just couldn't deal with my reality. *Maybe this is what depression feels like.* Bryan was a great colleague and saw me as an actual person, but I wasn't sure he was the one I wanted to talk to tonight. During training he often compared Morgan Stanley to his Merrill Lynch internship, thus making a point that our experience was perfectly normal. I was wearing a UT PLAY HARD sweatshirt and burnt orange sweatpants cut right above the knee. I lay on my side on the floor, as if I had just been watching television earlier, even though we didn't have reception.

"You left the door open. What is wrong with you? Are you drunk?" he asked, looking at the half-finished bottle of syrah sitting on top of the thick coffee-table book, *Parsis: The Zoroastrians of India: A Photographic Journey,* that Farah had brought on her two-day visit to New York last month. "Dad made me carry this ridiculously big thing all the way here even though I know you're too busy to open it," she announced as soon as she walked in. "My carry-on was crazy heavy, so you better appreciate it. Grandma sent four Tupperwares of cutlets and *biryani.* I negotiated her down from seven. And before I forget, she wants you to put this in your desk drawer," she said, pulling out a picture of a man with the sun behind him on a laminated card the size of a driver's license that she tucked in her wallet between her dollar bills. "It's that Indian prophet guy she believes in. She said he will take care of you."

"I don't even know who this guy is," I said, staring at the picture and imagining Luis or Michael finding it while they were looking in my drawers for binder clips or staples. "Plus," I said, "if someone found that in my desk, I'd be scared they'd think I was part of a cult or something."

We both started to laugh at the thought of me being called in to human resources to explain. I kept the prophet card in my nightstand, just in case. In the drawer below the prophet card was a homemade illustrated book Lena had given me for Christmas. I had skimmed through it without really reading it. "Thank you. I'll read it later in private," I told her. It had ended up in my carry-on, shoved in at the last minute as an afterthought. The only other thing in the drawer was the only family picture I'd brought.

I stared at Bryan. Days and nights had begun to blur. Other than seeing people sleeping under their desks and having a colleague leave the firm because he couldn't determine day from night and kept showing up to work drunk, I could remember little else than working. It was as if we were drowning for months and then suddenly, after about a year, one by one, analysts would come up for air.

"You are freaking me out," Bryan said, taking both hands and firmly shaking my arm harder. "Say something!" He looked around as if he were about to get help. "Where is your roommate?" he asked, as if she might pop out from behind the couch in this studio apartment.

"I'm not drunk," I said softly, fearful he would leave to get help. Somehow it felt like a peaceful break, being in this escapist state of mind, but with Bryan looking so frantic, I forced myself to snap out of it. "I don't know where she is."

He lifted me up and brought me over to my warm, cozy papasan chair, where I curled up in a ball. It was the only piece of furniture I had brought from home. Everything else belonged to my roommate. When we moved in, her parents drove in from Boston and scoured our entire apartment, carefully scrubbing every wall and baseboard while I helped her find a suit for our first day. That evening, around the coffee table, the four of us ate Zabar's spinach, sweet potato, and kasha knishes. When her mom kept trying to tickle her spontaneously to rid her of hiccups, I realized how much I would miss not having my family close by.

"I knew there was something wrong," Bryan mumbled. "You usually answer your phone right away." By now I was an hour late for the dinner Bryan and I had agreed to. "Did someone die?" he asked, bringing his hands to his heart. Bryan was one of the few people I'd met in training whom I made an effort to see every now and again even though we sat on different floors. His schedule was more flexible since his group was not nearly as busy. His fingers were often swollen, which he said was from the work stress. He'd been wearing his dad's ring on his middle finger since he was fifteen, when his dad died. We all admired Bryan's ability to double-fist drinks most of the night and still keep relatively sober. In his Analyst Facebook profile, he listed his favorite movie as *The English Patient*, unlike the other guys, who had listed *Top Gun*, *Goodfellas*, or *Star Wars*. Like many others in our analyst class, he was a Harvard economics major.

"Nobody died," I said, trying to sit up straighter. "I can't explain it," I said. "I just feel so burned out."

He put his hand on my shoulder and shook me in a teasing

way. "Don't let them get to you," he said. "It's just a job."

"It's *not* just a job," I said, holding both my knees close to my chest. "It dictates our life—when we can eat, sleep, and shower. Even who we have time to be friends with." My hands wrapped tighter around my knees, and I hoped Bryan was listening even though he was looking at the ground. "I was on the trading floor before where they screamed and threw phones. I could handle that. But in corporate finance, I feel like it's slow brainwashing. I'm being rewarded for being a monkey—for agreeing not to think, speak, or have an opinion."

"You're overthinking it," Bryan said. "Morgan Stanley corporate finance is no different from other investment banks. My summer at Merrill wasn't that different. Give it a little longer. Plus, what are you going to do, quit? The only one who loses if you quit is you. They could care less about you, me, or any other analyst who isn't a billionaire's kid. A million Ivy League kids would take your job in a second. You have to look out for yourself, and that means not letting them get to you."

As soon as Bryan said "quit," I felt a warm fear pour through my body. What would I do if I quit? How would I pay my college debt and my horribly high New York City rent? Would anyone in New York hire me if they knew I was a Morgan Stanley dropout? Todd would say no. I had no idea what I'd do. I'd focused on banking since my freshman year—every class I took was chosen depending on what banks valued on my transcript, and every club I joined was to show them my dedication.

We sat there quietly lost in thought. After many fears ran through my mind, I thought back to a question I had asked myself earlier in the day. I leaned forward in my chair and asked Bryan the same question, and I wished he'd say yes to it so I didn't feel so alone: "Do you feel like something in you is slowly dying?"

He scratched his thigh and then sat back against the futon, moving his head back and forth in contemplation.

"I know you're not like them," I went on. "When I first met you, you said you hoped you'd be a wonderful father one day. Who talks like that here?"

"I still want all that," he said defensively. "These are only two years of our life. Everything we do after this will be easy once we get the Morgan Stanley stamp," he said, shrugging his shoulders. "All we have to do is just push through." So little seemed to bother him. I was envious of his ability to shelve his feelings. Unlike me, he rarely judged our officers' ways. Their late-night strip club visits were the last thing he'd freely choose to do, yet he would join them to keep his team player status. "It's their way of letting off steam," he explained. "You and I are just here to get an experience."

"Bryan, I don't think you get it. Sometimes I hear myself thinking really sick things." My feet touched the ground and my hands were suddenly animated as I explained. "I've told you how Todd always has to impose his disturbing philosophies on us while we're in meetings. I swear he was an abused child," I said, pausing to shake my head. "Like the way he thinks anyone who's not a banker is a failure. The other night when the town car was taking me home, I was looking at people on the streets and I caught myself thinking, 'If I don't keep working hard, I'll live the insignificant lives of those people outside our building.' And then, like someone with a split personality, I was startled that I'd think something so evil. You see! This is changing me," I stressed loudly and sat up straight. "This isn't about *them*. I hate who *I'm* becoming."

"But you said you caught yourself, so you're not becoming

them," Bryan corrected me. "You know better. That's good!"

"I think if you stay here long enough," I said, staring at him in a fearful daze, "you become like them."

"Stop," he said, putting both of his hands on my shoulders. "I know you well enough to know that you'll regret it. You left Houston to make something of yourself just like I left Florida. You are way too driven to leave. Just push through."

That wasn't what I wanted to hear, so I involuntarily began closing my eyes again. "Nina," he said with a slight jolt on my shoulders. "Just push through," he repeated gently.

But I kept my eyes closed, not wanting to open them again. Listening to him made me feel worse—like there was something wrong with me. Everything Bryan said was similar to what I expected my parents to say. When things got difficult, my parents pulled out their tough-immigrant mentality and plowed through life's challenges. That was probably why I avoided calling them even when I did have time. I could already hear my mom reminding me: "The biggest problem your generation in America has is too many options. Maybe that's why you all can't endure difficulty as well. You should be grateful for what you have." Then my dad would add, "If your worst problem is having a stable job with good benefits, that's not a bad problem to have. Happiness comes through hard work and sacrifice." Once they got their jobs, they kept them, no matter how rocky things got.

"You'll be fine," Bryan said, reaching his arms out and, holding my head with both hands, firmly pressing his fingers into my scalp. "In a little over a year, when we throw our beepers into the ocean at our closing cruise, you'll laugh at all this. I know you will." He got no reaction from me, so he started to laugh loudly, hoping me make me laugh.

As if he were a father, he tucked me into bed, set my alarm, and sat in a chair next to me until I fell asleep at 11:00 P.M. As he waited I could see his eyes shift between my bare dresser and the floor, which was covered in clothes. The room looked like it was a generic hotel room with lousy maid service. It would be hard to believe a person with a family tightly linked with a huge community of aunties, uncles, and cousins lived in this space, devoid of any warmth.

Even though Bryan only waited there because he'd regret it if I did something to harm myself, I didn't dismiss him or reassure him that I'd be fine, since I didn't want to be alone. Bryan had a shaky past of his own. His father had amassed a great deal of debt and then drowned himself so that his large family could maintain the comfortable lifestyle they could no longer afford. Life insurance made Ivy League educations possible for Bryan and his two older sisters. Bryan's worst fear was to wake up one morning without any money. It was a fear that played into his work. Even when he wasn't busy, he stayed at work for hours, just in case.

Bryan came back the next morning to pick me up and escort me to my desk like it was my first day of school. As he walked away he said good morning to Michael with a longish stare as if to say, *Play nice.*

In pantyhosed feet, a couple of nights later, I scurried over to Daniel's desk on the other side of the floor. "Hey!" I said, relieved to see my fellow late-night worker.

"Can't break," he said. "I'm about to head out of here. One of my sister's friends has been in town for a week, and I'm supposed to take her out."

"Actually," I said, fiddling with the paisley scarf my

grandmother sent me, aware that I'd worn it too often. I really needed to make a department store run at some point. Another item to note in my Palm. "I'm getting off too. I came by to ask if you wanted to go out." *Please invite me*, I kept repeating in my head as I spoke with him. It didn't look like there were other people around, and the thought of spending the evening in my apartment sitting in front of a television that didn't really work wasn't appealing. You couldn't be picky as a banker. If you wanted to go out, you had to go out with whomever was around.

"Great," he said while flipping back and forth between two Excel pages. "Come along. We're just going to Merchants. I thought I could hook her up with a good-looking banker there," he said laughing. "Bryan and Ali are coming too."

"I'll just meet you there," I said as I bounced back to my desk with glee, relieved that I wouldn't be alone, feeling pathetic, like I had been earlier that week when I called Shyam.

At my desk, I prepared a couple of things for the next morning. While I was page-checking a presentation, Luis, who had been gone for a few hours, returned. I tried to look fully engrossed so I wouldn't have to listen to him spin fiction to hide the fact that he'd been out with his friends.

Even after working with Luis for almost a year, I had trouble understanding him. Considering he didn't get that much work from officers, he seemed to work late nights a lot. This couldn't be face time, since there weren't many people around to impress. It seemed like compensation for all the time he spent going out with friends. Maybe Luis was caught in a cycle: He needed to alleviate the stress of Morgan Stanley, but doing so only exacerbated the anxiety he felt about not getting his work done, which would drive him back to work at night. From what I heard, he'd run off to all these social events and try to play them off as work. It was clear that he was anxious about what our supervisors thought of him, but his concern would only kick in after he'd burned off the stress of working here. It wasn't too odd that he was doing this. None of us had mastered the ability to balance work and life. And Luis was a really fun guy, but I couldn't get involved with his pattern of mixed signals. I had enough to deal with myself.

"Did you hear who left?" Luis asked, standing next to my desk.

"Who?" I asked curiously.

"Remember Darren from M&A?"

"Hardly. I don't think I've seen him since training."

"He went through a really tough past three months. First he had a major breakdown, and then his group said he started bringing the Bible into work every day. They said he found God and decided to quit." Luis gestured with his fingers, highlighting the fact that this was crazy behavior.

"Wow," I said, wondering if he had tried antidepressants first, like many of the others. I paused, anticipating how our officers would use him as an example of someone who couldn't handle it. I thought back to an analyst who'd quit after a month. After weeks of late nights adjusting charts and doing unfulfilling number crunching, she announced she was leaving to be a production assistant for a movie. "Film is my dream," she explained to our bewildered faces. Deep down, many of us were envious that she had the confidence to do what she wanted when so many of us created stories in our heads that trapped us. Sadly, most of us would take antidepressants before finding the courage to do what we really wanted.

Luis walked over to his desk. "I have just had the craziest time in the copy center! They're just stupid," he said, setting down the fabricated paperwork he carried around the building.

"Not just dumb—totally stupid!"

"Yeah," I said, wondering where he went to eat.

"Can you adjust my screen and keyboard again?" I asked Luis. "My hands are stinging with the carpal tunnel feeling again."

"How does everything keep moving around? It's all out of whack again," he said as he carefully readjusted my computer and seat height.

"You're awesome. Thank you," I said as I tried out the new setup.

"How does it feel? It should lessen your backaches, too."

"Perfect. Thank you."

He was soon distracted again. "You see this?" Luis said, pointing to his bar chart, which ranked all the banks. "Morgan Stanley is supposed to be a higher bar than Lehman. It's obvious from the data points fifty-one and forty-five, but I swear they did it wrong about ten times."

"Oh," I said, uninterested in his guilt. If he was gone for less than two and a half hours, he would usually act as if he'd been upstairs dealing with graphics or copy center staff. "I'm leaving for Merchants. Daniel, Bryan, and Ali are going too. Any interest?" I offered.

"I wish I could, but I'm swamped," Luis said, swiping at his forehead as if it were sweating. "Well, maybe," he said, engrossed in thought. "Look at the blue," he said, pointing to his graph. "It's not even Morgan Stanley blue. How long have those stupid fucks been working here, and they still don't know Morgan Stanley blue!" I noted that he had borrowed Todd's favorite description of the copy center. Most of our team used it now.

I decided to get ready to leave rather than listen to Luis convince himself of his own stories. "Hey, if you want to go, we've got to go now," I demanded as I logged off my computer.

"If I go now, I'm definitely going to have to come back and work all night. I'm swamped!" he said.

He placed his charts on his desk and stared at the ground as he squeezed strands of his crispy hair, which made small popping sounds like bubble wrap. "Why don't you all come to *Apartment* instead?" he suggested. "We haven't hung out in a long time."

"Whose apartment?" I asked as I picked up my Morgan Stanley tote bag. Hanging out with Luis actually sounded like fun tonight. He really knew how to enjoy himself, which I needed.

"No," he said. "*Apartment* spelled A-P-T, the underground lounge that recently opened in the meatpacking district."

I shrugged my shoulders as I rested my tote bag on my chair.

"It has no address or phone," he went on. "You have to know the right door to get in. Once you press the hidden bell, the unmarked door automatically opens. We have a reservation upstairs. They only let funky, beautiful people in, so you don't have to deal with the everyday riffraff. I can't believe you haven't heard of it—for sure within a week or two it's going to be the place to see and be seen. It's supposed to be amazing! My friends went last night. It's set up like the ultimate bachelor pad. It even has two king-size beds."

"In the bar?" I asked. "That's weird."

"It's *the* New York three-story flat. Michael and I made reservations months ago. Before it even opened." He stroked his gold-and-cream tie tenderly. "I got this from Versace yesterday. The sales clerk said I looked like Raphael, you know the model with the longish brown hair."

"It is nice," I said picking my bag up again. "I need to leave. I told them I would be there soon. Do you want to join us?" I actually wanted him to go since he was fun to hang out with as long as he wasn't talking about work.

He still stood undecided. "They even have potato chips with crème fraîche and caviar," he tried tempting me. "And I heard they make a mean Pimm's Cup with a skinned cucumber."

"I won't make it. Have fun," I said, eager to get moving.

"They even have a host who greets you: 'Thanks for coming to my place.'"

"Have fun," I hollered as I walked away.

"Okay," he shouted. "I decided. I'll go to Merchants, then to APT, but then I'll definitely have to come back here and pull an all-nighter."

It was so frustrating not to know when Luis really had a lot of work. The less I had to hear about his workload, the better I felt.

We normally chose Merchants since its clientele was mostly bankers with a sprinkling of lawyers. Luis had the car wait outside of Merchants so he could take it to APT next.

Only a month ago we'd had a work function at the bar. That evening I handled everything perfectly. I knew it was one of my opportunities to network and impress the higher-ups. Steve warned me earlier in the week: "It's an opportunity. Use it!" I knew he was right. Most of the top people had made it at the company because they befriended the right people. Steve had trained me all along. "If they wonder why Times Square is called Times Square, find out. Then, the next time you see them, tell them." This was mere basics, and I nailed it. I went around the club taking turns talking to the right people. I had arrived at work at 6:30 A.M. that morning to do my research. I rattled off all the sports scores to Enrique, a VP in global equities; gave Marla, a managing director in capital markets, all the details on a golf course that was being renovated just a couple of hours outside of Manhattan; and discussed the economic effects of the taxi strike that would soon take place with a managing director in mergers and acquisitions.

Luis and I dashed for the bar as soon as we entered. I ordered a blood-orange martini. It took too long to feel a buzz since I had improved my alcohol tolerance so much. Usually, every gulp was building to an alcohol tolerance career strategy, but tonight my goal was to benefit from the numbness of each sip. As soon as the bartender placed the red concoction in front of me, I knocked it back like a shot. "Beautiful bloody," I said with a smile. "I'll have another."

"Easy, easy," Luis said, laughing as he swiveled back and forth on his plaid bar stool. "I'm glad you made it out tonight. We haven't hung out in a while."

"It's nice to be out."

"The last time I remember you so excited was when Andy came in with that Ibiza dance CD," he reminded me. "That guy is just crazy. I'm starting to believe all the rumors that he's on coke. He's got to be on something," Luis said, thinking back and shaking his head. Andy was the all-night clubber analyst who sat on our floor. He'd come into work a few weeks earlier at 2:00 A.M. He was between clubs—hopping from Pink Elephant to Marquee—and stopped by to send out a file to an officer on his team. "I got it," Andy shrieked in a childlike tone while jumping around our desks like a leprechaun and flashing a CD in our faces. Odors of smoke and citrus from Pink Elephant's scent machine that was rumored to send out pheromones breezed by us as he scurried around. "The latest Ibiza CD came out this week!" he screamed so loud I covered my ears. I had to jog my memory of Ibiza from when Luis had first told me about it: an island off Spain that has some of the most "outrageous" raves in the world and attracts thousands of people like Andy annually. Andy blasted the music and stood on Michael's desk chair, swiveling around as he danced with his hands in the air. At first Luis and I stared at his performance in shock, especially when he began screaming: We knew there were other analysts working on our floor. But it wasn't long before we were all standing on our chairs, spinning in circles, flailing our bodies around like caged animals. Slowly, we could see other analysts across the floor pop their heads up, joining us while we all screamed deliriously, "Woooohooooo!"

"Good times," I said to Luis with an uncontrollable smile. The sharp pain in my belly from laughing hysterically for so long was the only thing that made me sit down that night. It was spectacular, standing on that chair, feeling so powerful, and screaming whatever I felt like.

I grabbed my second drink and a glass of water, leaving Luis at the bar to decide between a lycheetini or a berry saketini. I walked over to our table and was excitedly greeted by Bryan and Ali. I had hardly seen Ali since training, even though we sat a floor or two away from each other. Their faces and bellies were swollen from too many corporate meals. Bryan's face had broken out in red stress welts.

"Godiwalla!" they screamed in unison as I approached the table.

"Double-fisting," Ali commended me as I sat down.

Like many of my colleagues, I had been isolated from others. Even if I hadn't talked to some of them since training, they were the closest thing I had to friends. Pleased to have people to hang out with, I leaned over and hugged each of them. The touch of warm skin was startling.

Daniel interrupted our reunion with an outsider. "Hey, everyone, this is my sister's friend Anna." We were rarely around nonbankers since most of our prebanking friends were tired of our unpredictable ways and inability to talk about anything other than work. It was never fun to be a nonbanker around bankers. It was as though you didn't exist.

"Hey!" we all said together, though our stares, which quickly sized up her faded REI fleece and jeans that made it clear she wasn't a professional, were less than welcoming. I tried to be a little nicer than the others, smiling more often. Not that long ago, I'd been that outsider, and it wasn't a good feeling.

"Where are you from?" I asked her.

"Maryland," she replied quickly. Her nervousness made her somewhat of a victim in our crowd since we sensed insecurity quickly.

"No," Daniel asked more directly, "where do you work?

"Oh, I'm a sculptor," she said timidly. "Mostly with black stone . . ."

Luis, who was just approaching the table, asked eagerly as he used his hips to scoot me over on the booth seat, "You're with Blackstone?"

"Yes," she said. "I use it to sculpt obelisks."

"Do you know anyone at Blackstone, the boutique investment bank?" Luis asked hopefully.

Daniel, Ali, and I would have interrupted to clarify, but we were confused ourselves.

"But what do you do during the day? For work?" I asked, wondering why my first question wasn't sufficient enough. We knew consultants, lawyers, and accountants, but being an artist as a profession was a foreign concept. I wasn't sure I'd ever met an artist, and in New York? How would you pay rent?

"I'm a sculptor," she said, smiling in amusement.

"Well, how do you make money?" Bryan asked.

"I waitress and sell my art."

"Oh, you're still in college?" Ali asked, still genuinely trying to understand.

She paused, not expecting the barrage of questions. "I'm actually a few years older than you all," she said as she stirred her Sprite with a straw.

"Do you know anyone who works for Blackstone?" Luis asked again, hoping there would be a small chance he could use this sculptor to expand his network.

"No," she said, looking terribly confused.

Luis looked at her, and then at Daniel, raising his left eyebrow. Daniel shrugged his shoulders, reminding us that it was a favor for his sister.

The lights cast a slight jade tint over the bar, and the sapphire liquor bottles lined up behind the bar glowed turquoise. I sat between Bryan and Luis. For the next several minutes, the three of us caught up while Daniel and Ali talked across from us. The sculptor sat on a low cylinder stool that was pulled up to our red velvet sofa. She sipped her soda as she looked around, thrown off by all the colored lights. Soon there was an awkward silence, which Luis broke by asking, "Does anyone know how to fix a circular reference on a dynamic balance sheet?"

"It depends what kind of circular reference," I said. "Sometimes it will tell you the cell reference and you can just go to it by tracing the precedents."

"What are you talking about?" the sculptor asked no one in particular.

Daniel looked at her and then at Luis and said, "Also, it could just be because it's not iterating enough times. Do: Control-Alt-O. Control-I. Then change the iteration to about a thousand. That usually works."

"The easiest way is to do Control-Alt-G with goal seek," Bryan offered.

"Is this some computer thing?" the bewildered sculptor asked.

"Daniel, it's not Control-I to iterate," I said. "It's Control-T."

"Bullshit!" Daniel said, slapping both of his hands on the table. "It's Control-I!"

He said it with a feistiness that set me off. Maybe it was because I hadn't quite forgiven him yet for punching me. "You are so wrong!" I said, moving forward and slightly jumping out of my seat.

"How much you want to bet?" Daniel challenged.

"I don't need to because I'm right."

"I'm never wrong about my shortcut keys," he said.

"Neither am I," I said, challenging him. My eyes met the artist's startled eyes for a second, and I suddenly felt my face flush, both horrified and certain that I'd just made a fool of myself. The way Daniel and I went back and forth at one another was just like our officers. Looking at her also made me aware that we had ignored her earlier questions. All of us. Like she was invisible. *Isn't that what our officers do to us?* Was this now acceptable behavior for us? What else would we start inheriting?

Bryan and Ali exchanged small smiles. Finally Bryan said, "If I could build a macro to record you two, I'd just laugh as I watched it over and over."

Ali closed his eyes and shook his head and said to Bryan, "Bad Excel joke." He then looked around at all of us and said, "We're out drinking. Please help me forget I work with a bunch of geeks who can't talk about anything better than Excel," which made our whole table shake with laughter.

"Hey," Bryan said, changing the subject, "I thought Brandy was coming."

"I think she's going to be here later," Daniel explained. "While we were walking out the door, Bob called her into his office to staff her on a new deal. She may not make it out. That sucks for her," he said with a chuckle.

"What's so funny?" Ali asked.

"Hey," Daniel said, leaning closer as if we should all huddle. "Did you all hear that she was making out with some guy at that Carbon Club? Some guy from Lehman. She didn't even know him."

"So what?" I said. None of the guys at the table had room to judge others.

"Dude, she was all over him! She's a slut, that's what," Daniel said. He, Ali, Luis, and Bryan all laughed at his lame rhyme.

Daniel went on, "Her whole group is talking about it. I found out from her associate."

"It's none of their business!" I said. I thought of Michael's vocal sexual excursions and added, "Anyway, that's really weird, since Michael came into work and buddy-buddied up with a senior officer, who now idolizes him because he hooked up with two random women at a work function."

"But that was totally different," Luis said. "Michael wasn't hanging all over them in public. Plus, they asked him."

I was relieved when Anna chimed in. *Finally, I'm not the only woman.*

"Don't you think your argument is a little flawed?" the sculptor asked Luis.

"It's different for men and women," Bryan explained sympathetically. "She shouldn't have done that if she didn't want everyone at work talking about her."

"So," I asked, squinting my eyes in disbelief, "if I go and kiss that guy over there, and you go screw that woman over there, tomorrow at work you're cool and I'm less responsible?"

"Yes," Daniel said in a calm, logical tone. "It's just a biological fact. You could get pregnant, and I can't. It says something about your judgment."

I began biting the inside of my cheek as I looked at each of their faces. *You all don't really believe this, do you?* "You guys are so disturbing," I said, finishing the rest of my martini in one swallow. *You too, Bryan?* The whole conversation was making me feel claustrophobic. I elbowed Luis in the ribs. "Move. I need another drink."

My excitement at seeing the few friends I had quickly turned to annoyance. I waited at the bar as I mangled my twenty-dollar bill and gawked at the hundreds of alcohol bottles. I thought of Brandy and this new dive in her status. Until now, she was only known for her sharp, impeccable work. Considering that another analyst the year before had been criticized for being "inappropriately flirty" after she wore a sleeveless dress to work, surely Brandy's irresponsibility would be indirectly addressed in her performance review.

Then I thought about how my officers would react if they had just heard me disapprove of Michael's sexual excursions.

They would crinkle their brows and say, "I'm surprised. Nina's usually not like that." This was starting to feel like a losing game. If I said, "I'm offended," they'd all crowd into Todd's office and leave me out of this rare opportunity to be part of "team bonding."

I thought back to how I reacted when Michael came into the office and announced one of his common hookups with random women he met at bars to everyone. "Don't you just love her," Todd, one of our senior officers, said to the group as I high-fived Michael. From then on Todd no longer started all his group jokes with, "Nina, are you going to get all offended if . . ."

I closed my eyes and shook my head as I wondered whether Luis would describe my non-team-player behavior to anyone in our group. Performance reviews were around the corner, and I'd worked way too hard this year to have something stupid like this work against me.

From the left, I saw the sculptor approach the bar. I kept staring ahead at the bar lights, not sure what to say. I couldn't remember the last time I had spoken to a nonbanker. I started to wonder what people talked about, as though I was socializing for the first time. *"Are you having a good time?"* Too serious. *"Do we seem like weirdos?"* What if she says yes? *"Have you been to this bar before?"* Sounds like a pickup line. I was curious about what kind of people she worked with, but I wasn't sure how to ask the question.

"Those guys are crude. I don't know how you deal with them every day," she said, shaking her head. "Daniel just said he'd love to throw that woman on the bar and fuck her. I mean—" she raised her hands to her head and shook them as if she were washing her hair—"couldn't he have just said he thought she was attractive?"

"You get used to it, I guess," I said. *Why am I standing up for those assholes?* Plus, when would I really get used to it? "I know it sounds ridiculous, but it's like dealing with full-grown children who didn't get enough attention as kids." *I'm just making this up as I go.*

"Are most of the guys you work with like this?" she asked.

"Unfortunately," I said, smiling to myself and wondering whether to be truthful. "You're talking to some of the nicer ones. I don't even associate with the really obnoxious ones. Well, outside of my officers; I don't have much choice when it comes to them."

"Does it bother you that they lack compassion?"

Compassion? The word sounded so foreign to me. I tried to imagine Todd saying the word—impossible. If compassion managed to get past our revolving doors, it would be squelched. Corporate finance was about breaking you down and destroying you if you complained.

"I've interned in groups that aren't nearly as bad as this," I said. "But the reality is that my only full-time jobs have been in investment banking. When I think about banking, the word *compassion* doesn't come to mind. And you only know what you know," I said, shrugging my shoulders.

After a pause, the sculptor stared at my profile and said, "So," in a new, chipper voice, "I knew a banker that worked at Bear Stearns."

"Yeah," I said.

"He was in corporate finance. He used to publish stuff."

As much as I wanted to avoid playing the name game, I couldn't help but laugh aloud. "Nobody in corporate finance publishes anything. Only a select group is able to write coherently. Trust me. I work in corporate finance."

"Well, he used to write these things called print books or something."

"Oh, he wrote a pitch book. It's basically a presentation telling your clients how you're the best bank through various bar charts and numbers that prove it. It's not complicated stuff. And trust me, it's no novel."

"That's so weird," she said. "He always acted like he was publishing articles or some official documents."

"I'm sure in his mind he was," I said, tapping my twenty against the bar and wondering what other creative things banker guys used to impress nonbanking women.

We both looked around as we waited for our drinks, and I knew I'd regret it if I didn't say it, so I abruptly blurted out, "Hey, I'm sure tonight isn't your idea of having fun, but it's just really nice to have another woman around. Thanks for saying something earlier at the table. I'm usually on my own."

"Sure," she said, glancing at me, and then looking away uncomfortably.

The waiter placed my *pomme*-tini and Jamaican sidecar in front of me.

"It's really too bad the lights here distort all the natural colors. These drinks must have vibrant colors, but you can barely tell what you're drinking."

I laughed. "It's weird to me that someone would even think up an observation like that. Why does it matter?"

"Don't you want to know what you're drinking?" she asked, looking at me in alarm.

"No," I said as we started walking back toward the table. "All I want to know is that it can do the job."

Though I was annoyed with my coworkers, I felt like they were all I had. When I got back to the table, Bryan suddenly reached across the table, wrapping one hand around my neck and using the other hand to give me a noogie, rubbing his fist against my head while he screeched in a high-pitched Alvin and the Chipmunks voice, "We're sorry, Nina. Don't be mad at us." The rest of the guys leaned across and rubbed their fists on my head and joined Bryan in the chant.

"Aaaaahhhh!!" I shrieked as we all laughed. Finally, I jabbed them with my elbows to get them to stop. When I sat up, I could feel my hair standing up all over the place.

"That's okay," I said undoing my rubber band and pulling my hair back into my signature tight, low ponytail. "It's my fault," I said with a tart smile. Then I paused, watching their confused faces. "I forgot I work with assholes," I announced as I began laughing even harder.

"Ohhhh. That hurts," Daniel said as they all joined in.

"Cheers to that!" Ali said, raising his glass; we followed suit.

"Okay," Bryan said in a back-to-business tone. "Daniel, you're not off the hook." He looked my way and brought me up to speed on the conversation I'd interrupted. "Daniel was telling us about his blind date."

Recently, many colleagues in the office had been pushing Daniel to find someone. He spent a good amount of his free time with his bosses at strip clubs that were conveniently located a few blocks away from our building. A couple of months ago, Daniel was harassing one of the strippers, almost making a scene, so his superiors thought it might be a good idea for him to take it easy on the clubs for a while.

His officers suggested to some analysts in the technology

group that they set Daniel up with one of their friends. We tried to find friends or friends of friends who were interested in the idea of dating a banker. Daniel liked to look like a banker all the time. He was never off. Whenever he had the opportunity to go home and change out of his suit, he would always come up with an excuse as to why he had to leave it on. He also needed his beeper to be visible. He thought it would be impressive if it went off. "Chicks dig it."

Ali, out of concern for Daniel, grilled him about his date. "Well, did she call you back?" he asked.

"No, she never called back," Daniel said, shaking his head.

"Do you know why?" Bryan asked.

"Well, I don't know," Daniel said in a higher pitch. "I mean, maybe I talked too much. I just hadn't talked to anyone in so long. I think I just rambled the whole evening, but she acted really interested."

"What did you talk about?" I asked, surprised to see Daniel so unsure of himself.

"Mostly?" he asked.

"Yes," Ali encouraged him.

"Well. . . ." Daniel's eyes shifted around as if he was about to change the subject. Then he gave in. "Mainly, I explained to her how our leveraged buyout Excel model works." He paused, but was caught up in defensive excitement. "I mean, she asked me all these questions. It's not like I just kept talking. She wanted to know!" He then bowed his head and created an eddy in his whiskey with his stirrer.

"What do you mean by 'mostly'? Fifty percent of the evening?" Ali suggested.

"More," Daniel said, in a tone that indicated he was taking

responsibility.

"Wow," Bryan said. "I could see how most people would be interested for maybe five or ten minutes. A quick overview, maybe, but not for hours. Well, unless she's a banker too," he said hopefully.

"No," Daniel said flatly. "Well, what the fuck am I supposed to talk about? That's all I had to talk about. People talk about life and this is my life. It's all I have to offer!"

"Next time," Ali said, putting his hand on Daniel's shoulder.

"Yeah," Daniel said, unconvinced. He sat for a few seconds considering the evening and then said, "Dude, at least I had something interesting to talk about. She asked me the most fucked-up question in the middle of when I was explaining debt ratios. The bitch asked me what I wanted to do with my life."

"What did you say?" Ali asked, hopeful again.

"I told her," Daniel said, "I want to start my own business and be a millionaire." Everyone was quiet for a moment, and then Daniel turned the question around. "Well, what the hell would you have said?"

"The truth?" Ali asked rhetorically. "I want to go back to my home country, Bangladesh, and feed the sad-eyed starving beggars. But instead, what will I do? I will work for the best LBO shop I can get into."

"Why?" the sculptor intervened.

"Because I can. And the majority of this world can't," Ali said with a shoulder shrug and then looked at Bryan. "What about you?"

Bryan smiled and said with confidence, "I want to make enough money to retire by the time I'm thirty and then spend all my time on a sailboat with my family. I will have a girl first and then a boy." We all shifted uncomfortably since we knew that Bryan's dad committed suicide over money.

"What about you, Luis?" Daniel asked.

"I'm only here so that I can go to Harvard Business School," Luis said, shrugging his shoulders casually.

The waiter placed a bill on the table for all the drinks we hadn't yet paid for. Ali asked, "Are you all expensing this for dinner?"

"How?" I asked, knowing it would be hard to expense a meal from a bar.

"They have food here," Luis informed me.

Bryan shook his head and said, "They'll find out."

"Our officers do it all the time. They got pissed off when I wouldn't expense their drinks last week," Daniel said. "Plus, do you think they pay for their strip club tabs?"

"They owe us," Ali said.

"A liquid dinner," Luis agreed.

I started to get up to go to the restroom and Ali interrupted with a laugh. "Nice try, Nina. You haven't answered the question."

"I came here because I wanted to be a banker," I said, looking down at our colorful drinks. "I figured it was a prestigious career that would introduce me to lots of smart, successful people." I paused since they started snickering at my idealist notions, which made me just cut to the chase. "I just want to be successful."

"What's successful to you?" Bryan asked with a sly smile.

It was clear to me that I was disenchanted by my onetime ambition of being a banker, but I hadn't thought past this banking experience. Unlike me, my colleagues had access to Ivy

League alumni with whom they could touch base regularly to get a feel for their future career paths. I was beginning to wonder how to redefine success. Until now, I'd just assumed that people who had money, prestige, and power lived perfect happy lives. If they didn't, why would so many people, including my parents and many from my Parsi community, spend a lifetime inching closer and closer to these things? I'd never been around people as powerful and rich as the ones I met at Morgan Stanley. Until investment banking, the closest I'd gotten to people like this was through soap operas. But I had no idea where to start in terms of redefining success. If my parents, my community, and now my colleagues weren't my role models, who was? The question seemed so daunting that I tried not to think about it. And I, like so many of my colleagues, now made a habit of avoiding rather than reflecting.

Under the table, I thrust my fists upward, joggling all our empty glasses, and said, "One last round—tequila washed down with double Goldschläger!"

"I'm in!" Luis agreed, getting up to find a waiter.

"Hard-core!" Daniel shouted. "Hell, yeah!"

Too impatient for a waiter, I ran over to the bar and returned carrying a heavy tray of colored potions back to the table. We all closed our eyes and gulped until we felt light enough. After each shot, we cheered, "Thank you, Morgan Stanley!" All the while, the sculptor watched us in motionless amazement, as if she were one of her own creations fixed in an exhibit.

CHAPTER 8 Application

"Mom, I feel like my head and stomach are about to blow up into tiny pieces like a cartoon character," I said, lying on the floor of a Kinko's in our Houston suburb with my head on top of a purple paisley Bombay Dyeing blanket folded tightly in Lena's lap.

"I'm so sorry, honey," she said. "Lena, adjust her head." Instead, Lena offered me the two-ply Walmart plastic bag.

"Not yet," I said, wishing I could throw up and relieve myself of the nausea.

"We're almost finished," my mom said. "Are you sure you don't just want to stop and go home?"

"No, the deadline is in two days," I reminded her. "Would you go home?" We were filling out the Morgan Stanley Scholars application that would guarantee me an internship and give me a large two-year scholarship. It targeted students from schools that weren't feeders for Wall Street. I'd taken the Greyhound bus home from UT Austin for the weekend.

"Why do you wait until the last minute! You used to do this to me with science fair projects, too. Tell me at ten at night you needed posterboard the next morning. How can I help you then? Your sisters never did this," she said, sitting in front of the computer monitor turning only her head and keeping the rest of her body in proper typing form with her index fingers positioned over the *F* and the *J*. I'd always been fascinated with her hands. Her fingers glided seamlessly back and forth on our piano. She was equally adept at speed-typing as she was at wrapping a fast-food burger back into its square paper, identical to the way it was served.

"It's easy," she would blush when asked to share her trick. "Lift up the near side and fold it on top of the burger. And do the same with the far side. Twist the side flaps away and fold under the burger."

This expertise came from previous jobs. Her first job in the United States was as a cashier at Jack in the Box. If you brought it up now she would wave her hand in embarrassment. "We went through tough times when we first moved to America." I was a toddler and only remembered that her fast-food colleague Linda would pick her up on a motorcycle so she didn't always have to walk the two miles. Both the motorcycle and my mother's fast-food days now seemed improbable considering that she had long since moved on to a corporate job as an administrative assistant. "It's a job that pays me well," she said, incapable of suppressing her disenchantment. This was not the same enthusiasm she had expressed at first when she proudly wrote to her parents back in India on a blue aerogramme that she sealed with a gold monogram G sticker. "I even have my own stapler!" All the little triumphs became so minor with time and perspective. Soon we became the embodiment of her success.

She often reminded us, "You must have an American degree in this country." Look at Jamshed Uncle—brilliant surgeon in India, but no one here acknowledges his ten years of practice. He had to start again and become a businessman. Look at me. No matter how hard I work, without a degree I'll only be an admin assistant," she would say with a fierceness I couldn't forget.

"The application is only last minute because I found out about it last-minute. In my business council meeting this week, I saw someone filling it out. That's how I found out about it," I said, holding one hand on my forehead to feel my 102.5 degree fever and placing the other on my stomach, hoping to keep from throwing up. "Thanks, Mom. You never let me down."

On Friday I realized the chills and waves of heat were not anxiety but a fever, and I called her out of desperation: "Mom, I only have three days, and I have to apply for this. Between the money from the Morgan Stanley scholarship and internship, it will pay for the rest of my education." Already I'd won most of the scholarships I'd applied for, but they'd all been relatively small. This scholarship was unbelievable compared to the rest. I'd be able to cut back to working just one job, and there'd be no threat of having to drop out of school. *I have to get this!*

"Come home," she said. "We'll all work together. You recite, and I'll type. Lena can be your nurse. Plus, you know how excited your dad gets when one of you comes home, running around to cater to your every want. He'll take you back to Austin on Monday if you still feel too weak." When it came to assuring our success, her energy elevated to a frantic pitch. She was determined for us to have the opportunities she never did.

"Did you wear earrings to the interview? Did you starch your shirt? Did you smile?" She'd pepper me with questions that felt like a secondary interview. So often I just wanted to forget about it, relieved the interview was over. It was as though she wanted to relive it alongside us. Through high school, my parents would leave work precisely on time, spending their evenings dropping

Shireen off at work, ferrying Farah and me to dance classes, and then picking up Lena from her study groups. All that commotion so that we could be one step closer to the American dream.

"I'd never let you down, but sometimes I wish I could," she said in a tired voice, looking at her watch and calculating how many hours we'd been at Kinko's.

"Mom, you said you were going to drop Liz and me off to see *Braveheart* by seven," Lena said.

"I know, Lena," she said sternly, now playing with the margins on the application, "but you know we're pressed for time." Though she seemed irritated, now that Lena was the only one living at home and her other three daughters were all at UT, it was clear she enjoyed the fact that her kids still demanded her attention. She was used to managing four, so today two kids were effortless.

Lena held a glass of Jell-O water, an Indian solution to any stomach sickness. "You need to drink this so you have some energy," she insisted, putting it up to my lips while cupping my head and lifting it with her other hand. "Grandma made the watermelon one especially for you."

I took a couple of sips as I stared at my mom's coarse hair, which waved back and forth like a wild, winding road. In India she would lay it on an ironing board and use a clothes iron to straighten it. On my head, you could pull out hairs that were exact replicas of her wavy hair and sitting next to them were straight, thin hairs like my father's. "The balance of two extremes," my mom would say.

While Lena was feeding me Jell-O water, she looked up and said, "Mom, look how vulnerable Nina is." Lena looked back down at me and pinched my cheek as she laughed and I continued to gulp. "I like you this way," she said. "You're always so tough. No one ever gets a chance to baby you."

"Thanks for taking such good care of me," I said, grateful to be pampered.

Seated next to my mom, a woman with blue patent leather heels too high for a Kinko's visit looked up from formatting her Janie's BBQ menu with concern. "Is she okay?" the woman asked Lena.

"She's applying for a Wall Street scholarship," my mom jumped in, as if that would explain it. "Her application is due in two days. I would never have made her do this otherwise." She went on, as she often did, to answer questions that were never asked. "I have four bright girls. My first one is premed, in the Peace Corps, and is applying to Johns Hopkins. The second one is studying engineering and spends all her summers at DuPont."

"How wonderful," the woman said, smiling broadly at Lena and me. "So you have four girls?"

"Here are the other two," my mother said, flipping over the back of her checkbook and showing the woman a picture of all four of us dressed up at the Persian New Year party.

"Wow, they are beautiful," the woman said, looking back and forth between the photo and us. As she studied the picture, my mom turned to us and silently mouthed, "I told you everyone says that." We both rolled our eyes in embarrassment since we'd seen this promotional scene so many times.

"Look at all that gorgeous hair," the woman said and then looked up at Lena's thick, permed fluffy hair you could lose a comb in. "Do you mind if I touch it?"

"Sure," Lena said. She then looked at me and we both started to giggle. Every now and again a Texan woman with thin, flat hair would ask us this unusual question that felt like a compliment but still made us feel like freaks. It was particularly frequent when I was in line at the grocery store or Target. Whereas on the New York streets, no one was ever interested in my hair.

"My whole family doesn't even have this much hair," she said, smiling.

"Mom, we need to hurry up," I announced. "Do you know how much this is costing?"

"Oh yeah," she said, putting a hand in front of me, letting me know she had it under control. "Calm down, *beta*. We only have one question left. Sit tight; I'm going to work out a deal with them," the negotiator extraordinaire said as she jumped up. I could hear her now: "Listen, my daughter is terribly ill and this is taking much longer than expected. We are loyal Kinko's customers. We're here at least once a month." She always followed with the hard sell, "Can't you give us some sort of discount?"

As soon as my mom walked away Lena looked at me and asked, "Why are you so serious?"

"Give me a break. I'm sick," I said, even though I felt buoyed by all the activity and attention. Slowly, I'd worked my way to sitting up, and now Lena and I sat in little squats with our backs against the wall—a seated position my grandmother would be highly offended by since it is the same as the squat-toilet stance in India.

"Not right now," Lena said, "but you've changed since you started college. You were all about having a good time and looking for the next football player to date before you left. Now all you care about are your grades and jobs. You barely even did your homework in high school. What happened?"

I turned to face her, surprised that it wasn't obvious to her why my life had changed. "You don't understand what it's like to support yourself," I said. As I spoke, I felt the same racing adrenaline my mom must have felt when I wouldn't stop begging her for a new, trendy leotard even though I already had too many. On a bad day, she'd fling her checkbook at me and say, "You want it that bad? Then show me how to pay for it with a negative balance. Show me!"

Overnight I went from being uninterested in high school work to being committed to a perfect college academic record. Not out of interest in the subjects, but more to prove to myself, and my dad, that I was worthy. I declined my dad's "deal" to stay in Houston under his roof, and instead I went to UT, which meant I was financially independent. I chose UT mainly because his well-intentioned, yet tight grip on who I could date and where I could go was suffocating to me, an-eighteen-year-old American girl. It took a toll on our relationship since I'm sure he saw it as the height of defiance when I once again ignored his advice. The first year after I left for college, our interaction was somewhat limited, but it improved each year.

"But don't you get financial aid?" Lena said. "It can't be that bad. Just take out a bunch of loans."

"Only a part of it is financial aid, and I have to make up the rest by my internships and working multiple jobs." My voice got louder, and now I was kneeling over her squat. "Sometimes I have trouble sleeping at night, wondering if I'll have to drop out each new semester. If you don't have the money, you can't enroll. There's no layaway program."

"Calm down or you're going to get worse. Lie down," she said, straightening out my blanket pillow, eager to defuse the situation. "You sound like Mom complaining about how much it costs to raise kids," she said with a throwaway laugh. "And you're way too bitter for a college student. You should go out to sorority events with your high school friends."

I didn't see much of my high school friends, since their sororities consumed their social lives. "Do you know how much it costs to go to a sorority event?" I screeched loud enough for a young couple wearing matching red Rockets hats to turn our way. As I said it, I realized how much I *did* sound like my mom. But Lena's comments felt so flippant to me. She couldn't appreciate how much it took to support yourself. *Is that what we sounded like as kids? So ungrateful!* "It's easy when you're living off other people's money," I said, staring at the Gucci purse my parents had bought her. Farah would call me to announce, "Did you see those Kenneth Cole shoes they bought Lena? Are they trying to spoil her? She needs to get a job, not hang out at the mall!" We were those older sisters with an "I worked hard, so you should work harder" attitude. We found it difficult to stomach the leniency that parents adopt by the time they're raising their last child, naturally growing tired toward the finish line.

"I'm sure Mom and Dad will give you money if you ask," Lena mumbled. She looked straight ahead and rocked back and forth in her squat. "Dad said he was trying to make a point by demanding you stay in Houston for college so he could keep an eye on you. Who would have guessed you'd just change overnight and become so responsible?" She stopped rocking and faced me. "You should just ask them for money and have a good time."

"They help me out every now and again, but I'm actually learning a lot by supporting myself. Plus, their money comes with rules," I said, eager to live on my own terms and prove to my dad that I could make it on my own, even though most of the time I felt completely overwhelmed with this abrupt new independent life.

"Isn't it ironic?" Lena asked. "Even though you still did pretty well in high school, you were his most challenging kid, and you left to get away from his strict rules, but you're doing everything he wants—getting perfect grades, working when you're not studying, and hardly dating or socializing."

Lena laughed at her observation, but I didn't find it as amusing, because it was true. So much of my energy in college was geared toward desperately trying to win his attention with perfect grades and accolades. Determined to prove him wrong, I wouldn't be his ungrateful daughter. Instead, I'd be his favorite, most successful daughter, the one he couldn't help but brag about at his weekend Parsi dinners.

My mom walked our way, pumping her arms up and down like a victorious cheerleader, and Lena and I both looked around, already embarrassed, in case anyone was looking.

"Mom, I'm never going to make it to the movie," Lena complained.

My mother pointed to Lena and her slight drawl informed us that she'd used her typical chameleon ways, changing her accent for the salesclerk and loving every second of it. "Stop whining, we're almost done! You'll be on time." Then, turning to me with a smile, she said, "We have one more question left, so pull yourself together and focus. By the way, he's only charging us for two hours instead of six."

"Mom, what did you say to him?" Lena said, laughing loudly.

"Your mother is a miracle worker," she said, shimmying her shoulders in pride. "I told him all about your first summer on Wall Street and how you impressed everyone, but that you need this scholarship to really make it. He wants to meet you, so go say thank you before you leave." She put her hands on her hips and added, "See how everyone in Texas wants to help you?"

Lena covered her mouth to contain her loud laughter. "I can't wait to tell Dad that you were trying to hook Nina up with the Kinko's dude."

My mom ignored her, still so pleased with herself. I could feel her confidence. "Okay, let's go," she with the same enthusiasm she had when she was near a karaoke machine. "Last essay question: biggest challenge you've overcome." She turned her head around. "What about going to Wall Street that first summer? You can talk about how your dad said you shouldn't go to such a dangerous city and wanted you to take that local job at Southwestern Bell corporate instead. Remember how hard you worked to convince him?"

A family meeting was in order: *Can Nina go to New York?* "Young girls are not meant to live away from home. And she's too disorganized. She'll get hurt," he insisted. "Stay in Houston. You already have a great job offer at Southwestern Bell. New York's expensive. You can save all your summer money if you live here."

But my motormouth didn't win me the New York experience; it was my mom who convinced him. She called every Parsi aunty and uncle she knew to see who could house me in New York City. "My Nina has a job on Wall Street. We are dying for her to go, but we need her to have some supervision." Ultimately she found an aunt who was there for the summer doing her residency in surgery and was stricter than my dad. The aunty insisted she was thrilled to help with this endeavor and housed me rent-free. I saved enough money to pay for tuition for my entire sophomore year. Every week I calculated how much I could save. At the end of the summer, I rewarded myself with a $10 increase in my monthly social budget.

"Well, in the end, you're the one who convinced him," I said. "What about the high school dance team? Remember how you said I could only join if I paid for it since it was so costly and it wouldn't be fair to my sisters?" She squinted her eyes a little and I could sense she wasn't wild about this example. "It was the first time I realized money could buy me freedom, and I didn't have to listen to everything you and Dad restricted me to," I said, my back straight with excitement.

"Watch it, missy. We are still your parents. Plus you don't want to put that in an application, because it sounds defiant. Even though you are," she said as she turned back to face the computer.

Though it was of no use, she played with the pencil she kept warm behind her ear as if jostling it would tickle her brain with ideas. Suddenly, the Texan accent was a thing of the past and she laid into me with her Gujarati accent: "Nina, don't get all worked up, but I want to remind you of your options. You saw how fast Farah got that top engineering job after Dad introduced her to Sorab Uncle. We can find you a top finance job in Houston. Zenobia Aunty works in finance at Shell in a high-ranking position, and she always says, 'Let me know when Nina's ready to work in Houston.'" She paused and I knew she, just like my father, was always torn between wanting me to live close by to them yet enjoying praising my Wall Street accomplishments.

No one could deny the power of the Parsi community. With their support, you could build a business almost instantly. There were only a handful of Parsis in Houston who didn't use Rustom Uncle as their accountant or depend on Yezdi Uncle's insurance policy, sticking a magnet with his big smile on their fridge.

But I was already taken in by New York's insatiable drive and ambition. "You know there's nothing that compares to Wall Street in Houston. Do you want me to be mediocre?"

She sat quietly for a moment, wrestling with the question. "Be with the best for now. When you are ready, you'll come back to Texas. I know you will." She looked at her watch and realized we'd have to leave soon to drop off Lena. She looked at me and said, "You're getting exhausted. Let's go. You can write the last question out by hand at home, and then I'll come back tomorrow early and finish typing the rest."

"Thanks, Mom," I said, getting up and kissing her on the cheek.

"Do I ever let you down?" she said as she shook her head from side to side, dancing to the sound of successful children.

On our way to drop Lena off at the movies, my mom did her usual grooving to Mix 96.5, "Hits from yesterday and today," in the car. She'd shout the lyrics she knew, then tap her index fingers on the steering wheel like drumsticks as she na-na-na-na sha-la-la-la-ed to the lyrics she didn't know. With her ear for music, she could play anything on the piano just by hearing it. She was never stingy, but one time when she bought Farah a karaoke machine for her birthday she ended up fighting Farah for the microphone.

"Mom, how come you didn't sing or become a pianist?" Lena asked.

"Because those are just hobbies and music doesn't pay the bills for four kids. Only in America do you get all this do-what-you-love talk. That's not how we grew up. For us, leaving for the

States was success and to get there you had to have a practical profession—doctor or engineer—or you could marry someone. For us, America was a country that had ice cream in gallons rather than spoonfuls."

My mom got married and moved to the United States when she was seventeen. Her grandmother got a call from a Parsi friend who said she knew of a boy coming from the States who was going to meet only eight women before returning with a bride. The friend asked my mom's grandmother if she knew of a young woman who'd be interested. She imagined it would be ideal for her granddaughter—a successful Parsi with an engineering master's coming from the United States for just a few weeks. She convinced my mother, a freshman in college, to meet him. After spending six weeks with my father, who was ten years older, my mom informed her strict father that she was getting married and leaving for the States.

There was something about my parents' life that terrified me. It was as if they were trapped into lives bigger than they were, with four kids with so many needs. When we asked my mom what she wanted in life she would hold our faces tightly with one hand, her thumb in one cheek and her forefinger in the other, and say, "You were my dream, *beta*." But only months before I left for college, while looking for whiteout in her desk drawer, I found a locked box labeled LETTERS FROM ZAL—EARLY YEARS. Next to the box was a folded-up sheet of paper with a list of American universities that looked like the colleges she planned on applying to. Maybe she wished things had gone as planned and that she had been able to go to college instead of getting pregnant on her wedding night. But when I confronted her, she said, "I would never have changed my life. I was dying to have you four girls. You are all the light of my life." It wasn't a direct answer, but I always wondered if she'd traded one dream for another.

It was a burden to live up to my parents' sacrifices. I could never be strong enough to live the lives they'd chosen. It wasn't in my nature to make so many sacrifices. I wanted a job I loved, a marriage I could leave if things were beyond repair, and kids despite my challenging career. Many Indians would consider this laundry list selfish. In this way, I was more American than Indian. I didn't know how to stop wanting these things. As an American, I had learned to bank on this level of abundance. Yet I knew that to my parents my inability to make sacrifices was an insult.

Tuesday morning I called Morgan Stanley to make sure they had received my application.

"I'm sorry, but the Scholars applications were due last week," the woman from human resources said in a confused voice.

I stared at the Xerox copy that my mom had made for me, *just in case*. "I'm reading it right here," I said. "It says October 23."

"That was the due date from last year's application," she clarified.

Sure enough, I was holding a copy of last year's application materials. I closed my eyes and tried with each word to calm down as I twisted the phone cord frantically. "But this is the application I got from the career office at UT. They only had this one application left. I didn't even think to check the year; all that mattered to me was getting the application just right." My tone became frantic as I rattled on. "Please, could you just look at my application? I spent my freshman year at JP Morgan." I paused, trying to gauge if I need to continue the plea, but she was silent.

"Please," I said, my desperation drawing out the word.

"I'll talk to the committee," she said crisply.

When I told my mother about this turn of events, her response was even more frantic than mine. "Did you tell them about your JP Morgan internship? Did you tell them that everyone at JP Morgan loved you?"

"Mom, I told them."

She interrupted me. "Have your manager from JP Morgan call them. Do you want me to call? They can't ruin this. You worked too hard."

"Mom, they were really impressed, but you know how these people are. One screwed-up deadline and—"

"I know you can get this one." She paused and I imagined her hand on top of her head pulling at a handful of hair, "Fali Uncle said his sister-in-law used to work at Barclays in New York. Maybe I'll have him call her?"

"No, Mom, that is a totally different bank. How can that help?" I said. "Please, Mom . . ."

"They are both in New York. You never know." She was so desperate. This wasn't just my application. It was our family's application.

"Please don't worry. It'll work out or it won't. She said she'd put it in with the other applications and mark it late. The committee will decide whether they want to look at it or not," I said with my hand on my stomach to temper my burning gut, and slowly falling to the floor in a squat to stop my legs from shaking. "I know. I have to get this," I said, imagining what it would be like to live my last two years of college not calculating every penny I spent. "I'm just so tired. Please, let it be. I feel like I've done everything I can."

"Your dad and I are sitting here praying for you. I bet you'll get it," she said.

"Of course she'll get it," I heard my dad correct her with a slight tone of annoyance that she didn't say it with more confidence. "Did you tell her to send her JP Morgan performance review?"

Several months later I got a priority envelope with an invitation to an intensive weekend of interviews and entertainment in New York, but it was as if a stubborn bull were standing between me and Morgan Stanley. After the application deadline scare, I couldn't afford to let anything go wrong. Normally I would have arrived at the airport several hours early just to be safe and walked through every potential interview question while waiting. I had a list of fifty-seven potential questions and wrote detailed responses to each of them:

Name three strengths and weaknesses. Give me an example of how you exemplify each.

Why should I hire you and not him?

How many gas stations are there in the United States? As you think through it, be sure to walk me through your logic.

Tell me a time you had to deal with an ethical issue. How did you handle it?

What is your biggest failure?

Because I had an accounting midterm that ended less than two hours before my flight, I had only a short window to get to the airport. Since I didn't have a car, one of my housemates offered to take me to the airport so that I didn't risk the chance of a cab leaving me high and dry without a ride. We packed my luggage in her car the night before and agreed to meet at the guard stand near the main library.

Ten minutes passed, and I started to panic. It was so wrenching to consider finding another ride, because my luggage was in her trunk and the interviews were at 6:00 A.M. the next morning. There'd be no time to shop for a suit. After twenty minutes passed, I ran to a pay phone and called a cab service that said they could be there in fifteen minutes. As I paced in wait, I started approaching cars, debating whether to walk up to strangers and beg for a ride, but I knew I was so frantic that if I started to explain, I would scare them.

I saw the yellow cab from afar in the congested campus traffic and sprinted a quarter mile to catch it. "I've got thirty minutes until my flight takes off. Take a U-turn here and get me to the airport. If you get a ticket, I'll pay for it. Please drive as fast as you can. This is my one shot to get into the best firm on Wall Street."

"Wall Street," he said with a smile. "I've never met anyone who's worked there. Put your seat belt on and let's go."

As fast as he drove, I still didn't make it to the airport on time. I ran through the concourse so fast that I started choking upon reaching the gate.

"Please," I said, but my words were inaudible. "I'm on this flight," I struggled to say, but again, no sound came out.

The gate agent shook her head, all too aware of the predicament I was in. "There's really nothing I can do at this point," she said, pointing to the doors. "Once the Jetway and cabin doors close, the flight is as good as gone."

"You don't understand," I said, holding my ticket and for the first time noticing the cost of the flight Morgan Stanley had paid for me, eight hundred dollars—nearly a full semester's tuition.

"I'm trying to get a job on Wall Street. This job will pay for the rest of my college degree, and the interviews start at six tomorrow morning," I said, pacing up to the gate door and looking through the window helplessly as I spoke.

"I can put you on a flight tomorrow morning, sweetheart—that's the best I can do," she assured me.

"Please," I said, swiveling around to look for anyone else who could help me. I accosted another woman walking by in a Delta uniform: "Can you help me?" Uncontrollable tears started to fall down my face as I pleaded for help. She froze and looked at the agent, who stood by speechless.

I looked back and forth between the two of them. "I have to get to New York! This scholarship on Wall Street is going to pay for my next two years of school. I don't know how I will pay for it otherwise." My face ached with desperation as the tears continued to stream down. The woman in the Delta uniform panicked and said, "Okay, okay, let's see what we can do. You *have* to calm down." I was becoming a security risk at this point. They whispered among themselves, made a call, and within five minutes, a stewardess from the flight opened the door to let me on the flight. Later, I found out my friend was waiting for me near another guard stand on the other side of the library.

We landed at LaGuardia at 5:12 P.M. I remembered that there was a Casual Corner near the Michelangelo Hotel in Times Square and took a cab directly there with ten minutes before it closed. Without trying anything on I grabbed a button-down shirt, a suit, and shoes and charged it to my credit card, knowing I'd have to return all of it before the bill was due. When

I returned to the hotel, the interview candidates were dressed in strappy heels and shiny tank-top shirts to head over to Webster Hall, a nightclub that had a cover of twenty-five dollars, which was practically my monthly social budget at UT. Just as I did when I interned at JP Morgan, I excused myself with lies. "I'm too tired tonight. Have fun!"

I was unable to sleep that night, so I walked around the expansive three rooms in my business executive suite. I watched *Letterman*, spun myself around in circles to make myself dizzy, and even picked up the room service menu and read every word out loud, hoping it would bore me to sleep.

The next morning was a series of back-to-back interviews. My first interviewer had credentials that alone made me feel small. "Good morning, I'm Laura Smith. I graduated at the top of my class from Harvard undergrad and then Wharton School of Business. *Fortune* has ranked me one of the Most Powerful Women in Business." While she spoke, I wiggled in my suit, hoping the price tags I tucked into my clothes and shoes would not slip out.

"You have As in all of your economics classes. I was an economics major, so explain to me the law of marginal utility, then explain to me what happens to the quantity demanded and the price of an inelastic product when the demand curve shifts up. Finally, give me a real-world example of when this might happen.

"What would your ideal obituary say?

"I see on your transcript you have some solid As here. Unfortunately, that means that the few Bs in your record stand out and look like Fs to me. Especially this one psychology class called Personality? Tell me, why I should hire someone with a B in Personality?

"What is thirty-five times twelve?" Right after she asked, I started to pick up my pen and write "35 x 12." But she lightly placed her hand on my tablet, showcasing a diamond that looked more like an ice cube. "No need. Do it in your head."

At the close of the interview, she looked straight through me and offered the same spiel she'd shared with every other unnerved candidate: "Annually, we hire about twenty scholars from across the country. The majority of the people I'll see today won't make it. This is a chance of a lifetime. Best of luck, Ms. Godiwalla," she said as she locked her eyes on mine and shook my hand firmly.

CHAPTER 9

Naked Ambition

Pam, Leanna, and I were at dinner celebrating our "almost only a year left" anniversary, an impromptu celebration after Leanna walked around our office floor looking for other analysts who could get out before 9:00 P.M. Like several of my colleagues whom I'd met briefly during training, they seemed like people I'd like to know better, but I'd hardly seen them since. I had just finished working several eighty-hour weeks in a row, and finally, for a couple days, things had slowed down.

Pam insisted on Balthazar, the quintessential fin de siècle Paris brasserie, since she had recently discovered their three-tiered seafood tower and Côte-Rôtie. Even though Pam would have much preferred to sit next to the soaring windows into which voyeurs glanced in awe as they walked along Spring Street, I was relieved when they sat us on the leather banquettes in a quieter corner so we didn't have to shout over the buzz-ing socialites. As soon as we sat down, I nestled against the wall under the lazily spinning fans and admired the fresh-cut flowers in oversize vases.

Not long after we sat down Pam announced, "Those two girls look like my investment club friends from Mount Holyoke."

Leanna just rolled her eyes and later explained to me that

she remembered from training that Pam often imagined she was seeing her college friends whenever they went to a supertrendy place she wanted to be seen.

Even though we were all thrilled to have a girls' night out, as at most dinners with bankers, we mostly complained about how inconsiderate our officers were, how mundane the work was, and how unbearable the hours were. But then the subject abruptly changed. Midway through dinner, while a littleneck clam slithered in her mouth, Pam casually announced that Luke, one of the analysts on her floor, had posed nude in a porn magazine.

"Wow!" said Leanna, who worked in the finance group. "That's bold."

"No way," I said, shaking my head. "That's got to be a rumor. Have you seen it?"

"No," said Pam, "but I heard someone in the office talking on the phone to a friend about it. He said Luke took these pictures a while ago, and then this magazine published them. . . . I don't know, his story went on, but I only heard the beginning."

"Do you think it's true?" I asked, staring at the aged mirrors reflecting rows of French wine bottles. "Or is he just looking for attention?"

"I think he really did it," Pam said. "He said it was in *Playguy.*"

"You mean *Playgirl?*" Leanna asked.

"No," Pam said. "He said *Playguy.* I think it's gay porn."

"Never heard of it," I said. "This month's issue?"

She nodded her head as she pushed the foie gras mousse toward Leanna, letting her know she should finish it. "I'm saving room for the profiteroles," she said. "I dream about that chocolate sauce." She looked straight ahead at the mirror with pensive eyes. "Hey, there's Spike Lee!"

Like true New Yorkers, Leanna and I looked up and over discreetly, and then quickly looked away, reminding ourselves that celebrity spotting was commonplace in New York. "You're such a good celebrity spotter," Leanna said, commending Pam. "I've seen Kevin Spacey near the Morgan Stanley building several times when I walked out of Starbucks. I'm pretty sure he's in a Broadway show nearby. Nina, didn't you say you saw Seinfeld right next to your apartment?"

"Yeah, my doorman sees him all the time. He must live pretty close by," I said, before changing the subject. "So back to Luke. If he told you he's in the magazine, why haven't you gotten a copy to see if it's true?" I challenged.

"I won't be able to work with him if I see him all oiled up," she said. "He sits on my floor, for God's sake. Plus, he's so scrawny. Can you imagine it?" she said, bending her pinky back and forth. No one wanted to say what we were all thinking: Luke was one of the few African American analysts in our program at Morgan Stanley.

Finally, Leanna said, "Okay, I'm curious! We all know that once you go black you can't go back."

"But I think he's only half black, or at least he looks only half," Pam said. "So I'm not sure where that leaves him."

We all snickered. "Isn't he scared everyone he works with will find out?" I asked.

"Who knows?" Pam said. "Don't forget, he's a celebrity analyst who doesn't have to do that much work to stay here. Remember, his dad is that well-known surgeon guy? Haven't you heard him talk about how he wants to be a model? Well, now he's a model. Plus, Morgan Stanley can't fire him for posing in a magazine. It's none of their business," Pam confirmed.

"I'm pretty sure that would be illegal," Leanna agreed. "Plus, I don't think Luke would tell anyone if he thought he'd get fired."

"I'll have to find this *Playguy* mag. The newsstand near my house is already closed, so I'll get it tomorrow."

"I want to see it!" they both screeched simultaneously.

I ran my fork along my duck confit, now less interested in it, and fixed my eyes on them, wondering how they could be so curious yet not act on it. It was almost impossible for me to stay put. *Did he really do it?*

The next morning, a cloudy Saturday, I bought a copy at the newsstand nearest to my apartment.

There was Luke. In the first photo, he leaned his neck back and gazed my way in a euphoric daze. Wearing only white ankle socks, he was a mere foot away from me. He sat on a small rug against a door. Like an innocent child exploring, he spread his legs and used one hand to stroke his nipple and the other to stroke his curled, solid hard-on. His moist, half-parted lips begged for attention. I looked at his fully oiled limbs in disbelief and then turned the page to find him on all fours, arching his back and thrusting out his butt, pleading for takers. I sat on my sofa and flipped through all twelve of his spreads in *Playguy* before I reached the Fresh Pricks page, which featured men together, creatively consuming one another.

Luke's pictures in *Playguy* captured a desperate bursting feeling too intimate for a magazine. Each new provocative position stunned me. But soon I was distracted by an impulse to compare *Playgirl* and *Playguy*. Digging through my bottom dresser drawer, below my socks, I pulled out the handful of *Playgirl* issues my college roommates and I used to ogle in our dormitory and compared them to this new porn where everyone stood proud and erect. I found it hard to believe that this was the same guy who sat next to me during training. I remembered Luke leaning over and remarking on our accounting instructor's pathetic attempt at a comb-over. In fact, other than in the cafeteria, I couldn't remember seeing Luke that much since training.

I drank a glass of ice water slowly to calm myself, but I couldn't keep this news quiet. I called Pam, who was at work. "Are you busy? Is anyone there?" I said in a quick whisper even though I was alone.

"Just doing an LBO model," she replied. "What's up?"

"Oh my God!" I screamed, like a hysterical child, laughing at the same time. "You have got to come over and see this! I got the magazine. It's nothing like the soft *Playgirl* models. He is totally hard!"

She sat silent on the other line.

"Is Luke right there?" I asked.

"Basically," she said.

"When will you get off?" I asked impatiently. From her curt tone I could tell someone else was there, probably her associate. It was clear she couldn't talk.

"Not till late," she replied.

From her rapid rhythmic motions, I could tell she was inserting five-millimeter-width columns between twenty millimeter-width columns into a spreadsheet, Morgan Stanley format. "Okay, your loss," I said. "Talk to you later."

I called several other colleagues, but everyone was too busy working. I eagerly needed to share this dirt. It didn't take much to make me childishly giddy now that, outside of work, socialization with others was limited and sporadic.

Saturday was considered a workday for most of us analysts, so I was getting a rare Saturday off that most of my colleagues weren't. I spent most of my evening on the couch flipping through *Playguy*, frustrated that none of my friends were free to hang out with me on one of my rare, quiet weekends. Around 9:00 P.M. that evening, Steve left me a voicemail. I needed to be in early Sunday morning. A sales memorandum had to get out for Project Clue by 6:00 A.M. Monday. On Sunday morning, I slipped naked Luke into my tote bag for work. As far as I knew, I was the first one to get a copy. Several had heard about it and speculated, but no one I knew had walked around the corner to see if it was true. Or maybe I was the only one who admitted to it. While most of the analysts were stuck working weekends, our supervisors stayed at home, so we'd be free to react as we pleased. I couldn't wait to round everyone up and share this amazing news.

As soon as I arrived, I walked around and gathered all the female analysts I could find from different floors: "Meet me in 32G. You don't want to miss this." The next half hour was filled with screams, groped pages of the magazine, and silent moments of awe. People rounded up groups to come see Luke's naked ambition. At 10:38 A.M., fixed income came; at 11:54, equity capital markets; at 12:35, mergers and acquisitions. All day I had visitors. For us, it was astounding to see a colleague break out of the restrictive corporate mold. Most of us had an "I'll believe it when I see it" attitude. And even though this behavior was just a step above middle school antics, it was an opportunity for us to be immature and break out of our pathetic, monotonous lives of nonstop work.

Luis and Michael stopped by the office around three o'clock.

"What are you doing here?" Michael asked, surprised to see me. "Just Friday you were complaining you were bored."

"I got a phone call yesterday from Steve," I said. "They want this Project Clue stuff out tomorrow morning."

They both approached their desks and began turning on their computers.

I couldn't hold my surprise long. "Luke posed nude in a porn mag. I've got it right here." My eyebrows raised, crinkling my forehead, and my mouth remained half-open as I eagerly anticipated their reaction. I was in my typical weekend work wear—jeans and a long-sleeve T-shirt. Hair pulled back in a tight ponytail high enough to look like I was about to work out rather than the low ponytail I would normally wear to work. Once during my summer internship at Morgan Stanley I stopped by work on a Sunday evening all made up, wearing a fitted dress and my hair down since I was on my way to a friend's party. I didn't expect anyone to be at work, but as soon as I entered the trading floor I saw two guys in my intern class sitting at their desks. "You're a babe!" one of them shouted across the floor. Some women would have taken it as a compliment, but after working with so many men who saw women as either either sexy or smart, I was sure to carefully choose what I wore to work on the weekends going forward.

"You are fucking lying," Michael said, looking around my desk to see if he could see the magazine.

"No big deal," Luis said. "I've heard people say Luke wants to be a model, and posing nude is how most of the Versace models make their way to the top." He fondled his Versace belt.

"Why do you even know these weird things?" Michael said, shoving Luis's shoulder.

"I lived in Italy for four years growing up," Luis snapped back as he brushed back his carefully groomed hair.

I wondered if our metrosexual Luis had posed nude, but the thought was too unappetizing to imagine. "Look at this," I said, bringing the magazine to their desks.

They huddled around it and flipped through it, saying, "Oh my God!" with each new page. After they closed the magazine Luis said, "They should have shaved him more." Michael was paralyzed, shaking his head. "He's totally going to get fired!"

"You don't know the laws," Luis educated Michael. "They can't fire him for modeling."

"Yeah, Leanna and Pam said the same thing," I agreed.

I was surprised not to hear from Luke's group until 4:00 P.M. I got a call from one of the analysts in his group. "I heard you got a copy of Luke's photos," he said.

"It's here on my desk," I replied. "You're welcome to see it, but I need to get my stuff done. I've been playing with Luke all day."

"I'll be down there soon," he said.

Within seconds, there was a group of around twelve Project Finance guys in front of my bullpen. The largest group of voyeurs yet.

"Well, you guys must not be too busy in Project Finance," I said, glancing at the herd approaching. "Traveling down eight floors just to look at porn?" I kept on typing since the excitement of sharing the magazine was over and now I was feeling the urgency of my twenty-four-hour sales memo deadline. "It's over there," I said, tilting my head toward the magazine on the corner of my desk.

Everyone stood quietly without a sound until I looked up. "Hurry up and look at it. I've got a lot of work to do," I said.

"I'm not going to touch it," said a tall blond kid who looked like the representative for the assembly.

"Well, then, it will be difficult to see it," I said, continuing to type.

Several others in the back were standing on their toes to see Luke on the front cover. Three of them walked up to the magazine to get a closer look. Luke stood bare-chested with one hand on his hip and the other leaning against a wall. He looked at ease, with a baseball cap on sideways, even though his jeans were sliding down so low they revealed his Speedo tan marks on his slender hips. The caption over his chest read, "Special Delivery: Our messenger boy brings booty right to your door."

For several minutes they stood silently staring at Luke's picture. Then they began pushing each other just to get a glimpse of the untouchable magazine. My back was to them as I tried to keep working, but I was distracted by the ridiculousness that surrounded me.

"You know," I said, annoyed, "he actually has a hard-on inside."

"I don't want to see him naked," a guy holding a golf bag said.

"I'm not going to fucking touch it," another guy said.

"You're right," I said. "That would make you gay." I turned around to face him with a lingering smile that I knew would make him self-conscious. "And of course you're not."

"I'm not!" he cried as he backed away from the magazine. He looked around at his colleagues to make sure they didn't suspect him.

This crowd was nothing like the earlier, fun crowd of

women in the conference room. Eager to get rid of these people so I could think through Project Clue's risk factors, I stood up on my chair and grabbed the magazine. "Back up!" I shouted. While organizing themselves, they speculated on Luke's future.

"Wasn't Luke born on Christmas?" a guy wearing pennies in his loafers asked. "He shouldn't be doing stuff like this."

A couple of guys looked his way, but no one responded.

"He can get fired for taking on two incomes at one time. Doesn't our contract say that you have to inform them before taking on another job? He'll probably get fired," one of them said.

"No, he can't get fired just for posing nude. It's not a big deal to be naked," another said. "People do it all the time. It's Luke's personal life."

"Yeah, but didn't some guy get fired for saying to a magazine that he bought expensive clothes and went on extravagant vacations? I heard that the article said he worked at Morgan Stanley, and he got fired just for making us look like we just throw money around carelessly," he said.

"Oh yeah, I heard about that guy," I said, remembering that an associate had told me the same story when I first started working there. Who knew if it was true or just another urban legend? The only thing I knew was that stories like that kept us on our toes.

"But Luke didn't say that he works at Morgan Stanley," another offered. He looked at me and asked anxiously, "Did he?"

"No," I said. "They use some other name." I couldn't hide my smile since it was so funny to see several of these guys, who were usually incredibly arrogant, absolutely out of their element.

Amused by their troubled, contorted faces I went on. "He is a bicycle messenger who happened to stumble into our office one day," I said, reading from the caption. At the entrance to my bullpen, I held the magazine up over my head like a librarian at storytime and flipped the pages. "They say he was sweet, willing, and"— I flipped to his spread, where he was holding his testicles and completely erect—"able. You will also be proud to know that they reported your colleague never got soft throughout the photo shoot. Furthermore, according to the magazine, Luke's reply to the question, 'Were you impressed with your stamina?' was, 'It was kind of fucked-up and kinky. It turned me on. One day I'll look back on these pictures as an absolute adventure.'"

Besides the gasps and "oh my Gods," I heard little from my audience. Only the guy with the golf bag kept shouting, "He is totally going to get fired! He is totally going to get fired!" The rowdy group that had entered my cubicle left in a silent single-file line.

By 6:00 P.M., more than thirty people had come by. Since I knew I would be at work late, I went home to shower and to get rid of the magazine that was causing me to waste so much time. I left it on my roommate's bed.

When I returned to work, I was only halfway through my selling memo when I got a call from an officer in Luke's group.

"A few of my analysts have informed me that you have a copy of the *Playguy* Luke is in," he said.

"That's correct," I said.

"I need it," he said.

"I don't have it with me. I took it home earlier today."

"I need you to go home and get it," he replied.

Irritated by this man who I'd never met, who had no direct

authority over me, I replied, "It is ten thirty at night, and I have to get a selling memo out to the sales force by six o'clock tomorrow morning. I'm not going home now. They sell them at every newsstand in the city."

"I couldn't find any," he said. "Maybe they're sold out."

Is he lying or did everyone else really go out and buy a copy? "Well, if you need it so badly, you can have one of your analysts go to my house and get it," I offered.

He paused for a moment and then in a softer yet threatening tone said, "Whatever you are working on is not more important than this. I promise you. I'll expect to have the magazine within an hour," he said and hung up.

Annoyed by his bullying, I fooled around for five minutes debating what to do. At first, I rationalized that Luke's hard-on was not more important than my $500 million deal. I ignored his threat until it hit me—this guy could get me fired for bringing porn to work. I reprimanded myself the whole way home for my poor judgment. Within twenty minutes, I delivered the $6.99 magazine to him, which he never returned. Later, I bought a new replacement copy from a newsstand and, now intrigued by gay porn, I also picked up a copy of *Inches*, a magazine that caught my eye during my last visit.

The day after I brought Luke's pictures into work, I was back to working long hours and wouldn't hear until much later that Luke was fired because, according to Morgan Stanley, he committed expense fraud. According to rumor, Morgan Stanley said that it was purely coincidental that he was fired not long after the magazine came out. My friends and I were shocked, as I assumed Luke was, since our understanding was that legally they had no grounds to fire him. Who could have foreseen they would fire him for alleged expense fraud right after the magazine came out? I felt bad for bringing in the magazine until many of my colleagues agreed that if I hadn't brought it in, someone else would have.

Not long after Luke was fired, people hardly mentioned his name again. Instead, the focus shifted to expense fraud. Analysts were getting called in for random expense audits. Rumors circulated that they were just doing it to make it look as if they regularly checked our expenses and were not just singling out Luke. From what I'd seen, many analysts felt comfortable taking advantage of expense accounts. Some would even just stop by the office on a Saturday, scanning their ID to show proof that they were in the office, and then expense their meals for the whole day. After an intense expense audit, Pam called to tell me that she would be resigning soon since they had called her in and interrogated her about her expenses.

Luke's entrance to Morgan Stanley was almost as dramatic as his exit. His father was close friends with the head of Luke's group. In New York City, many of the very wealthy African Americans stayed in a close-knit network that spanned industries. I'd heard that both Luke's father and his boss were at the forefront of this network. Luke must have known he was an anomaly, a minority who had celebrity analyst status at Morgan Stanley. Some people he worked with said he had no problem taking advantage of it. Rumor was, he'd waltz in after 11:00 A.M. at times. My first memory of Luke was during training, when, with a blasé attitude, he plopped down his massive four-hundred-page manual in front of the instructor and said, "This is a waste of time."

During training Luke invited Leanna and me to a party at Columbia University, his alma mater. I agreed to go since

I figured Luke would know some interesting people. He was attractive, connected, and irreverent, all of which made me curious. Unlike many of us, he was used to the luxurious life Morgan Stanley tried to sell us. Already, he had the glamorous existence that I hoped to achieve.

Toward the end of the party, comfortably inebriated, Luke started talking about his desire to be a model.

"So what's an aspiring model doing at Morgan Stanley?" I asked. "Why aren't you out making the real bucks?"

"I've done some modeling. I mean, I could go professional, but I just chose to do this first."

I imagined him walking down the catwalk in a tight shiny silver tank top as he twirled his sunglasses. "Modeling for what?" I asked.

"Different things," he informed me. "My girlfriend is a model too," he said, fondling his corduroyed thighs. "So did you notice what Pam wore today?"

Leanna and I looked at each other in confusion since we all wore uninteresting suits to work daily.

"The black ultrasheer pantyhose and slightly slit skirt," he said.

"And your point is?" I said.

"I just love that type of light sheer," he said, closing his eyes.

"How do you even know what's light sheer and what's ultrasheer?" I asked.

"There are different levels," he informed us. "And why do you wear your skirts right below your knees, Nina?" he asked.

"For the same reason you insist on hiding your lean thighs from us on a daily basis," I said, laughing yet annoyed. It was early enough in our careers that our male colleagues, who were too ambitious, tried to mask sexual comments about their female counterparts. Luke, on the other hand, was fearless. I was astonished at his indifference.

"But not all of you wear them that long," he said. "A lot of you don't."

"I've never noticed," Leanna said, uninterested.

"I think you should stop wearing such opaque hose," the model advised me.

"Luke," I said, "maybe you should have been a model. It appears you are in the wrong business," I recommended firmly.

"I could've been a model," he said defensively.

"I'm sure you could have," I said. "I'm saying you *should* have."

"I will be."

CHAPTER 10

The Printer

We all gathered at a huge table at a printer's office in downtown Manhattan to create Moon Company's financial documents. There were two representatives from Moon Company, the company issuing stock; two of Moon Company's lawyers; two of Morgan Stanley's lawyers; and two hired accountants. Since Moon Company expected to raise a lot of money, it used two investment banks, so there were four bankers, two each from Morgan Stanley and Lehman Brothers. Every couple of hours huge plates of extravagant food were delivered. For lunch, there was octopus in tomato cream topped with caviar followed by molten chocolate custards. Just outside our conference room door were two refrigerators: One contained every variety of ice cream you could dream of—cone, cup, or sandwich—and the other was filled with alcohol. This excess reminded me of my mother's stories about how small dessert portions were throughout her childhood in India. When my father visited her family's home in India, as the guest he was offered the serving bowl of custard first. To his hosts' astonishment, he began eating directly out of the serving bowl. He looked up and asked, "No one else is having any?" to mouths that were agape. His face turned bright red as he tried to explain: "In America the portion sizes are so large!"

Several years in the United States had made him forget Indian portions. He'd grown accustomed to American abundance.

The printer is a place where deal teams collect to draft a document for the Securities and Exchange Commission that explains all the details of the stocks or bonds a company plans on issuing. The company gathers its investment bankers, lawyers, and accountants together and, over several days, everyone writes up a painfully long document called a prospectus. Going to the printer is a notoriously long, grueling, and tedious experience. That's why they try to trick you by making the atmosphere resemble an all-inclusive resort with unlimited alcohol, food, pool, video games, and television. Our small group would spend thousands and thousands of dollars on food and entertainment in only a few days. *Wouldn't it be more efficient to just focus on the task at hand rather than surround ourselves with so many distractions?*

Today was my first time at the printer. Only Todd and I represented Morgan Stanley. Even though Todd wasn't my favorite person, I was curious to see him interact with professionals outside of our office. Would he be extra nice and thoroughly unrecognizable? According to Steve, this was an opportunity to impress Todd without having what he considered a middle manager there to interfere. It was a chance for me to "step-up," as he called it. I knew the hours were going to be long at the printer, but I was excited to get out of the monotony of the office and maybe even meet some new people.

Being at the printer reinforced the fact that we were investment bankers, the most respected of the high-powered executives. There was a strict power hierarchy that was based on our paychecks: bankers, lawyers, accountants, and the company executives. If you went around the table and added up the value of each individual's tie, briefcase, pen, and cuff links, and then arranged each person's total in descending order you would get the same order: bankers, lawyers, accountants, and the company executives. The hierarchy continued: Harvard and Wharton were the top MBA programs for investment bankers; investment banking the most sought after industry in top business schools; and Morgan Stanley and Goldman Sachs the most prestigious investment banks. Our officers made it their highest priority to maintain this rigid hierarchy. If you chose anything other than "the best," they would make you feel subpar until you started to question yourself. When one of our interviewees explained that in addition to Morgan Stanley he was considering Salomon, Ken asked, "Now, seriously, why would you downgrade your Yale degree like that?"

Analysts a year ahead of me explained that each person saw the drafting sessions as an opportunity to impress others. Going to the printer was a moment for bankers to strut their power in front of an audience, which made the competition to impress others more exciting. However, no one was mistaken. The bankers had the power. Somehow this power was supposed to justify all our personal sacrifices and gave us rights—to intimidate, to have the last word, to never be wrong. Bankers were regarded as the most confident and most intelligent in meetings. I knew this because I consistently saw others defer to us. This extended slumber party at the printer taught me that the *illusion* of power trumps knowledge.

For analysts, it was our superiors' duty to teach us how to carry that authority wherever we conducted business. Today was our first day of drafting the prospectus, and throughout the meeting, I closely watched Todd speak against anyone who tried to challenge him. At first, I was relieved to be on the winning team, and eager to learn how to mimic Todd's quick retorts, so that later on I'd know how to defend myself.

Paul, one of Moon Company's lawyers, asked why the equipment had not depreciated over the first five years and was therefore never noted as an expense. We all sat waiting, realizing that this was a legitimate point since not accounting for depreciation would make the profits look much larger. But soon after Paul raised the issue, he was silenced by Todd, who considered the comment paranoid.

Most of us at the table were still trying to understand whether Todd's comments were clever or just intimidating. It was my counterpart from Lehman Brothers who helped enlighten me. She looked Indian, which was exciting in one way, yet unsettling in another. At work, we were all business with little time for small talk. I couldn't think of anyone who knew much about my personal life. I never purposely hid that I was Persian-Indian, but it had now started to feel like a secret. My ethnicity had become unidentifiable to my group, which left me privy to office conversations about people from other cultures. We had a fresh-off-the-boat coworker named Raju who failed to fit into this culture because he couldn't trade in his familiar Indian tendencies for an ethnicity-free corporate persona. Officers often took notes on his downfall. They said just enough about him to make me fear what they'd say about me one day.

Very soon after I joined my group, I ran into Larry when I was in our lobby cafeteria picking up lunch. He asked me how my work was going as we walked through the seating area. We stopped briefly as we passed by Raju. He sat by himself in the corner with a contented smile on his face as he lapped up hearty servings of vibrant orange fish curry, spinach, and naan. With only his hands, he broke off pieces of naan and dipped them in the curry.

"Looks like you've got quite a feast there," Larry remarked.

"Please try some. It's delicious!" Raju said.

"It looks great, but I'll leave it for you," Larry said with a smile and a pat on the back.

As we walked away Larry took a long, deep breath and said, "With the strength of those spices, it's no surprise that he has to eat alone. I almost stopped breathing back there."

"It is definitely stronger than most curries," I said, nodding my head. I almost launched into an explanation about different curry spices, but I decided not to since I'd just joined the group and Larry hardly seemed interested in learning about anything he'd consider "ethnic." Maybe it was silly of me, but I assumed we'd get to know each other better working long hours together over a year. Maybe we'd learn a little about each other's families and backgrounds. Looking back, I realized that this curry conversation may have been the last time there was a natural segue to discuss my Indian heritage.

"Hope we don't have to smell that on him. It amazes me how many people feel the need to bring food from home. Don't you think we have good food here?"

"It's great!" I said. "I always get the food here. I love the pot pies."

"It's even subsidized," Larry said. "Too bad not everyone appreciates it."

Unlike the others, Priya knew I was Indian right away because she recognized my last name. She wore a boring black skirt suit, in line with the uniform that most women wore, but her funky black glasses with tiny white polka dots showed she had a little more style. She wore a short bob haircut that made her look sophisticated. We clicked instantly. She was one year ahead of me and she knew the ropes. She was witty and critical, which enchanted me because it was a side of myself that had been slowly silenced in this confining environment.

After our drafting session, I met her in the pool table room.

"Pretty sad the way Paul was shut down, isn't it?" Priya said.

"Isn't it just a judgment call?" I asked. "It doesn't seem clear what industry rules we're supposed to apply."

"Yeah. Neither of them is wrong per se," she said. "We had a similar issue on another deal I did last year. Paul and Todd just have different opinions, and Todd's is more aggressive."

"But Todd said there was an exception to Paul's argument," I defended, still trying to understand both sides since I was quite confident that it wasn't clear to most of us at the table.

"Not exactly," she informed me. "It depends on the industry, and since Moon Company is a conglomerate the judgment call can get messy. Anyway, do you know anyone who reads the whole prospectus?" she asked.

"Yeah," I gasped at the stupid question. "Tons of people: the traders, the salespeople, the investors."

She laughed aloud at my naïveté and said, "But hardly any of those people will ever understand the accounting going on in there."

"They're not stupid," I said.

"It's not about being stupid. In general, bankers take aggressive stands and then make strong arguments to back them up," she said. "I'm not saying anyone is lying. Bankers convince themselves, and then reinforce it while they are convincing others. Have you noticed Moon Company's CFO defers to Todd? Everyone in the room wants the CFO to be relatively happy since Moon Company is the one that has the right to hire and fire most of us sitting there."

"That's a weird power dynamic," I observed.

"Don't think too hard about it. We're just here for a couple of years," she said casually. "I'm not one of them. I'll get my MBA and open my own business. My group at Lehman is so quiet right now that all I do is sit around writing my business plan. I couldn't care less what they think. Plus, we're analysts here; nothing we say matters. Don't let this stuff bother you either. "

"Hmmm," I said, bowled over by her casual attitude.

"It's going to be hard to keep myself from cracking up laughing if Paul presses the issue any more." She shook her head and smiled. "It's the only thing that keeps me awake in these horrific meetings. Paul went to law school, but he's also a finance undergrad. Unlike most lawyers, he gets all the financials. He knows way too much, but he can't win an argument with Todd. Todd has his Ivy League MBA, which trained him to never say 'I don't know' and never be wrong. He can win almost any argument with or without the knowledge to back him up." She laughed and added, "That's the best education you can find."

I stood there pensively as I thought back to Todd's cryptic comment to me months earlier. He asked me if I had completed the projections he requested. "Not yet," I responded, "because I'm still waiting on some reports that I planned to base the numbers on. I'll give them to you as soon as I get the reports." Without looking up from his computer screen, he responded, "Wrong answer." When I asked an analyst a year ahead of me about it, he explained, "I'm pretty sure you shouldn't say you can't get something done."

I shook myself from these memories and asked Priya, "Speaking of bored, what are we supposed to be doing anyway? I can hardly stay awake."

"As analysts, we have one job—to make sure the company's name is printed in the right font, color, and indentation on the front cover. After we're done here, you have to go back and design a cool deal toy for everyone. That's the real way to differentiate yourself as a star analyst. Every now and then you can make a comment to show you are 'engaged,' but no one will listen to you. If you're asking me what I would do, I'd tell you to download a bunch of video games. I already mastered the chess game on my Palm today."

"I can't believe you're doing that," I said. "You look so diligent when you are on your Palm. I thought you were taking serious notes. You even made all the clever comments on the risk factors."

"It takes skill," she said, "but if you pay close attention, you'll see that most people are playing games or surfing the net. The accountant Chris is on his computer playing 3D Tetris—you can see it through the reflection in the window. What an idiot," she said as she shook her head. "Everyone knows not to sit on that side. You know that older lawyer with the bow tie? He gets up every forty-five minutes."

"I noticed," I said, laughing. "I think he has a bladder problem."

"He does, but it's because he drinks a beer every time he walks out, which is just in time for him to release the previous one. Of course, he's also going out to see the updated score of the Red Sox game. This is the second deal I've worked on with him."

After a few more beers and games of pool, we stopped talking about the deal and started playing the name game. After I went through the handful of Lehman people I knew, she turned it around and asked about the Morgan Stanley people she knew. She was still playing the name game, long after I was done.

"So you must know Michael and Luis," Priya said.

"Of course," I said. "They're in my group. How do you know them?"

"I met them at Spy Bar with Larry," she said. "My associate, Ben, the short ugly guy with thick glasses who's sitting closest to the door, and Larry went to Dartmouth undergrad together. Larry and Ben go to Spy pretty often, and Larry's invited Michael to join a couple times. But now that Michael already got his promise for a business school recommendation, we haven't seen him around much."

"Business school recommendation?" I asked.

"It was one of those nights. Michael hooked Larry up with this woman he could never otherwise get and Larry hooked Michael up with the recommendation that he's here for. Michael already got Larry's promise," she said enviously. "Isn't that sweet? I tried to get Ben to do that too, but it's still a work in process. He's not nearly as easy to persuade as Larry," she said, putting her hand over her mouth and snickering.

"What?" I asked. At this point, I wasn't surprised to hear Michael would get the business school recommendation he wanted, but it still annoyed me to hear it. *Don't let it bother you. It's probably just a rumor. There's no proof.*

"You've got to swear you won't tell anyone this," she insisted.

Even though I was curious to know what she was laughing about, I could tell I wasn't going to like it. "I swear," I said, dumbfounded that she knew more about my group than I did.

"I mean it. Don't even tell Luis or Michael," she pressed. "Did you hear about those airplane deal toys that were broken?"

"Yes," I responded. "They were my associate's, Steve."

"Larry actually broke them. Isn't that hilarious?" she went on laughing. "Larry told us how he cut off the wings and took out the pilot and broke his head off since he was the one that deserved to work on that deal."

"Seriously?" I asked, trying to figure out how an adult would do something like that. I knew Steve worked extremely hard on that deal and had been really upset when it happened.

"You better not tell anyone," she reminded me.

"Don't worry," I said. "No one would ever believe me. Everyone just assumes it was some barbaric worker from the copy center who came up to our floor." I took a big gulp of beer and asked, "You sure mingle a lot. When do you have time to do your work?"

As she spoke, I pulled nervously at my eyebrow hairs. I pulled harder and harder. Michael was in a different category than the average analyst, so I knew I shouldn't compare myself, but it was so hard to watch him get whatever he wanted. There seemed to be little payoff in being a star analyst other than that, hopefully, people wouldn't talk about how stupid you were. The hours I wasted at work felt futile, and it was very frustrating that I didn't know what I wanted to do after this Morgan Stanley experience.

"I manage both—work hard, play hard. My group has only been slow for about a week," Priya said. "You don't succeed here just because of good work. You've got to mingle to really move up the ladder. If you don't, you'll end up like Paul there in the corner, frustrated as hell."

But I couldn't imagine spending my spare time with Larry or Todd at a bar on a free evening. The thought depressed me even more than being at work all night. I felt a little silly asking so many questions since I'd already been there a year, but Priya was so open that I figured I might as well ask. "Don't you find it tiring spending your evenings with officers? Isn't it bad enough having to be 'on' all day? They're so judgmental—especially toward women. I feel like I have to constantly think about every move I make: Did I laugh too much? Did he misinterpret that smile? Should I say I'm sad we lost the deal or will he think that sounds too weak? By the end of the day, I just want to stop worrying about sticking to the script."

"Well . . . " she said with a long pause. "The challenging part of this job isn't building a model or pulling together bullet points for slides. It's knowing the right script to use and when to use it. That *is* the game," she said before she ran off to the bathroom.

She returned with a broad smile before she asked, "You don't happen to know a Bangladeshi guy?"

"Ali?" I asked.

"I think that's his name," she said. "I only met him once at CRY, a South Asian fund-raiser. He seems like such a great guy."

"He is wonderful," I confirmed. "He and this other analyst, Scott, are planning to start a fund that invests in nonprofits in Asia when we finish our two years. They're going to raise a bunch of money from the loaded American bankers and take it to Asia. But I don't know when they'll be able to start the business plan. For the last few weeks, Ali has been really fucked up. He was diagnosed with vertigo about a month ago. It's this disease that's usually associated with the elderly. Doctors think it's due to the severe stress. He can't see clearly or walk straight. It took him a long time to figure it out because he was always sleep-deprived or buzzed, which the doctors say feels similar. Everyone is so fucking jealous of him. He got to miss a month of work."

"Too bad that shit is not contagious," she said. "Well, you'll have to hook me up with Ali sometime. He is definitely a hottie. Speaking of, did you know the shafted boy?"

"What?" I asked.

"Luke," she said. "Wall Street's porn star? Is he actually that hot in real life? I hope he's not gay."

"I know him," I said. "But not that well. He's not bad looking in real life. I'm surprised other bankers know about it."

"Everyone knows about it!" she screeched. "I heard he's going to hire a publicist and hold a press conference with CNN. I also heard he's going to have the Reverend Al Sharpton lead a protest outside Morgan Stanley."

"Are you kidding?" I asked, shocked, since no one at work had mentioned him since. "For what?"

"Why are you Morgan Stanley folks so tuned out?" she said, shaking her head. "You're the third one who didn't know."

"No one at work talks about it that much," I said. "It's simple. He posed nude, and soon after, he got fired. I heard Luke was filing a lawsuit for racial and sexual discrimination since he thinks they fired him because they thought he was gay. But no one at work thinks much of it since most of us assume he got fired for posing nude. He hit on so many women at work, so we aren't really wondering whether he's gay. Plus, he didn't have many friends at work since he wasn't around much. I'm surprised CNN would care."

"You're really out of the loop," she said, with a look of both surprise and pride, excited that she was the one to share this juicy gossip. "My first year I worked really hard, but now I realize you can do better here by working less and hanging out with the right people. You've got to play their game to succeed here."

But it wasn't just me who was out of the loop. Most of my colleagues were too. Everyone seemed too busy to be interested. Since Luke was known to be arrogant, and since it appeared he really did submit fraudulent expenses, many just felt like he deserved whatever he got and were less interested in questioning Morgan Stanley's way of handling the case.

Priya and I agreed that it would be good to hang out again, so we exchanged e-mail addresses. On the one hand, I liked her frankness, but on the other hand, I had no interest in playing "the game" right now. If I'd met her early on when I started working here and wasn't so skeptical of the people I worked for, I would likely have been open to it. I wasn't Michael, but I knew how to be social when I needed to be. At this point, my goal was to have as little to do with these people as possible, finish my two years, and leave this place.

In the following years, I've read updates on Luke's lawsuit in several New York newspapers and magazines. Through those stories, I learned that not long after Luke filed a discrimination case, Morgan Stanley found Luke's college nemesis and paid him ten thousand dollars to help them set Luke up. His former classmate went to Luke and said he'd help Luke with his discrimination case by planting racist and homophobic e-mails on Morgan Stanley's computer system. As soon as Luke agreed to it, Morgan Stanley busted him. When Luke found out the company was trying to frame him, he busted Morgan Stanley for setting him up.

Later, when the case was finally settled, I read in *New York* magazine that Luke and Morgan Stanley publicly announced that their common goal was to help minorities, so they both settled by giving the Urban League a one-million-dollar donation. According to the article, Morgan Stanley claimed that Luke didn't receive money from the settlement. But the way the article read, it looked like Luke couldn't openly admit to receiving money, so instead he insinuated that they paid him fifty-two million dollars. The magazine said he started his shopping spree by buying two Ferraris, a Porsche, a Range Rover, and a Mercedes. He also hired a personal secretary, a publicist, and a bodyguard. And obtained a large stake in a modeling business. After I read all this, the same question kept running through my mind: How can you trust any of these people?

The next day, we returned to the drafting table at the printer for the second long, tedious session. Surprisingly, Paul revived the depreciation issue. Even the Tetris players and web surfers raised their heads.

"Paul," Todd said, pointing his pen at him, "what part do you not understand? It's obvious," he continued. "We're dealing with basic accounting here. We have accounted for equipment this way in several other situations. We even have the accountants' support on these numbers. Are you challenging them?" he said, opening his hand out to the accountants as if to let them defend themselves.

"But this instance is different from the others," Paul insisted as he crossed his hands over his chest and let out a deep breath of annoyance. "This isn't transporting equipment."

"But they're based on the same structure," Todd interrupted impatiently.

"That's not the point," Paul said, in frustration. "It's a judgment call, but that's not how I'd account for this type of equipment."

Todd began throwing out numbers and calculations to the point where it was almost impossible to follow. "So it's simple," he concluded as he ran a sleek hand over the part in his hair and narrowed his eyes as if he were trying to get a better look at himself in the mirror. "Paul, I would really rather not waste any more time on this. I've dealt with it many times in the past and would be happy to explain it to you in private, when we're not wasting other people's time." Todd looked at the company's CFO for his consent, which he readily gave since he knew he wouldn't understand what Todd just said even if we all walked him through it.

The company had one goal—to raise money. They hired investment bankers to do just that. The lawyers and accountants were watchdogs hired to balance the bankers by making sure that everything in the document was "realistic." The only problem was that each group—bankers, accountants, and lawyers—were hired by the company. If you disagreed too much, there was the chance that you could be taken off the deal. But since most were intimidated by the bankers, including the company, they often looked to the investment bankers to make the judgment call as to what was "too much."

"Well," the CFO replied, "I think Todd has a good point. I'm sure Morgan Stanley has done this before, and it doesn't appear to be a problem. Paul, I can't understand why your firm would challenge it. How about we just resolve your issue in private after lunch? It sounds like it'll just take a little explaining."

Meanwhile, the accountants sat silently. Out of courtesy, the senior accountant looked down and played with his cell phone as if to give Paul's humiliation more privacy. In an effort to better understand Todd, I copied down all his numbers as he spoke. While the meeting shifted to discuss other issues, I spent the rest of the time trying to make sense of Todd's calculations. Later that afternoon, I approached him with questions about his numbers. He blatantly avoided my persistent questions, and quickly rattled off numbers that were in no way relevant to the issue at hand. "I thought you were a finance major. Don't make us look bad," he said, lightly hitting my back and shooting me a smile. This was one of his greatest tricks, which seemed to work effectively when someone challenged him—make the other person feel stupid so he or she would give up and leave you alone. It seemed to work beautifully on this high-achieving crowd.

Later on, I tried again to catch him in the general seating area, but he kept interrupting me with phone calls and finally said, "Listen, Nina, I appreciate your enthusiasm, but you're going to have to think through this on your own." Before he got back on the phone, he stopped to stare at me with cold eyes and warned, "No one better waste more of our time on this issue today."

The purpose of the prospectus is to fully inform the investors of what they are getting into. If at some point in the future the company goes bankrupt, the entire team—the company and its bankers, lawyers, and accountants—can point to the prospectus and show how they fully informed investors of all the risks. Part of the strategy is to provide so much information that no one reads the dense hundred-page document; in this way, investors tend to miss out on the negative data. The section on risk factors, seemingly the most important part of the deal, is typically inundated with mundane risks such as "competition from existing players and new entrants" to explain that the company has competitors and may get new ones, or "exposure to foreign exchange rate" to explain that the company makes an annual immaterial purchase in yen. Unable to read through the innumerable risk factors with long explanations, instead investors only flip to the few key pages that the bankers recommend. The bankers spend hours cleverly crafting these small yet crucial sections.

The section titled "Selected Financial Data" is the most important, and it is an opportunity for bankers to use the creative thinking that they're paid to employ. In this section of the prospectus, if a company has no revenue for the next few years, the revenue numbers will not be shown. Instead, the revenue's extraordinarily high projected growth rates might be flaunted. Even a salesperson at the bank who sells the stock or bond directly to the investor wouldn't be able to explain all the details of the prospectus. But that might be irrelevant since, often, other than a lawyer, very few ever read a prospectus in full, including the team that creates it.

The third day dragged even longer, and we were stunned to see Paul bring up the accounting issue again. Priya set down her newly downloaded Conquer video game rather than pausing it. This time Todd's lashing was so brutal that we all knew Paul would not speak again. "Paul!" Todd responded loudly in a tone that startled me into sitting up straighter. "Enough is enough." This time, Paul sat mute throughout the rest of the meeting. Was he worried his job might be on the line? After his scolding, Paul looked at me, and our eyes linked long enough for me to express my empathy. Immediately, I panicked, shifting my eyes to the windows in front of me. It was humiliating to be part of Todd's team. I didn't agree with his aggressive ways. The oppression that seemed so natural in our building suddenly felt even more overbearing and embarrassing in public. As a first-year analyst, I knew that my opinion didn't count at this table, but how could Todd silence an intelligent senior lawyer? *We're not on the same team! I'm not like you!* I wanted to shout. I directed my focus out the window, fearful of meeting anyone's eyes. I wished that I had a video game to consume me. Distraction arrived in the form of a building plastered with advertisements. Across the street, a billboard for HBO had a muscular boxer punching out someone's head. The caption read, FIGHT WITH ALL YOUR MIGHT. Underneath that was an ad for Stephen King's book that flashed *Dead Zone* beneath a picture of a woman whose eyes welled with blind terror.

The final billboard was the most confusing. It had large black printed letters that read IMAGINE LIVING LIFE IN PEACE against a simple white background. That was the entire billboard, written in huge type. In the corner of the billboard was a tiny logo, but too small for anyone to read. *Who paid for that?* I wondered. Everything I did at this job reiterated the lesson that money trumped everything. *How would they make any money?* I leaned forward in my seat and strained to take a better look at the logo. *Are there people out there who care about something other than money?* My confusion settled into a deep, mesmerizing haze. Soon, I could no longer see outside. I could only see my pale reflection in the window: an image I had not stopped to consider in almost a year. I couldn't stop gawking. For me, there was no recognition. My face looked swollen and bruised; there were heavy bags under my eyes. Slowly, everyone else's reflection along the elongated, stiff table surfaced—Todd, Priya, the lawyers, the accountants, and the company's executives.

On the outside, I carried myself like an investment banker. I rattled off random knowledge to impress others and spoke about things I didn't really know about with boldness that would convince anyone. I wore the harshness of a New Yorker, helping tourists who needed directions without eye contact or a smile. But seeing my reflection, I felt like a flamingo at a table of giraffes. It just felt wrong. I had already succumbed to performing many of the actions that once disgusted me. I made people around me feel like they were wasting my time. I ordered work clothes online for several hundred dollars since I couldn't make it to the store. In a week, I'd wasted enough expensed food to feed a family of six.

As I looked at the crowd, nobody's image terrified me more than my own. For the rest of the meeting I sat silent, absorbed with this new onlooker who burned me with a gaze of betrayal. The person I knew who started working here a year ago was suffocated by layers of suits, annual reports, spreadsheets, judgments, and so many other things that, deep down, I knew were unimportant. But how could I escape this? I kept hearing Lena's advice to Shireen during my visit home for the holidays. Still in the Peace Corps, Shireen was struggling with the local hospital's bureaucracy, frustrated that the villagers might not get the best health care available. Shireen said she didn't have the authority to change the hospital administrator's decision, so she wasn't going to do anything about it. "Is that who you want to be?" Lena asked her. I was annoyed when I heard it. Instead of suggesting a solution, Lena would often ask these directly personal questions that left me adrift. Today her question ran through my head over and over. *But how do I know who I want to be if I can't even remember who I am?*

During one of our short breaks I called home and my mom answered. She and my grandmother were about to leave for the grocery store, which was a terribly exciting outing for my grand-mother. Her best matching suit-and-skirt outfit was probably being ironed as we spoke. My mom began telling me about an injury my dad had sustained last week in karate class.

"After his class, he walks in the house with blood splotches all over his eyeball. Like some kind of horror movie!" she explained. "As if nothing was wrong. When I asked what happened, I find out the wooden staff, you know, those thick, long poles they use as a weapon, went straight into his eye. His opponent accidently jabbed him. But of course your father tells his opponent, 'That's okay. Let's keep going.'"

"Oh my gosh! Is he okay?" I asked.

"No, he's not okay! He doesn't know when to quit! The man thinks he's Chuck Norris, but he's not. There's a chance of partial blindness. I rushed him to the emergency room as soon as he got home. On top of that, after he gets stabbed in the eye, he didn't even come straight home. He said he stayed to work out for another hour. Seriously, the man just doesn't know when to quit!"

"What was he thinking? Can I talk to him?" It was so *him* to keep fighting. No matter how much pain he was in, he wouldn't dare quit.

"Today's not a good day. Call later tomorrow. So what's up with you, Ms. New York?"

I wanted to show him I was concerned, but I knew he wouldn't want to reveal that he was vulnerable or anything less than invincible.

"All's well. We're at the printer working on a stock offering. I'd say more, but I can't talk about anything. It's all confidential."

"All you do is work and you can't even talk about that! Well, are you at least working on important deals?" she asked.

"Yeah, they're big deals. But whatever, I don't even care about that anymore. This place is wearing on me."

"Why don't you take a vacation and refresh yourself, sweetie?"

"I really need it, but it'll be a while because I can't travel while I'm covering this deal. I'm working with this officer right now who has four mouths and no ears, so I'm just annoyed." As I spoke, I looked around the room for video cameras, in case I was being taped. *This place has made me so paranoid!* "He can't hear anyone but himself. A good part of me wants to just not show up to work tomorrow." For about the last month, I'd casually thrown out hints that I'd been unhappy at work to my parents, hoping they'd say, "Well, you can always get another job. No need to be unhappy." I had never explained to them what the culture was like—violent tempers, drug addicts, alcoholics, porn, strip clubs. *Does my dad even know what a strip club is? We don't ever discuss anything sexual in my house. In all these years, I've only seen my parents kiss a handful of times.* They only knew bits and pieces about my work experience. If I had to guess their opinion on whether I should stay or leave, I'd say the conservative Indian part of them would tell me that it was not an environment with a solid set of values, but the tough fighting immigrant side would come to the fore and they'd advise me to stick it out.

"Don't talk like that," my mom said. "You don't want to get fired. You've worked so hard to get there. And what about your school debt? Do you think you could make six figures in Texas?"

"I can't think about that anymore. I'm beyond it. Something has got to be better than this. The number one thing I'm learning here is how to work while sleep-deprived and emotionally exhausted from dealing with these people."

"You just sound tired, honey," she said. "Can you hear that? It's your granny shouting from the car. We're late for her grocery store outing. They have fresh lychees at Fiesta this week. Sorry, honey, I'll call you later. You just need a vacation. Come home for a visit, and you'll be brand-new."

After talking to my mom, I spent the rest of the evening during our long meeting wondering if it would be so difficult to leave. *What if I just didn't show up tomorrow?* At 2:00 A.M. the meeting ended for some of us. The lawyers would be up all night changing "in order to" to "so that" and aligning the ones digit columns and the tens digit columns precisely. Even though I'd had only six hours of sleep in the last two days, I was wide awake. My chest smarted with pain, and I was breathing as if I were on a treadmill. The only thing I could do with this painful energy was run. I headed straight to the extravagant gym at the printer even though I could have gone home. But even after running miles, my body could not calm down. My heart raced in a panic beyond my control.

While I was running, all these stories ran through my head like a reel of film that wouldn't end. I saw my officers in a conference room all hanging out together: "I told you we shouldn't have chanced it by hiring a girl." Then I saw the head of our Scholars program shouting at us: "If one of us looks bad, we all look bad!" My dad looking at me with his bloody eye, asking me, "You're not going to be a quitter, are you?"

I kept increasing the treadmill speed, faster and faster, hoping I could shake their faces for a while. I looked around to see if there was anyone else in the gym. I was alone. I ran so fast I thought my heart was going to pop. But I still couldn't leave them behind. I increased the speed even more. I was running so fast I couldn't catch my breath; my chest rattled. I listened to myself gasp several times before I flipped off and heard the cracking sound of my tailbone hitting the floor. I lay there for a few minutes, partly in pain and partly from exhaustion, but I felt calm. I looked to the doors to see if anyone would enter, but I only saw flashing signs: EMERGENCY EXIT. ALARM WILL SOUND.

Lying on the ground, I could hear my beeper vibrating against the wood. I grabbed it and saw a Morgan Stanley number. Steve had beeped hours ago, but I never saw it. I checked my voice mail. "Nina, this is Steve. I've been trying to beep you for hours. Where are you? I hate to do this to you. I really do." I looked at the ground and tried to remember when I took my last shower. "But I just found out myself. Tomorrow morning Project Gist will need a one-pager for the hundred-million dollar debt offering. It won't take that long to do," he said, trying to alleviate the guilt. "I'd ask someone else, but Larry insists that you should do it since you've worked on other tech deals. It has to be done by tomorrow morning. You could work on it overnight and still make it back to the printer by 7:00 A.M. We trust this to your capable hands."

I stepped outside the printer and saw the sickly familiar row of black town cars. They followed me everywhere. "Morgan Stanley, Times Square," I said to the driver in a defeated, soft voice. Rather than throwing my neck back against the headrest like usual, I craned my head to look out the windows. Swarms of people headed home after a long night at the local SoHo clubs. A couple playfully fought over the last bite of their late-night falafel, reminding me that the last person I felt so blissfully close to was a high school boyfriend. This severe loneliness grew larger every day. I watched a woman in a black Lexus blaring "Baby, I Got Your Money"; she wore a white fur hat and while talking on her cell phone, she used her car to nudge a group of slow-walking tourists crossing the street. They were so focused on the sky. Did all New Yorkers see it in only small blue rectangles and triangles? One of the guys had a shabby head of dirty blond free-flowing curls, and as we got closer I spotted his Longhorn sweatshirt. "Slow down," I said to the driver, remembering what I'd seen Central Park runners do when they saw the horns. I rolled down the window, and as we passed them, I stuck my arm out and gave him the "hook 'em" hand gesture, making horns with my index and pinky fingers. He screamed out "Hook 'em, baby!" with a smile that was so wide-mouthed that happiness surged through me for a moment.

For the first time since I arrived in New York City, I was envious of its inhabitants—people who knew how to enjoy life. At work, these people were deemed lazy. I left the window open and stuck my head out, feeling the wind on my cheeks and forehead. I closed my eyes and said an *ashem vohu* prayer my grandmother had taught me, hoping the car would crash so I wouldn't have to go into work tomorrow.

CHAPTER 11 Step Up

I'm not the biggest fan, but how about the Rainbow Room?" I suggested even though I could only remember the bland, rubbery red snapper I got last time.

"It's so uptight and the food is so-so. Hold on," Natalia said, shuffling through a manila folder she was balancing on the side of my desk as she flipped through printed menus and restaurant reviews. She was an analyst a year ahead of me who sat on the other side of our floor. "Here it is! I've got this listing of New York City's most expensive restaurants," she said with excitement. "How about Le Bernardin?"

Michael's typing slowed to three letters a second and his ears perked up. "I've been there a few times," I said, shrugging my shoulders, not wanting to go back since it would remind me of the nerve-racking lunch where I had to keep going outside in the rain to check whether our client's town car had arrived. "I wasn't in love with it. But I'll go if you really want," I offered halfheartedly. I reached for a Kleenex since her musky perfume had started to tickle my nose.

"Le Cirque and Nobu are here too, but like everyone else, you've probably been there too many times. Skip." She flipped the page and asked, "What about Aquavit or Union Square Cafe? I've been to both but . . ."

"I have too," I said feeling ungrateful that we were looking through the top restaurants in the city and could only find reasons to complain. At one time, I'd relished the novelty of going to nice places, mainly because it made me feel important, but while I was there I often realized I was just as happy with the Pongsri Thai food around the corner from work.

"Let's try and find one we both haven't been to," she said hopefully. "Windows on the World, Gramercy Tavern, Daniel . . ."

I could sense Michael had been holding himself back; his eyes kept darting our way and back, but now he couldn't contain himself. "Nina, you would love Windows on the World! The view at night is unreal."

"I know. I do love the view," I replied. I could see his disappointment that he couldn't be the authority figure. "I've been there twice." I looked at Natalia, "I've been to all of them, but I'm happy to go to Daniel again." I shuffled my feet on top of the stacks of annual reports and financials piled on the ground, the perfect height for a footrest.

She carried on, determined that we both go somewhere new. Natalia now started mumbling to herself, "Peter Luger, Balthazar—way too casual." Then she lit up, opening her dark-brown-lipsticked mouth so wide she looked like a scary clown. "Hey, how about the Four Seasons Restaurant?"

"The hotel?" I asked with a shriveled face of disappointment even though less than a year ago the Four Seasons Hotel was one of the fanciest places in Austin where I could hardly even afford a breakfast taco.

"No, the name is the same, but it has nothing to do with the hotel," Natalia explained.

Michael looked at Natalia, and now I could tell by his unusual interest in the activity at my desk that he was eager to get an invitation to join. "You two will love it," Michael said, "Make sure they seat you in the Pool Room. Don't do the Terrace."

"Great," Natalia said looking at him briskly to politely acknowledge him, and then turned to me. "I've heard great things. This review says it has one of the most expensive foods in the world, a baked potato for two hundred dollars," she said with glee. "Let's try it. Midtown, Fifty-second and Park."

"See you there at eight," I said. I was less excited about the restaurant and more relieved it would not be another lonely evening. The last couple of nights I had left work at eight, and since most of my friends were traveling, I was alone, falling asleep on my sofa partly out of boredom and partly out of exhaustion. I knew this break of leaving work early would only last a few days before I'd get staffed on another project that would take over my nights and weekends.

Though Natalia looked and acted like any other American, her parents were Russian immigrants who had settled in Boston. We met over the Xerox machine, where she helped me troubleshoot a Tab-A error. Since there were so few of us, there was often a spirit of camaraderie among the professional women on my floor. Natalia stood out, and I was drawn to the confident way she pulled her shoulder-length hair behind her ear and took the liberty of wearing red suits in the summer when most women shifted to pastels. I took no risks, wearing mostly black and navy year round. She was a Harvard economics major and according to our Analyst Facebook her favorite cartoon was *Calvin & Hobbes*. In two months, she would be free from Morgan Stanley, having lined up a position at a local investment fund.

Without much enthusiasm she mused that it would be "more money with fewer hours."

Natalia had been part of the oil and gas group, a much smaller team than our blue-chip group. Her counterpart analyst was a guy and for their analyst going-away event, the team decided that the guys would play golf and she and her manager, the only two women, could go to a spa for the day. The head of her group must have felt a little guilty, because he told Natalia she could also go splurge on a dinner. After wandering around the floor looking for people who weren't busy, Natalia settled on me, a mere acquaintance.

Like many, I had gotten used to sharing evenings with people I didn't know that well, knowing I might not talk to them again for months. Even when I met people I wanted to get to know better, like Priya, by the time I was free, she was already staffed on a new deal and was working most nights and weekends. "Friends" were people I spoke to about once a month. It felt isolating at times, but there was also the excitement of learning about someone new, like having a series of affairs with no commitment. Relationships had evolved from insufferably close ties to fairly shallow connections. Who knew where it would lead, but the expectations were low.

We both arrived promptly at 8:00 P.M. for our dinner. Though we both lived on the Upper West Side, we met at the restaurant. When alone, I'd often take the subway, excited to see everyday people and wonder what their day was like. I'm sure Natalia took a cab, since most of my colleagues tried to avoid the riffraff subway types.

A waiter with an eastern European accent escorted us to the Pool Room, which seemed crowded for a midweek dinner hour.

The tables and small delicate trees surrounded a glistening rect-angle pool of water. The room shimmered with soft lighting that created a soothing atmosphere. Since we'd had time to go home and change before dinner, gone were the stuffy work pantsuits. Instead, we were draped in silky tank tops and flowing black pants. Somewhere in between finding time to curl my eyelashes and digging up some dangly earrings, I'd somehow slipped into an uncontrollable smile that I shared with people as we breezed through the dining room. We were two attractive, seemingly carefree women together in a room filled with couples on dates and executives.

Ordering was easy. "Bring us the best you have," Natalia told the waiter. She smiled at him so many times that I won-dered whether it was because she thought he was Russian or whether she was just lonely like me. Like good waiters often do, he paid attention to her eyes and quickly picked up on her need for attention, giving her a wink after describing the "luscious smooth buffalo meat that will give your taste buds a buzz you won't forget." I'm sure he'd seen many lonely women walk in and out of these doors, and there was no better way to maximize your tip than to flirt.

We wasted half a table full of appetizers that our waiter carefully chose. My stomach turned as he walked away with full plates.

He brought over his recommended entrée: bison, foie gras Périgord, truffle sauce. I was concerned he'd only chosen it because it was the most expensive, until I tasted it. It was the first time I'd tasted red meat in New York that I could say was better than Texas beef. Natalia and I savored the soft, juicy meat in complete silence.

Natalia kept swirling her glass of burgundy with loose hand motions as if she were rolling dice. She asked about my last name since she was friends with someone in high school whose last name ended in *walla*.

"Not all but most of the *walla*s are Parsi," I explained. "We practically all know each other since there are only a couple of hundred thousand in the world. It's a crazy tight community." Our waiter came over and laughed with us when I told Natalia there was even a Sodabottleopenerwalla family.

My cheeks were warm and ached from the long overdue laughter. I could feel them blush red just like my father's would.

"What's your friend's last name?" I asked.

"Shanaya Colabawalla."

"Of course," I said. "I spent some holidays with her family during one of my internships." I went on to explain, "Whenever you move somewhere new, your parents put you in touch with someone in the local area so that you feel welcome." I could see her surprised face. "This one New York family even threw a big birthday party for me, and I'd only met them once before. It's crazy!"

"If your community is so small, how do you meet people to date?" she asked.

"You either grow up in one of the four major cities where Parsis flock to, or you attend World Congresses to meet people your age. It's different from your average dating scene."

"Sounds like a sweet setup. Our Russian community is tight, but not quite like that." She went on to explain the Russian name endings of *vich* and *ova*.

I leaned back in the velvety lounge chairs and kicked off my heels. The more burgundy we drank, the more unwieldy her wine swirls became. Our white tablecloth was stained with red splashes that she didn't notice. Appearances weren't important for the first time in a while. Judgment had lifted too. I wasn't worried about what she'd report back about me to others. Since she was leaving for a new job, it was clear she felt the same way.

I flagged the waiter down for a final bottle. He uncorked the Veuve Clicquot La Grande Dame and filled champagne flutes.

"Nice choice," Natalia said. "I was worried you'd choose the rosé, which would remind me of our Project Ball closing dinner."

"I much prefer this vintage. It has a silky texture that I adore," I said as I raised my glass and made a toast to her two years, asking if she had any lessons to pass along. I expected a one- or two-sentence answer, but she leaned in and offered much more.

"I've made some great friends here. They basically bring a bunch of successful, interesting college kids together—valedictorians of countries, world champions, royalty, you name it. I'll stay in touch with a bunch of them for life." She put down her wineglass and began rummaging through her purse, and I wondered if she was looking to retouch the bright red shiny lipstick she wore, which I imagined was called Red Patent Leather. She went on, unable to find what she was looking for. "After my two years here, I could feel during my interviews that everyone wanted me. We're at the top Wall Street firm, and we'll always have that gold star on our résumé. Focus on that and don't let the fucked-up culture distract you. Use them like they use you."

"Words of advice," I said nodding my head, wondering if I had already become as hardened as she was even though I'd only been there half as long. I didn't realize it until she said it, but there was a part of me that didn't trust the majority of my colleagues. And it wasn't even because I thought they were all inherently untrustworthy. Rather, something about this competitive, fear-driven culture seemed to bring out the worst in people, including me. There was something exhausting about it, too.

I watched her as she continued rummaging through her purse, and I hoped I wouldn't be Natalia a year from now: spending my good-bye dinner with a virtual stranger, and getting satisfaction from spending as much of the company's money as possible to get back at them. But part of me knew that I could easily be her if I hung around for another year.

A shout broke into our intense conversation. Scanning the room, we saw heads turned to a guy in a light gray suit on his knees, holding a small velvet box in his shaking hand. "She said yes!" he shouted with relief as we all clapped.

Natalia clapped too, but her drunken, glazed-over stare revealed that she wasn't paying attention to the romantic moment. My question about what she'd learned at Morgan Stanley had struck a nerve. She stopped short and placed both hands on the table. "The second month I started here," she went on, "I worked really hard on this deal, and when it came time to do all the cool work like the road show, the client told my VP that he didn't want any women traveling with them. My VP framed it like this: 'Natalia, I'd hate for you to be with clients who don't want you there.' So my counterpart analyst went instead of me." She began pouring more burgundy into her wine glass even though it was already three-quarters full. I was surprised to hear her rattle on like this, since she was usually so contained. But this may have been the first time someone asked her about her experience and she felt she could answer honestly.

After word got out about what happened to her, many other female analysts shared their difficult work experiences with her, she said. The women analysts didn't want to admit it to others because they just blamed themselves. Excited that some women were open to sharing their experiences, I asked Natalia for their names in order to start a women's committee so that we didn't have to all feel so alone. Even though there were hardly any senior women, I imagined we could invite a few of them to offer us advice. During my summer internship I worked for Laura Smith, one of the most powerful women in the company. I could start with her. From our table, I looked at the shimmery silver beads that covered an entire wall of windows, excited at the idea of having a support network of women at the firm.

After Natalia and I eagerly discussed the women's committee idea, she gave me some contacts for post–Morgan Stanley jobs. The most intriguing was for a prestigious investment firm that invested in women- and minority-owned companies. As soon as she suggested it, a comment Farah made to a staunch environmentalist, who had condemned her for staying at her firm after a huge chemical leak, ran through my head. "Well, I could stay at my firm and be the chemical engineer who makes a positive change, or I could leave and lobby my firm to change. And I choose to be the change." I couldn't see myself staying in the Morgan Stanley environment much longer, but something about helping change the power dynamics for those underrepresented in the business world sounded appealing to me. In college, I would've laughed at the idea that being in business could be different for women than for men, but only a few weeks into my Morgan Stanley experience, I completely understood. I had to admit, knowing that I had something to look forward to after

Morgan Stanley put me in a much better mind-set. The last few months, I'd felt so lost without having something I was working toward other than finishing two years here.

Our waiter came over with a longing smile directed to Natalia as he explained the desserts, and I knew she'd tip him at least a couple of hundred dollars for all his attention. The vanilla-poached pears, tarts, and cinnamon-pumpkin crème brûlée all sat in front of us patiently. We tried only a bite of each of them since we were too full for more, and it wasn't long before Natalia grew sleepy from all the burgundy.

"Thanks for the invite," I said to Natalia. The waiter held the door open for us as we left the restaurant. "It was really great!"

"Thanks for the company!" she said graciously. "We should do it again sometime."

Right after she said it, I felt this empty feeling for all the times I'd met people in New York I liked and hadn't ever connected with them again. We all kept so busy that there was no time to reconnect. No depth. "That would be great," I said in a less enthusiastic tone, knowing it wouldn't happen.

Natalia automatically lifted her hand to hail a cab.

"I think I'm going to take the subway. Any interest?" I asked, even though I knew the answer.

"Are you joking?" she said. "It's all going to be expensed."

"It's not about the money," I replied, shrugging my shoulders.

"Suit yourself," she said with a confused smile as she shut the cab door.

The next day after dinner with Natalia, I was already back to working around the clock. For the following weeks, I hardly spoke to anyone other than the few people on my deal team. For this transaction, I was working with an associate outside our blue-chip group who was new to the company and trying hard to prove himself. He'd keep me and the other analyst on his team around all weekend and most nights doing inefficient tasks like poring through annual reports page by page looking for acquisition targets he could suggest to his officer.

Almost a month into the project, I was excited when I got off before midnight one night, so I walked across the floor to look for other analysts. I found Daniel inhaling a S'mores Pop-Tart on his way out with some mergers and acquisitions analysts to Whiskey Bar, so I joined. After stumbling home from drinking that night, I woke up in the middle of the night convinced that I was drowning. The water would come out of the walls and choke me. Every time I closed my eyes, I started to gag. I went over to my roommate's bed, but she was still at work. I picked up the phone to call Ali, but he was having his own vertigo crisis. Daniel would tell me I was not drunk enough. Everyone else was working on deals out of town. My parents would not greet a 3:00 A.M. call warmly. But I could not be alone.

I had to settle for images. Rummaging through my nightstand drawer, I found my family Christmas picture from when I was still in high school, and the homemade card that Lena made me last Christmas, decorated with my dance picture.

My body felt embalmed from the earlier tequila shots. I'd managed to get into some flannel pajama bottoms, but I was still wearing my dress blouse, decorated with the whiskey Daniel and I had thrown at each other earlier that night. In this mess, I sat on the floor in front of my refrigerator with the door open and propped both pictures next to me. The cold kept me alert enough to remember that I wasn't dreaming. The murmur of the fridge kept me company. Balled up with my knees to my chest, I continued sweating and shivering as I drank all my emergency vodka. My fridge was generally empty, but my freezer was stocked with vodka for these very nights.

With every gulp, I struggled to shift my focus from one photo to the next. In our family Christmas picture we all had to choose one gift to show off to the camera. My sisters and I all squeezed together atop my mother's, father's, and grandmother's laps on our sofa, which had a string of rotting vitamins behind it. My dad held up *Controlling Cholesterol for Dummies* and my mom her Danielle Steel book, *The Promise*. Farah sat upright on my father's lap holding her new Palm Pilot organizer. Lena squished her tiny figure into a ball between my parents as she held a book of Donald Hall poems. Shireen sat in a squat on the floor in front of my parents, holding a box of organic chocolates. Showing off a suede, knee-length jacket my friends would envy, I lay sideways, sprawled across my mother and Farah, my feet dangling over my grandmother's lap. My grandmother didn't hold up a gift since doing so was obviously ill mannered. We all laughed as I insisted my grandmother say, "Bite me, chutney!" to the camera.

Clinging to my sticky kitchen floor, for the first time, I read the card Lena made me. The front page read, "To Nina, From an angel." And underneath it a warning: "This book is based PURELY on fiction." Her book consisted of only a few pages, with some pictures and a few words. Her story tracked the progression of a once cheerful, determined, charismatic young girl who, once she had escaped her home, had successfully made it somewhere that she wanted to be—wowing everybody. She then described how the once-fun fictional character was now incapable of making anyone laugh. But worse, it was impossible to make her laugh. Her fictional character isolated herself from everything that meant anything to her, and consequently failed herself.

Six months ago when she gave this to me I wouldn't have understood any of it, but tonight, it all made sense. Perfect sense. I wanted to call her, eager for any human contact. But then I remembered a month ago having to let her go abruptly because Todd needed to speak to me urgently while she tried to discuss her boyfriend crisis. "Sorry, I've gotta go," I said, hanging up the phone as Todd stared me down. *I forgot to call back*, I thought, as I kicked the crisper drawer.

I grabbed a pen and made a list on my hand. "More V, G, & W," I wrote. Vodka, gin, and maybe whiskey. Then, after contemplation, I wrote down, "Scott—antis." He looked happier now after taking the antidepressants. He said it was easy. On his first appointment, as soon as he entered the doctor's office, before he even sat down, she asked, "Where do you work?"

"I'm an investment banker," he replied.

"Antidepressants," she diagnosed. "What kind do you want?" And that was it. Scott paid two hundred dollars for the four-minute visit and said it was worth it. The medication completely numbed him.

The next day, on Saturday, I was supposed to meet Steve at 9:00 A.M., but I didn't wake up. After he beeped me several times, he called my home at 9:10. I was still on the floor in front of the fridge. "Nina, where are you?" he asked surprised.

"Oh my God!" I said. "Sorry. My beeper is in the bedroom, and I was in my kitchen . . ." I explained. But he was uninterested in explanations. "Glad I caught you. I'll see you in fifteen minutes," he said.

After throwing on a pair of jeans and a new shirt, and

dousing myself with my roommate's Vanilla Bath & Body Works body spray, hoping to hide the stench of alcohol, I went downstairs to hail a taxi. My Upper West Side neighborhood swarmed with smiling couples pushing their jogging strollers on their way to Central Park. I stood on Broadway for several minutes watching the cars go by. I stepped closer and closer to them as they passed by at forty miles per hour. *What if it were just a leg? Would I get a week off? But Jessica in mergers and acquisitions came in the whole time her leg was broken.* I walked closer and closer to the curb as the cars breezed by, kicking up wind. A few cars honked. Drivers even screamed, "Get the fuck off the road," but it was still the most peaceful moment I had experienced in so long. It felt safe, comforting.

Though I still felt low and my head vibrated, I did not feel that different from when I had not slept in days. In fact, this feeling was better. I felt a little less concerned, a little less anxious. Much less aware.

As I rode into work, all I could remember from the night before was an image of me banging my head against the mirror as I brushed my teeth. I kept my eyes in contact with the mirror the entire time. Never letting myself escape, I hit my head harder and harder as I held onto the hot and cold water faucet taps to keep my balance. In the cab, I squinted my eyes in confusion and looked in the rearview mirror for bruises on my head as I wondered whether it was a dream.

When I came into work, it was obvious to Steve that I was hungover. He had never seen me this way. He passed by my desk several times and took long stares.

"I'm going downstairs to get a bagel," he said during one inspection. "Do you want anything?"

"Water!" I said longingly. "Water!"

"I'll get you a big bottle," he said as he shook his head. "You should turn on the light so you can see properly," he suggested.

"That green lamp is an annoyance," I said without looking up.

"Suit yourself," he said, as he raised his eyebrows in surprise.

Luis walked in and passed Steve. "Good morning."

"Good morning," Steve replied as he walked off.

"Nina, your hair is all sticking out over here," Luis said, motioning to the whole right side of his head.

"I know," I responded. "I'll fix it later."

"I hate being here on Saturdays," Luis said. "Michael just took off for the Virgin Islands, so I have to pick up his Project Runner. He got hooked up with a three-day, two-night resort in St. John. Poof, he's gone overnight while we're here working our asses off. He just called yesterday and left Todd a message. Can you believe it?"

I looked up, highly agitated. "Seriously, he's not around?"

"I am dead serious," Luis said as he stood up from his chair.

I picked up my ringing phone. "Morgan Stanley."

"Hey, it's Daniel," I heard him say in a faint whisper.

"I can hardly hear you," I said. "Are you at work?"

"I'm calling from conference room 32B. I can't talk from my desk or they will hear me. I got great news. I just had a huge breakthrough. You know that health-care deal I was working on? They want to create new software. They just got a bright CFO and they want me to join. They already started Starfish, the other big health-care venture. They're promising me a bunch of shares. I can't go wrong. I'm going to be loaded!" he said, now speaking in an ecstatic whisper.

"Are you leaving?" I asked.

"No, it's all under the table until I finish my two years," he said. "Yikes, I just saw my associate walk by, I'll call you later."

As soon as I hung up the phone Luis asked, "Do you think that Todd thinks I'm lazy?"

"I don't know," I said. "I've never thought about it." My head was so cloudy I was hardly listening to Luis.

"After they staffed me, he told me to make sure I take care of the deal properly," Luis said. "What do you think he meant by that?"

"He was just reminding you," I offered.

"What did he mean by 'take care of it properly'?" Luis said, hands on his hips. "Here I am, working on a Saturday. Obviously, I deserve more credit than that."

I just wanted him to be quiet and go away. I covered my head with my hands and took a deep breath. As my head throbbed, it became clear to me: Not seeing any of these people for a day, a week, anything, was exactly what I needed.

"Have you ever heard him say anything about me?" Luis asked. Not getting a response, he looked up and asked, "Are you okay?"

"I'm fine," I said, irritated, as I kicked the wall under my desk and gawked at my computer screen, resenting the fact that I wasn't the one chosen to start a company or get vertigo.

Steve handed me my water and walked away. Within seconds he returned. "Nina, I didn't want to say anything, but it's a little difficult working with you when you're not at your best. I would never have expected this from you."

"I'm taking a vacation, not this week but next week," I said, unaware of my words.

"Are you okay?" he asked. He placed his hand over the low barrier in front of my desk with genuine concern.

"Yes," I replied. Not knowing what I meant, I said, "I just need to go home."

"Well, you realize that Project Kama is coming up and you could miss out on an opportunity to step up," he reminded me as he straightened out his polo shirt collar.

"That's okay," I said as I picked up the phone to call the copy center, purposely not making eye contact. "I'll e-mail you dates," I said to him. Automatically, I thought back to Leanna, who flew out for a week long vacation with her boyfriend to Hawaii. As soon as the aircraft landed, she was beeped, and had to catch the next flight back. I added, "And I'm purposely going when it's not busy so that I won't need to come back early."

"Good idea," Steve said, surprised at my new assertiveness.

We left the office at 1:00 P.M., since Steve thought it was a good idea to call it an early day. On my way out, as I walked through the lobby, I found the scattered overhead lights unbearable. I looked down to shield my eyes from the flaming lights that were thrown in so many directions they distorted the ground. For only a second, I felt compelled to look at the ceiling's unusual formation. There were thousands of lights ablaze; each one was tucked away, covered by blinders. Though they were surrounded by others, they lived an isolated existence where they would never see or reflect on one another.

This time when I returned to Texas, my dad came alone to pick me up at the airport. He greeted me wearing a loud Hawaiian shirt that he had picked up on vacation ten years ago on a "Buy 20 shirts, get a discount" deal. "How is my little Wall Street Mickey Mouse?" he said, greeting me with an endearing whack on my head.

When I got to our house, Farah and Lena were there to welcome me. Shireen was still abroad in the Peace Corps. My grandmother had prepared my favorite shrimp curry. It was the same dish she used to ease me out of my "no Indian food" phase in high school when my mom had to show her how to make "shortcut" enchiladas with Cool Ranch Doritos for me instead. We all sat in the living room drinking tea while my mom was in the kitchen engaged with some last-minute dinner preparations. On principle, my grandmother wouldn't stay in the kitchen when my mom was cooking with her Heinz ketchup added to curry or potato flakes added to the lentil soup shortcuts. Farah, Lena, and I all sat on the couch, propping our feet up on the coffee table while my mother was not around to scold us.

"Nina, I'll come visit you in New York," my grandmother said, holding the television remote in her hand even though the television was off. "I already stayed in Farah's home for two weeks and cooked one month's food. All covered in saran wrap," she explained, showing me with her hands how she covered them neatly, "and then in nice Tupperwares to keep it fresh. We can invite Siloo Aunty and Jamshed Uncle over. I told you they're my sister's brother-in-law's first cousins. They want to meet you."

Farah leaned over to me. "Oh, good, you can finally meet more of our hundred million relatives we've never met." She held up three fingers and mouthed, "Three months' worth of food," as she rolled her eyes. She pinched me, warning me not to say anything, as she whispered in my ear, "If you don't carry back Tupperwares of food to New York, she's FedExing them to you. The FedEx boxes are already in the garage."

"I don't know if you'll like New York, Grandma," Lena said. "It's not like Texan comfort."

"Now, Nina," my grandmother explained, "I've been to New York many times. I've lived in Bombay, so you don't need to tell me about flats. I know it's not a house."

"You've only been to New York in transit," my dad interrupted, talking over her.

"Zal, be quiet," she said, lifting her hand so sternly I could tell she was still angry at him for not taking her to H-E-B Grocery for the one-day "Six Dancing Tangelos for $1" sale. "I'm talking to Nina." She spoke in Gujarati even though she knew we understood. It seemed to make her feel like she had more privacy.

My dad just laughed as he sipped his tea, amused at how unnecessarily excited she got.

She went on ignoring him. "Nina, I'll cook for you while you are at work, and we can play cards when you come home. I'll be happy once I see my Nina settled down in her own home. I've already seen Farah in her lovely home. Shall I come for two or three weeks?" she asked, looking at me. "I don't want to stay too long. You tell me."

I warmed my hands on my cup of Darjeeling tea with mint and lemongrass as I looked at my dad with "help me" eyes so familiar to him. Even though my grandmother had lived in the States for years, my parents were our liaisons in explaining any American ways that were unlike her soap operas.

"Mummy, she has a very small place," he pleaded with her.

"Now stop it!" she said loudly in Gujarati to him. "Zal, I told you to keep quiet."

He looked at me and shrugged his shoulders with laughter that was now annoying her enough for her to send him dirty glances.

Farah jumped in with a clever visual. "Grandma, she lives in an apartment that isn't much bigger than your bedroom."

"Such a small apartment!" she said, covering her mouth and gawking at me. "I thought you have a good job." She looked at my dad and said in Gujarati, "What are you doing telling people she's working on Wall Street like some crazy man?"

"I do, Grandma," I explained. "It's different in New York. Everything is expensive. People think my place is fancy because I have a doorman, like a security guard."

"How will we invite Siloo Aunty and Jamshed Uncle over from Flushing?" she said, still planning out the visit. "We will have to go visit them. It will be an embarrassment the way you are living."

We all laughed as she carried on, which worked her up even more.

"Grandma," Farah added, "you won't want to have people over at Nina's place. You may not even see her. When I went for two days we only spent about five hours together."

"Six," I corrected her, as I got off the sofa and lay down on the comfortable rug, just like Farah and I used to while watching our back-to-back television shows.

"She has four plates, six forks, and four spoons. No knives. It's not exactly entertainment-friendly," Farah explained. "Plus, New Yorkers go out all the time. Maybe because their apartments are so tiny?" she said looking at me, pleased with her hypothesis.

Quickly the conversation turned from playful to serious.

My grandmother glared at my dad as if I were his fault. In Gujarati she said to him with disgust, "Why did your father and I give up everything to send you to the best education in India if your daughter is living worse than our family in India?" She took a flat fist and hit the arm of her chair. "Tell me." The whole room went silent, but she insisted on an answer. "Tell me!"

"Mummy, please," my dad said, turning red with embarrassment. "Enough." It was a trade-off for my dad, being the oldest son. He got the best education, and in exchange he was expected to take care of his parents later in life, be successful in the United States, ensure his younger brothers became U.S. citizens, and breed successful children.

It was rare to see my dad so uncomfortable. The first time I saw my dad embarrassed was at the doctor's office. He took us to the doctor for any complaint, including headaches. My mom said it was the idea of insurance that excited him in America. "You could keep going back for free, like a buffet. It's not like that in India." While we were at ShowBiz Pizza the night before, I was leaning up against the Donkey Kong machine and felt a bump behind one of my nipples. It didn't hurt, but it felt like a tiny pinball. My dad's eyes were bloodshot, and he looked terrified as we sat waiting for the doctor. He hadn't slept all night, and I heard him tell my mother I was too young to know what a tumor felt like. The appointment was quick. After explaining to Dr. Gomez the pinball feeling, he said, "Raise your arms," and looked at my armpits. After seeing thin black hairs starting to grow, he looked at my father and said, "Your daughter is going through puberty. One day she will have breasts, like other women." We might have both laughed if we were more comfortable with each other, but instead my dad walked out of the room, turning his head away from me, while I put my shirt on. For the first time the doctor didn't give me a lollipop on my way out and my dad didn't hold my hand as we crossed the street.

My dad's embarrassment made my sisters and me uncomfortable. Eager to avoid an argument between my dad and my grandmother, we started eyeing each other, thinking of ways to defuse the tension just as we did when we were younger. Suddenly Lena screamed, "Get her!" and she and Farah charged at me. Farah grabbed my arms and Lena seized my legs, and they lifted me in the air, letting my body hang like a hammock. Then they began swinging me back and forth as I wiggled and screamed. "Tell them to stop! Somebody tell them to stop!" My grandmother covered her mouth as she laughed privately, and my dad kept his red shade, but this time he was in for a long laughing fit.

After a few minutes my mom called from the kitchen, "Stop all the horseplay and come set the table, girls." Farah and I put our teacups in the kitchen sink and helped my mom lay the table. I carried two pots of hot orange shrimp curry to the table. "This smells amazing!" I said, holding my head over one and taking deep breaths. "I could eat coconut on everything."

"Don't do that," my mom said. "You kids have long, thick hair that falls everywhere. I even saw one of Lena's hairs in the fridge the other day."

Sitting together at the table made me feel like we were on *The Brady Bunch*. With so many different schedules growing up, we often ate separately. "What are you eating in New York?" my mom asked me as she passed the *kachumber*. She would have called it *pico de gallo* if we had an American visitor over. "You look chubbier and paler."

"Sushi when I have time, but I don't get away from my desk much, and I definitely don't get out in the sun."

"You really eat the raw stuff," Farah commented. "When you left Texas you hadn't even heard of it. Now it's your favorite meal?"

"Well, eat real food now," my mom said as she passed basmati rice my way. "Your grandmother has cooked your favorite. In the freezer she has pans of everything she could ever remember you enjoying. Including *burfi*."

After a few minutes, my dad left and came back with a picture. "Did you see the picture of me and the mayor? He gave me my promotion during our event at the Convention Center downtown. Everyone in the office was hoping I would get it. Even the girl who's the head of aviation wanted me to get it."

"Zal," my mother said, "why are you doing all this in the middle of dinner? Wait until we're finished."

"Dad, if she's over eighteen, she's a woman, not a girl," I said, embarrassed. During my visits, I couldn't help but notice the way my dad spoke to me like I was an equal. After all these years, I'd finally earned his respect.

"The mayor knew all along, but he never even told me about it. Did I show you the letter he wrote praising my excellence?" he asked, knowing he had not. He went to the wet bar, where he had already laid it out for me. "Here," he said. "Read it carefully. He says my work is unparalleled. Can you believe they knew about my promotion three months before and never told me? He's a disciplined man, Nina. After twenty years in the military, he knows to keep things close to his chest. Do you know what that is called?"

"What?" I asked.

"Discipline," he repeated.

"That's impressive, Dad." My dad now seemed to need my approval just as much as I needed his. Somehow our relationship had become this exchange of accolades.

"Ladies," my dad said in an announcer's voice, "keep Friday night free for our annual Rockets game."

"Annual? We've never been to a game together," Lena said.

"It's new," he said.

"Zal, explain it properly!" my mom said to him in an irritated tone, and then immediately carried on as his translator. "It's a new father-daughter outing," she announced as if he weren't in the room. "This is his way of saying he misses you all," she said, looking directly at me.

My sisters and I all looked at one another in complete surprise. It was so out of character for him to make *any* plans outside a Parsi function, much less father and daughter? *Wow!*

My sisters and I all exchanged excited smiles.

"Sounds fun!" I said.

After a long silence and several half-eaten plates of curry, Farah asked me, "So, how's life up north?"

"It's okay," I said.

"What have you been doing for fun?" Farah asked.

"Nina," Lena interrupted excitedly, "I saw Jennie and Summer at Blockbuster the other night, and they were asking about you. They said they haven't heard from you in ages. I told them you were busy but that you'd try to call them." She put down both her fork and spoon as she spoke.

"Yeah," my dad added, "I always see Kara and Hannah outside doing the lawn, and they always ask for you, too. You should call them. You shouldn't forget all your high school friends."

"I will, I will," I said. I turned to Farah and answered her question. "Well, we go out to bars and clubs sometimes. It's cool to check them out, but they all look the same after a year. It's getting old."

"But," my mom interjected, "I thought you loved New York City. You always said it fit your personality much better than these boring suburbs."

"I do love New York's pace. There are so many different people from places I've never been. Plus, it's fun being somewhere where everyone is trying to make it. Most of the time I thrive on it." I paused before I admitted it. "But I'm getting tired."

"Did you ever look into taking dance classes up there?" Farah asked.

"I can't really get out of work that early. I always miss them. I definitely need to find something though. Work is getting to me," I said. "I'll look into dance classes when I go back."

"Farah is right," my dad agreed. "Exercise is important for your muscles, heart, and blood circulation. Your mother and I have always encouraged you all to keep in shape with dance," he said.

"But Nina, you are still doing well at work, aren't you?" my mom asked.

"I'm doing well, but I'm getting tired of it, so I'm not sure what I'm going to do," I explained.

"You're not going to leave, are you?" my dad asked, putting down his fork and knife in surprise.

"Remember how terrible she looked when she came home," Farah said. "Does it look like she's having a good experience?" she said to our parents. "She looked like she was half-alive."

The first couple of days after I arrived, my body shut down in complete exhaustion. I was asleep for most of it. Too tired to sit up at the dinner table, I lay down on two chairs as my mom fed me by sliding miniballs of rice and dal that she formed with her fingers into my mouth. My dad watched in shock, hardly able to eat his food.

My grandmother began shaking her head and pointing at my cheek, mumbling, "Boils."

"Grandma, it is called a zit in America," Lena educated her.

"You enjoyed your internships," my mom reminded me. "Maybe you just need to adjust to this new group slowly. Give it some more time. It would be so sad for you to just give up like that."

Lena, as usual, sat quietly at the table. Since she was always around people who were much older, she was rarely heard. She learned to be the interpreter of our lives.

"You know, Nina, with all that stress you should be careful," my dad said. "Have you gone to get your heart murmur checked out recently? I told you when you left for New York to get it checked once a year."

It was something I never even thought about. "Dad," I said, "you know it's minor and doesn't even affect me. Getting to the doctor is very difficult. Sometimes I don't have time for a shower. Do you think I'm going to be able to keep a doctor's appointment when I have to plan it weeks ahead of time? It's not Texas, where I can call the doctor and ask to stop by sometime today, and be greeted by smiling nurses who call me honey and notice that my hair looks cute pulled back in a barrette instead of down. This is New York, where if I show up eight minutes late for the appointment, my appointment's canceled."

"Nina," he said, irritated with my rationale, "your health is your wealth. How many times have I told you that? You can't neglect it."

"Well," I said, "my company doesn't give a damn about my health, and they own me. Mom, look," I started, hoping to come up with some explanation she could find satisfying. "It's difficult to explain, but sometimes my choices may be disappointing to you," I said, knowing that I had no intention of really explaining to them what my job was like. There was no way I'd use the words *strip club* in front of my parents. I wasn't even sure if my dad or grandmother knew what they were. But my worst fear was to explain to them what it was like and still have them recommend I stay. To them, I imagined, a long workday with a few abusive comments here and there was child's play compared to things they'd dealt with in life.

"They just burned you out," my mom said, shaking her head.

"Okay," Lena interrupted. "Nina doesn't need everyone weighing in on her life. It's not our decision, it's hers. She's smart and will figure it out."

This was my problem: I couldn't think clearly. What I wanted and what they wanted for me was all jumbled together in my head. *Did I take this job to win over my dad or for me? Should I stick out the two years because otherwise they'll think I'm a failure or because I'd feel like a failure?* I couldn't answer any of these questions with confidence.

"We're just trying to help you," my grandmother said, reaching out to hold my hand.

My mom put her warm hand on my cheek. "We all just want you to be happy, *beta*. Lena's right—you do what you like."

"Her health is the most important thing," my dad said. He looked at me and said, "You finish your job there, and then you come back to Texas and find a good job here. You can make good money here, too. Plus, money won't buy you a new heart or lung."

I took a deep breath as I thought about what he said. Just hearing him say my health was more important than the job made me feel like I had so many more options than I'd limited myself to before. At Morgan Stanley we were reminded that work came before our health, family, and everything else. It sounds like basic knowledge, but I'd forgotten.

I slept better that night knowing that in the rooms around me lay sleeping bodies who could save me from drowning. When Lena offered me my own room, I insisted that I sleep in the spare bed next to hers. "I don't want to mess up a whole new room," I said. But she knew. Being able to hear my parents' bellowing snores all the way upstairs in Lena's room no longer disturbed me as it had growing up. Instead the noise lulled me into a deep slumber.

My grandmother had an unparalleled determination that I paid keen attention to while growing up. From the moment she arrived in the United States, she saw how easy it was to win a fortune through *The Price Is Right*. Since then, thirty years later, she tried not to miss a single show. Even if she was up cooking all night, she would not be late for the 10:00 A.M. showing. Every morning, she sat googly-eyed in front of the television with her orange binder and red ink, good-luck pen in hand. In her binder, she documented a short description of every item on the show with its corresponding price. She knew the prices, makes and models of every doghouse, popcorn popper, daybed, car, tent, you name it. Over the years, she diligently documented and memorized thirty volumes of pricing information—498,250 products and 19,950 showcases. She and Bob Barker grew old together. Using the *National Enquirer* as a trusted source, she compared his ailments to hers, informing us all that his arthritis kicked in before hers. We had already taken her to California twice to be a contestant on her beloved show, but she was never invited to "come on down." Still, she never lost faith that one day she would claim her deserved winnings. When my father mocked her pipe dream, she'd quickly retort, "It will happen. You watch and see!" slapping his shoulder with a turmeric-stained wooden spoon while he shook with laughter.

My grandmother remained fiery like that in my memory, so during my visit home I was struck by her loneliness. But her lonely life seemed only marginally different from what I'd escaped in Manhattan. Now that my three sisters and I had moved out, the hours spent braiding our hair and dancing with us in the living room were now silent ones that she spent sitting in her chair alone. Trapped in our house, she either spent her days cooking, pacing, sitting in heavy silence, or watching *The Price Is Right* and *As the World Turns*. With no one to speak to, she even began to forget much of her English. I guess it shouldn't have been too surprising since she had always found our suburban silence frightening and our large house alienating compared to the commotion that stirred her former home in India. Her life in India was the antithesis of this pacified existence. In India, she resided with extended family and innumerable servants in a home overflowing with visiting friends and extended-extended family. If she left to go to the marketplace, for a walk or on the bus, she would be closely surrounded by sweaty, breathing bodies.

I spent the first couple of days of my visit catching up with everyone. A few days in, I was so worn out by the rare interaction with people that I went into the game room to start reading the many *Investor Business Daily* and *Fortune* articles my dad had clipped out for me with a sticky note that said, "Let's discuss after you read these." My grandmother approached me in the game room, put her hand on my arm, and said, "I just want to spend time with you. You don't have to talk to me."

"Grandma, is everything okay?" I asked.

"Everything is fine," she said, while inching her chair closer to mine. Then she began her food monologue. "At nine o'clock, after I had tea with some ginger, cloves, cardamom—I didn't add lemongrass today—and two percent milk, I ate porridge with a little bit of the raspberry jam. Not the big teaspoons we have with the flowers on them. That is too much. The smaller teaspoons, the ones with the G initial on them. I put only two-thirds of that teaspoon. Just enough to add flavor, but not too sweet. In the afternoon, I had the lemon chicken, shredded, not cubed. I didn't cut it. I just tore it. Maybe half a centimeter, each piece . . ." She showed me the size with her index finger and thumb. After delivering an excruciatingly detailed report, she concluded with a description of how the food had affected her day. "But it was only leftovers, so the day was not so good."

I sat quietly, taken aback by all the details, but she didn't pause for my response. I hadn't met anyone in New York who talked in such detail. Who would have the patience to listen?

"Nina, did I tell you about the time I served the queen of England and the duke of Edinburgh?" she'd ask rhetorically.

In India, she catered meals for the dignitaries and executives who frequently visited the headquarters of Tata Corporation, India's most esteemed company. She mingled with the Tata family, one of the most well known Parsi families, and other elites while working there.

"Tell me," I said. Even though I'd heard the story every few months growing up, I listened intently as if it were brand-new.

Her eyes fixed on an object behind me, and suddenly she was in a trance, reliving the dream. But her fascination with her food overpowered her interest in the dear queen and duke. "I made minced lamb stuffed in fine crisp patties with a mango chutney and also leavened bread with nuts, raisins, and cherries. This was just the appetizer. For the patties, you take finely shredded ground lamb and marinate it overnight in a paste of cumin, coriander, garam masala . . ."

"Do you wish you were still there instead of here, Grandma?" I asked, wondering if she dreamed about going back and escaping this boring suburban life.

"This is my destiny, Nina," she responded with puzzlement at such an odd question. "You don't question fate," she reminded me.

"Oh yeah," I said, feeling silly for forgetting that she and my dad tended not to regret things very often. It was evident that food and her television shows were the main things that kept her going these days.

We chatted for a while, and then I decided to start reading again. "Do you want to watch television with Mom and Dad?" I asked. "You'll be bored with me. I'm just reading."

Ignoring me, she sat right next to me and put her hand on my knee. "I'm most happy like this." In my peripheral vision, I could see her extensive smile. Her dentures were almost falling out of her mouth in euphoria. I read for the next thirty minutes, and we never exchanged a word.

As I moved outside to the patio, she followed me. She came in a *kaftan* dress bearing two cups of masala chai and said, "I won't interrupt you again, but I just want to tell you I've made chai so it will cool your body while you read. If you drink it, you won't overheat. Also a few snacks," she said, placing string cheese, nachos, Cheetos, and Cheese Nips on the table. We both had a weakness for cheese snacks. When I was younger and we would fight, we sometimes would punish each other by hiding the Cheetos from the other person. Within minutes, her smile returned as soon as she sat next to me and placed her hand on my knee. Over the next hour, I periodically checked to see when it would fade. But it never did.

We talked on the patio for a while and then we went back inside and sat in the living room. Across from me, she sat hunched over on our gaudy pink-and-green flowered recliner. She firmly dug her elbows into her knees and used her palms to prop up her head. In profile, from where I was sitting, she looked like a bicycle U-lock. I remembered this bored look growing up; it lasted from noon until 1:00 P.M. as she waited for the next soap opera to start. "Grandma, didn't you miss *The Price Is Right*?" I asked.

"I'm taping it because you are here," she said.

The rest of the afternoon we spent together, frying eggs and stuffing them neatly into fresh hot *rotli*. Only she had the skill to make it look like the fried egg had always been secretly stashed inside the tortilla-like whole-wheat bread.

That night, I woke up to the sound of banging pots and the heavy smell of cloves and chili powder from my grandmother's self-imposed cooking goals. I came downstairs and found her in the kitchen. Her scarf attempted to restrain her hair, but it had defiantly escaped from the back of her head in unruly waves. For the last ten years, her back had failed her and forced her to lean forward 25 degrees. When she stood over the stove her head was directly over her concoctions, as if slowly merging with them. When she lifted her powerfully built arms in her *kaftan*, she looked like a tie-dyed indigo and magenta butterfly. Tonight, she was in an absolute panic.

She could not sleep and would cook all night because she was overwhelmed by the unrealistic amount of food she had decided to cook.

"Come quickly and hold this pan," she commanded in an irritated tone, as if I had arrived late. Her appliances and utensils were monstrous, heavy, and industrial.

"What are you doing?" I asked, confused by the spaceship-shaped bread that filled the kitchen. There were at least forty freshly inflated puri, puffed Indian bread fried and filled with potatoes, green lentils, sprouts, mint leaves, and spices, sitting on tiers of cooling shelves.

"What, you can't see?" She gestured to the trays. "I have to make eight dozen puris for tomorrow," she said.

"For who? There are only a few of us. Who will eat so many?" I asked.

"We will just freeze them if we can't finish them." She suddenly realized she was even further behind. "I haven't even started the tamarind chutney. Stop distracting me and help. Hold this!" she demanded and pushed a pot into my hands. My arms quivered as I held the massive vessel while she poured some of its contents out. Before I could put down the empty pot, she shoved a spoon of chutney in my mouth and asked, "Too much cumin?"

Though I wanted to tell her that my unbrushed palate was not a good taste tester, the vibrant chutney warmed my mouth. "It's delicious, Grandma. The best I've ever had," I replied, impressed.

She shook her head without hearing me. "Must be too much salt. A little extra fell in because you came in and surprised me."

"Grandma, it's perfect. Seriously, don't change a thing."

"Move, Nina," she said, pushing me to the side and walking over to dump out the chutney into another big bowl. "Now look, I have to start all over. This batch was ruined. We'll have to eat this batch, and I'll make a new one for your dad. You know he doesn't like salty food because of his high blood pressure."

I wanted to laugh aloud because my father eats everything and never complains. "It's perfect," I said. But she was too busy to hear. Her frantic, obsessive pace seemed totally irrational. It was as if she had convinced herself that my dad wanted all these things that I was pretty sure he didn't. Was she trying to prove something to him? Whatever it was, it was hard not to notice that we both craved his approval. Since my dad didn't have her around during his childhood, maybe she was trying to make up for it by doing everything she could for him and his family.

"The puris must be done by tomorrow," she said to herself. She had decided to make them, and they would be cooked.

The next morning, at 11:30 A.M., I woke up unexpectedly, but this time it was to loud voices. I stood at the top of the staircase that led down to the living room and saw my grandmother on the sofa in tears with my dad talking loudly. "Why do you need to talk to them about everything? Now they have told you he is dead. He's dead!"

"Who is dead?" I asked, gripping the staircase banister.

"India called and left a message saying your grandma's oldest brother is dead, and now your grandmother wants to call. They are busy with so many things. Tell her not to bother them, Nina."

"Dad!" I screamed, looking at my grandmother shriveled on the sofa. My father's minimalist approach to life could be a bit much for the many women he lived with. He would particularly get frustrated with my grandmother since she could be the other extreme. He just accepted life as it came and couldn't understand our need to analyze and discuss everything.

My grandmother's last surviving sibling was presumed dead. The message from India said her brother, the only one left of her twelve siblings, was missing. He was an Alzheimer's patient and wandered off into the bustling streets of Bombay while his wife was shopping. They waited two days before they called us. It was the third day, and they were confident that he was dead.

I often seemed to be around when she heard of deaths. Once in junior high, while my grandmother prepared my peanut butter sandwich, she got a stealth call from India. Her siblings were not as wealthy since their kids were not educated in the States, so they could not afford to make international calls. We would only get a recording that would start: "Telegram from India." As soon as I heard it, I bellowed, "Grandma, India! India! It's India," and she came running, grabbing the phone with her sticky peanut-buttered hands. She was just in time to hear the recording, "Your sister has died. I repeat, your sister Goola has died." Click.

I was the only one there to console her. "Grandma, we still love you," I said as I tried to lift her head, which hung in devastation. She grasped my little hand so tightly and used her other to keep her glasses from falling. I offered her my other hand too, and she squeezed them both as I wondered about these mysterious people with whom my grandmother shared her curry and love.

Now, with her last brother dead, those prior brushes with death seemed easier. My grandmother came lunging toward me as soon as I made it down the stairs.

"Are you okay, Grandma?" I asked. But her wails were too extreme for her to speak.

"He's dead, Nina," my dad said. "There is nothing we can do here in America."

"I'm the last one," my grandmother said in a distant voice through sobs.

As she spoke, I realized I hadn't even met or seen pictures of most of her siblings. They were strangers to me. "Let's go to a pay phone," I suggested to my grandmother, thinking maybe I could cheer her up by taking her out to eat. Plus, it seemed easier to walk out of the house than to be an intermediary between the two of them. I went upstairs to change and get shoes for her.

While she cried, I packed her in my dad's car. Before I started the car, she kept motioning to the napkins tucked into the side of my door. I handed her a big stack of Long John Silver's napkins, which she began tucking into her collar and putting over her head. Behind them, she hid her weeping face from any potential onlookers as we drove through our neighborhood.

After we used 7-Eleven's pay phone and found out her brother was confirmed dead, she became talkative. "Why is your father like that? He thinks everything in life is so easy. So what if I get upset!"

In the car, I stared at my grandmother and said only what I could. "You know he likes to keep things simple."

"I sold everything I owned to educate him," she said. "Your father went all over India to the best schools. Every month his papers were sent by ship to be graded by Cambridge University in England. Do you hear me? The best schools! Four diamond bracelets and two necklaces just for his high school. What more could a son want?" she asked.

I shook my head, not knowing what to say. The arguments that used to be so normal during my childhood were now more than I could handle. My limited relationships left me drawing blanks even with my own family. I had grown used to the greeting of a small empty studio apartment. Feelings were now things that sneaked up on me, and I'd worked hard to smother them. I looked at her napkin-decorated body helplessly as I tried to think of something comforting to say.

Once we reached Long John Silver's, her favorite neighborhood fast-food joint, she was back in full form as if nothing had happened. As I was ordering her favorite fried fish, chicken, and shrimp platter, she lunged over the counter, ready to announce her three-minute rule. "I want it fresh," she explained, pointing her finger at the juvenile, underpaid staff. "Absolutely hot and fresh," she went on, moving her hands in circles to show the steam. "And you all really need to use beer in the batter," she advised them. "Right now your batter is okay, but it needs beer to be superb!"

I smiled at the staff as they stared back and forth between us. "She loves food," I explained to them with a slightly embarrassed smile.

We sat at a table near the window since I thought all the kids near the play area might cheer her up.

"I'm saving these for you since they are your favorite," she said, pulling out all her hush puppies.

My favorite? Oh, yeah, I forgot. Eating fast food felt strange. Since I'd lived in New York, sushi in a plastic container was the closest thing to fast food that I ate. Even though I grew up on it, all this fried food had started to feel foreign to me. But I ate it quietly as I wondered for the first time, what is a hush puppy anyway? Bread? Are those onions?

"Do you have a Long John Silver's in New York?" she asked.

"No," I said. "We order food at work or eat at restaurants like you see on *The Bold and the Beautiful*." I had to provide a caveat so she didn't think I was richer than I was. "We don't pay for it. We charge it all to the company." Saying it made me feel guilty since she adored food so much and for me it was now a casual thing.

"My God," she said, dropping her fried shrimp and covering her mouth with her hand since her jaw involuntarily dropped. She paused and I knew she was imagining me at one of the tables in my suit with a scarf wrapped neatly around my neck. She went on. "I'm sorry I said that yesterday, about your flat being too small. You must be doing well. We just want you to be happy, settled down in a nice big house with a good-paying job. And later, a nice Parsi boy. That's all."

"I know," I said. I was pretty clear about her and my parents' idea of what would make me happy.

After rummaging through her purse, she pulled out a prescription pill box that she'd filled with cloves, making it clear to me that she had overeaten. Unlike us, my grandmother mostly used Indian herbal remedies. As I watched her suck on her clove, I realized that most of what I knew about Indians was through her. She was my window to India, the country most of my family grew up in and I still knew so little about. I was in my twenties, and I had only visited a few times in my life. I barely knew my hundreds of relatives. "My little India," I mumbled, smiling her way, but she didn't hear me.

We sat quietly watching a woman pry a GI Joe out of her son's hand. My grandmother broke the silence. "That's okay that he didn't come with us. Your dad has a different way, Nina. He likes to be alone. He has his own way of showing love," she explained to me, even though it felt more like she was explaining it to herself.

It did seem like we were both waiting for my dad to be someone he wasn't. Just like I used to wish he'd say "I love you" like my friends' dads, but when I asked him why he didn't, he said, "Talk is cheap." It just wasn't his way.

"I'm glad you're here," my grandmother said, looking at me and smiling.

"I'm so glad I came home," I said, putting down my spork and reaching for her hand. I grasped it tightly, realizing that I needed her today more than she needed me.

*

After my five-day visit, my dad drove me to the airport. The whole family crowded the driveway, standing outside waving until we reached the end of the street. My mother and grandmother were dressed in their bright flowery *kaftans*. The neighbors were already accustomed to this show every time a guest came over.

As usual, when my dad and I were alone neither of us talked much. He only interrupted the silence a few times. "Did you brush your teeth and say your prayers?" Since we were little these had been his standard questions. By now I was confident that he knew that when we said yes, we weren't always being truthful, but asking seemed to make him feel better.

"Be sure when you get on the subways that you check that your foot doesn't get caught in the gap," he said helpfully. "Perin Aunty visited New York and said it can be dangerous."

"Maybe for old people, but it's really hard to fall through," I educated him. "You should visit sometime. You'll see."

"Let me jog your memory, since I've told you before, but you must have forgotten. On January 19 of 1965 the *Queen Elizabeth I* ship dropped me off in New York City right on the Hudson River. Bombay to New York City in only three weeks. So don't think I haven't been to New York. It was my first stop in this country."

But you said you took the Greyhound bus right away to your college in Missouri, so you didn't really see New York. Plus, I didn't mean visit New York a hundred years ago. Did they not even have planes when you were my age? If I were younger, I'd have blurted my thoughts out uncontrollably, but by now, I'd learned that sometimes it's better to keep quiet.

In his last attempt to parent me, my dad pointed out the

roads. "This road was made using a new technology I developed, polymer-modified asphalt. You want to increase its strength and flexibility by adding a polymer called SBS, styrene butadiene styrene, or polyethylene. The asphalt alone is not strong enough. We also use this new technology on runways and taxiways. See," he said pointing to the ditch. "These road slopes are not done well so the water is accumulating at the crown of the road." Then, interrupted by a marvel, he turned his head completely around to engage me, as if he weren't driving. "Remember I told you about the beltways." In awe, he stared at the intersecting freeways. "Beautiful," he said. One of the only times he would use the word.

My dad and I shared a tendency to lose ourselves deep in thought. We'd have in-depth conversations with others in our heads that were often more fascinating to us than those with real people. I'd become silent and stare in a trance, but my father was more physically engaged, particularly in the car, where he didn't have to take his eyes off the road.

During our ride to the airport, I was reminded of my dad's conversations. When we were younger, a car ride with my father was an experience. Once he was at the wheel, he was engrossed in conversation with others, but no one we could see. His lips and his hands would move in response to these other people he was speaking to. But he made no sound. His most frequent hand gesture was taking his right hand and turning it over, palm up, as if he were about to catch something. With this gesture of puzzlement, he would raise his eyebrows and firmly squeeze his lips together. When I was little I couldn't help but stare. I would lean my head against the window, acting as if I were asleep, and through my slyly slitted eyes I would watch his conversations and wonder whom he was talking to. But as an adult, I felt compelled to stare out the window. The intimacy of catching him with those he thought were secret was just too much.

During our ride to the airport, he continued to make these upward-palm hand motions while his lips moved and his head shook. I looked out my window, deep in my own conversations with him as I wondered whether he was telling me all the things he wished he could say too.

As I watched the strip-mall shopping centers pass by, I couldn't help remembering how afraid I used to be at the thought of never getting to go out and explore beyond these confining suburbs, imagining how exciting it would be when my life *really* started. I worked so hard to leave here, hoping to finally feel free and independent. But at Morgan Stanley, I felt more trapped than when I started.

After we reached the airport, as always, my dad insisted that he come in and drop me off at the gate even though we didn't speak to each other much on the way. I imagined he was appalled by parents who would drop their kids off at the door of the airport since he would never leave us until he saw us walking all the way down the hall onto the airplane. Whether or not we looked, he waved the whole time.

We sat in silence for an hour until my flight was called. When they announced it, he reached over and pulled out a plastic Eckerd Drugs bag. "I bought you these ayurvedic medicines. I would have imported the real stuff, but you will like these better since they're American. Only just recently the Americans are catching on to the ancient Indian traditions. This new American company Pure Planet is now making them. I am giving you Amla-C Plus. It's known as the Indian gooseberry. Research shows that it can be absorbed twelve times faster and creates more potent medicinal effects than vitamin C. It will help your immune system. You need to take one every day. Without fail."

"I'll try and remember to take them," I said as I thumped my heavy bag onto the chair.

"I'm telling you, you need to take one every day," he insisted. "If you need to make a note in your Palm Pilot, then write it now." I could see fear in his eyes, as if he were wondering whether I'd be okay.

"Sure," I said, wanting to make an effort to take them and hoping I wouldn't let them rot just like the ones I'd let rot behind his sofas at home. From his shaking hands, I could see he was desperate to give me anything that might make my life better.

"Dad, it's not like my lung is hanging out of my stomach or something." Even though I was touched by his concern, I had to make a funny comment to defuse the intensity, which was making me feel uncomfortable. "You look so serious."

"Okay," he said, ignoring my smart-aleck comment and hugging me so tight I thought he'd break my ribs. Just as I was about to leave, he put a firm hand on one of my shoulders and with his other hand pointed a finger at me. "You are always welcome in this home. You can come back whenever you want." He pointed at my other shoulder. "This is your home."

As he spoke I tried to look at him, but instead I was so overwhelmed that I acted as if I hadn't heard him. My mom's translating voice echoed through my head. *"What he's saying is that whatever you do, he'll still love you. So do what you want and stop worrying about what he'll think."* I was aware my dad was giving me an out by saying this, because I was quite confident that if he were in my shoes, he would stick it out. But I wanted an out so desperately. I wiggled around, adjusting the Morgan Stanley tote bag that hung heavy on my shoulders as I realized I had come home to hear exactly what he had just said. At that moment, as I stood there in front of my dad, anything work-related seemed like a distant thought—completely insignificant.

"Don't forget to call home when you land."

"Dad, I'm not going to call you in the middle of the night. I come home late every night, and you all have no idea where I am."

"Don't be cheeky. Your mother will stay up all night wondering," he said, even though I knew it would be him. If I'd been younger, I would have reminded him that Americans don't say *cheeky*, and he'd have reminded me that the English language didn't originate in Houston. But we were beyond that.

I plopped the bag down on the ground and said, "Maybe I shouldn't have brought this as a carry-on. It's too heavy."

"Check it in," he suggested. "There is no purpose in carrying it around if it hurts you."

"But, Dad, you are the one who always used to say, 'You shouldn't have brought it if you can't carry it yourself.'"

"I never said that," he said innocently. "Now don't be silly," he said, grabbing the strap. "Check it in."

"No," I said. "I decided to carry it, so now I will."

"Nina, don't be silly! Check it in now," he said, desperately pulling the bag from me. "It's not too late."

"No," I said, forcefully grabbing it back. "I'll carry it this time. I already said I would. Next time, I won't make the same mistake again."

Red wine," I said to the bartender at the Nuyorican Poets Cafe, who wore a nose ring and had spiky blond wisps of hairs flying out of her headscarf. With my first sip, I was overwhelmed by its vinegar taste, sure that it had been opened at least one day earlier. Over the last year I had become far more educated about wine, so I knew this bottle had cost less than eight dollars, but I was so excited to buy any drink in New York that was served in a plastic Dixie cup and cost only four dollars, it didn't matter.

Soon after returning from my visit to Texas, I had gotten a call from a friend, Ashley, whom I had met while studying abroad in Australia. Instead of using his summer in law school to intern, he was coming to New York to do an intensive film class. "Film is what I'm most passionate about, but my father's law firm is where I'll end up working," Ashley explained over the phone. We met up a couple of times and were a perfect match. Ashley had little money but loved fine food, and I had enough money for a nice meal and wanted to be around someone who could talk about something other than banking. He spoke with such intense emotion that he gave me the chills. During our last visit, he had given me a gift, a *Time Out* magazine with stars next to interesting cultural and artistic events around the city. That was how I'd ended up at the Nuyorican Poets Cafe weekly poetry slam. "Powerful storytellers and poets who keep it real," the description said. "People you genuinely want to get to know." It was easier to go on my own than to try to convince one of my banking friends to join me. It would have felt like I was asking a favor.

This evening was my third visit, so I wasn't as taken aback by the homespun feel of the place—the hand-painted sign on the door that resembled graffiti and the bar that was covered in papers, not unlike my cluttered desk. The café was intimate, about the size of a New York City loft apartment, and scattered with tables. No more than forty people would fit comfortably, but they packed in about three times as many. Too self-conscious to sit alone at a table, I clung to the bar like a child not quite comfortable with its surroundings.

The staff remembered me each time I visited because, unlike others, I left generous tips. She passed me the sign-up sheet as it was going around.

"No, thanks," I said.

"I know your type," she said, as if she knew all about me. "It's my job to help you break out."

"Break out of what?" I asked with a laugh, straightening my jeans uncomfortably.

"Break out of your shell," she said loud enough to embarrass me. "You've been here a few times now, and you just quietly listen to others rant about their lives. I know you've got something to say. You're one of those closet poets?"

"Definitely not," I said, shaking my head and looking around to make sure no one else was listening. "I hardly know what poetry is. I couldn't imagine going up there and saying stuff. All I know is that I really like to listen."

I enjoyed being invisible there. People didn't seem to ask or care where I worked. Only once a guy at the bar asked, and I said I worked at a bank. "Like a teller?" he asked. "Something like that," I responded. I could tell by his sour facial expression that he was completely uninterested in such a boring background and he quickly scurried off. Knowing that people in this room would not be impressed by the name Morgan Stanley put me at ease.

"So you're not a closet poet. Then who do you read?" she asked.

"Oh, I don't read poetry," I replied, feeling uncomfortable— she was reminding me how far out of my element I was here.

"What about books? Who's your favorite author?" she pressed.

I knew it was a basic question, but the last book I could remember reading was for a history class. Eager to come up with something clever, but only able to think about how ignorant I was about to sound, I settled for "I try not to pick favorites." My hands nervously began clutching each other. Looking around, I felt like I was in a United Colors of Benetton ad, with gray-haired regulars standing right next to teenagers. The room was filled with so many languages and shades of skin.

"Okay, maybe next time you'll get up there," she said with a smile, letting me know I was off the hook for now.

To my relief, the lights dimmed and the show of poets began. But none of this was classic poetry—this was an urban, expressive crowd. A woman dressed in a red hat that looked like a plastic pool float rapped in Spanish about her life as a teacher in the Bronx. The crowd screamed, "Represent!" Though I didn't understand it, she was so passionate I could feel her excitement.

Next a student from Columbia University stepped up with a thirty-second poem that kept the guy next to me snapping to the beat of her rhyme. Then there was a preppy guy in his twenties who could have been a lawyer, who sang in French.

Before the French song ended, Daniel called, so I stepped outside. "Hey, I can't talk," I whispered, even though I was outside. "I'm at that place where they read stuff out loud. Remember, I told you about it."

"Again?" he said surprised. "You went last week. Why would you go all the way to Alphabet City again?" But there was no pause for me to respond. "I guarantee you're going to want to leave. We're going to an underground private party—Claire Danes and Gwyneth Paltrow—tons of celebrities," he said with a laughing scream. "It's all underground, so this guy is coming over to take us. We only have one spot . . ."

"Thanks, but not tonight," I said, cutting him off. All these evenings sounded fun and were the kinds of things that would impress my friends back in Texas, but the reality wasn't that amazing. It often took thirty minutes of waiting in line for a drink, and most of our evening was spent trying to meet all the important people around us. Luis and Michael would see who they could get pictures with, and I'd go home feeling pathetic. It was the bragging about it later that usually gave me the thrill, but I didn't even care about that part anymore.

"Are you crazy?" he said in a serious tone. "This is a chance of a lifetime. Plus, those two Rockefeller dudes are going to be there too. You said you thought one of them was cute."

"I'm just not in the mood tonight. Next time," I said.

"What?" he said, but again, he didn't wait for me to respond. "What is it about that place? You said they don't even serve martinis," he said, stressing the *tinis.*

When I walked back inside a guy in a Knicks baseball hat and polo gently touched others' backs, making way for me to walk by. I hadn't put words to what it was about this place that kept me coming back. Everyone was welcome here. I was in a room of strangers where I hardly spoke, yet I was moved. In this environment, completely foreign to me, I felt some sort of connection. I felt closer to these utter strangers than to the people I'd spent the last year working countless hours with. I knew I had something to learn from these people, but I wasn't sure what it was. That kept me coming back.

The following week at 9:30 P.M., I got a beep from Todd. "Nina, I know this is last-minute, but we need a sales force memo for tomorrow morning." Throngs of people walked past me in the hotel hallway as I leaned forward and shoved my finger into my ear harder, as if that would make Todd more audible. Determined to get back to the dinner table and not miss dessert—chocolate marquise with cherry sauce—I contemplated how I could bring this conversation to a quick end.

"I'm not even in town," I said, shouting over a couple hundred voices. "I'm at that strategic finance conference event two hours away in Stamford. Call another analyst." My last few weeks had been quite manageable, making me forget the late nights. After experiencing the good life, it made a call like this from Todd even more annoying—a reminder that I was still under their claws.

"No, we need you on this," he said firmly.

"Please call someone in Manhattan," I said, lightly kicking my heel against the wall. "By the time I get back it will be 11:30, and I'm not sure I'd even get it done."

"I know you can," he said, switching to his baritone voice that would have normally made me start cracking a few knuckles. "Let me be frank. This is a big opportunity for me, and I want no mistakes."

"Did you talk to Ken about this? We had a conversation about workload last week." After vacation, I came back and confidently discussed with Ken making an effort to better manage our team's workload. He said I should be flattered to be so busy but that he'd talk to others about making an effort.

"Look," Todd said in an unyielding tone undercut with anger—this wasn't a request anymore. "There is no client at that strategic finance event. I need you to think about your priorities. I know we have a big team and things can get hard, but you are part of our team. I've been in your shoes. But look where I am now." He paused and then shifted his tone to that of the inspirational sales guy: "Nina, this is where you can be."

I winced at the thought of being him—that person. The moment I hung up, I tried to reach Steve to see if he could intervene, but he was out of town. Standing with my back against the wall, I thumped my heel and blankly stared at all the rushed, suited bodies passing by me.

"Nina," a Merrill Lynch analyst I'd met earlier during dinner screeched from across the hall as he held up a duffel bag. "Don't forget the free bag! It's worth at least fifty dollars." When we played the name game I realized he knew Daniel, Ali, and Bryan, and I knew several of his colleagues who were prep school friends with several of my colleagues. My world felt small.

I smiled and waved good-bye; then I walked downstairs to get a town car to take me to Morgan Stanley.

It would be a long night, so I decided to pick up sweats from my apartment before heading in to work. As I turned the knob to my apartment door, I was greeted by the scent of fresh basil—something unheard of in our apartment. Equally surprising was the fact that my roommate was actually home. "Yaaay! We get to hang out," she screamed and rushed toward me as though I was visiting from out of town. "I got off early tonight and actually cooked some spaghetti," she announced. "What are you doing here? Bryan said you were in Connecticut."

"I was two hours ago, but I got a call from Todd about a new project."

She rolled her eyes and put down her vodka tonic. "That sucks."

"I know," I replied, frustrated that our roommate relationship felt like a bad game of phone tag. "Sorry, we'll hang out next time. I'm on my way out—long night."

As soon as I got into the office, an associate from another group asked for my help sending a fax to Argentina since he didn't know how to use the machine.

"First, you need to put a name on it," I said, pointing to the title page.

"Just write Jose or Mario," he said. "Don't they just keep using the same two names over and over?"

He said it so seriously that I looked at him intently, trying to figure out if he was kidding. I hardly knew him, so it was hard to tell. I even paused, waiting for a response. But my typical scripted "work-appropriate" talk wasn't working tonight since Todd had already pissed me off.

"I hope you're joking," I said with squinty, annoyed eyes. I paused again to let him answer, but he just looked at me and then at the fax machine. "How do you know I'm not Hispanic?"

I asked, aware that there were very few Hispanics other than the cleaning staff within these walls. In my small suburb where I'd grown up, people were labeled black, white, or Mexican. Like the rest of the dark-haired people, I was used to falling under the Mexican category.

"You said you're from Texas," he snapped confidently as he laughed at the thought. And from the way he said it, I could tell it wouldn't have bothered him even if I were Hispanic, which annoyed me even more.

"You do realize that you can be from Texas and still be Hispanic, right?" I said as more of a statement than a question. "I'm from Texas, but I'm also Persian-Indian," I explained.

"I knew it! You're not Hispanic," he said, sounding pleased with himself for being right. "Who are you anyway, the PC police?" he asked with a big smile. "Don't get too cocky, because I know you're right up there with me, annoyed that a bunch of them are taking a big chunk of our paychecks so they can stay lazy on welfare."

From the smile on his face, I could see that he thought he'd won me over with his clever statement. "You have no idea how absurd you sound," I said as I left him standing at the machine by himself.

Even though I was annoyed, I was grateful we'd had that exchange, because it gave me a great idea. Performance reviews were due soon. I could write voluntary performance reviews for officers who I found offensive. I focused on officers who I thought were "lawsuits waiting to happen." I purposely worded it that way because officers were more likely to listen if money was at stake. Anything else would have just been whining. Even though analysts' opinions didn't matter much, writing them gave me great satisfaction.

Later that night, bundled in my cozy sweats, I downed several cups of coffee while poring over annual and quarterly reports. Though Andy wasn't around, I played his Depeche Mode CD to fill the stillness of the quiet office.

At 4:22 A.M., I walked into Todd's office and sat in his tall, black cushiony chair as I looked at the vast Hudson River. The whole back wall was a reflective window. I wondered if he ever stopped to appreciate the view.

Directly across from his office was an apartment building with all the lights blacked out except for one square. I almost looked away, embarrassed at invading someone's privacy. But then I remembered the public nature of New York. A father paced his living room holding a toddler, snuggled into a bright yellow sleeper with duck feet. The father's eyes chased sleep even as he walked, but he kept his tight grip.

This is where you can be, I thought as I looked at Todd's astounding number of prominently displayed deal toys, one in a huge trophy-cup shape. "This is the payoff," I muttered. He had a four-by-six photograph of his wife and three kids near his phone, angled so that only he could see it. I squinted and looked at the children, wondering if any of them looked like him.

The sleek tower that housed us was peaceful at this time of night. Besides my humming, I could only hear the murmur of the copy machines down the hall. There was a faint scent of left-over Mexican food in the trash. I didn't run around in a frantic state like I normally would, desperately trying to get out of there.

I placed the memo on Todd's chair and smirked, knowing he'd be annoyed by the subtitle a half centimeter off-center. I'd had a song stuck in my head all day, but I couldn't place it. Finally, a few words came to me—in Hindi. It was a song from a Bollywood movie, which was odd since Parsis rarely watched them and I had only seen a handful of Bollywood films through-out my life.

The one and only time I heard the song was at my Parsi friend's wedding, which was during my summer internship in New York. We weren't close; I'd only met her a few times through annual congresses over the years. Her father had threat-ened he would not speak to her again if she married outside the community. "He'll come around by your wedding day," we all assured her with smiles without teeth. Each week before the wedding a new aunty or uncle would try and convince him to attend and not give up his only daughter. As the day came closer, fear shifted to, "Will he show up at the last minute and make a scene?"

I had come straight from work and missed most of the cer-emony. The majority of the guests were excited for the happy couple, but there was a small group of overly concerned guests between whom I happened to be sitting during the reception. I was solo—no date or family to accompany me. My table was filled with couples who ran back and forth to the dance floor. Every now and again, one person would stay back, feeling sorry for me. While I sat alone at the table, I couldn't help but hear the commentary on both sides of me.

To my right was a table full of Americans. "What type of family is she coming from if her own father would shut her out like that?" a woman with a bleached-blond bob who hadn't got-ten around to touching up her roots announced loudly. "Did you know that they let vultures eat their bodies when they die?" a man with dirty blond wispy hair said to two college-age girls. Both girls wore their red hair in similar tight updos—likely they shared a hairdresser. "You know how I know?" he asked them, nodding his head and covering his lips with two fingers, though neither girl acknowledged him as he went on. "I read it on the Internet."

To my left was a table of Parsis. "Can you imagine that they may even raise their children Christian," Purvin Aunty said, fiddling with her pine tree brooch that held up her hand-embroidered sari. As per her request, Indian designers had copied the brooch from page twenty-three of the Zales holiday catalog. "Can you believe that? I pray for her mother." "They didn't even do a proper prayer ceremony," Minoo Uncle said, still wearing his blue velvet yarmulke-like prayer hat. "That Christian part must have been twice as long as the Parsi prayers."

I sat alone at my table, shifting around half a piece of *burfi* and leftover buttercream icing on my plate and wondering which table I'd rather be sitting at. But I couldn't relate to either table. Listening to them back and forth reminded me that I wasn't just Parsi or just American, but something in between.

After "Dancing Queen," the DJ played a popular Bollywood song. Parsi kids started screaming and hit the dance floor. Bollywood had only just become popular among them. Before that, Parsi kids thought it was something that just their parents might enjoy. The American kids were so enamored with the funky head movements and wild arm swings that they walked up, eager to learn the moves. Kids from all around the room slowly started to join, forming a circle of dancers so big the adults stopped to watch. At first, the Parsi kids were teaching the Americans. But it wasn't long before the Parsis began picking up interpretations from the American kids. They were all having so much fun that it became hard not to stop and stare. These kids' open-mouthed laughter was what silenced the ping-pong chatter between the two tables on either side of me. It was so contagious that all three of our tables started looking at each other, laughing and clapping loudly. As I craned my neck to see all the kids, I could hardly keep myself from leaping out of my chair.

Sitting in Todd's chair while remembering the wedding, I realized I'd need to pave my own route to happiness, like those dancing children. I knew I needed to leave my team to be happy. What were my options? If I were my parents I imagine I'd tough it out in corporate finance, and if I were the main character in a Hollywood movie, I'd just walk out. But both of these options were too extreme for me. I wasn't just Parsi or just American. What I'd have to do would be something in between, like Farah's calculated risk of studying both engineering and dance. It was a tightrope I was willing to test.

"I wanted to let you know, I'm planning to leave this group and go back to capital markets, where I interned." It wasn't until I said these words that I got Steve's full attention. His shifty eyes were now completely focused on me; he was no longer distracted by the thought of his long day of meetings ahead. I had thought about making the shift for weeks now. When I'd reached out to Laura about forming the women's committee, we had also discussed my switching groups. After I successfully kicked off the women's committee, I shifted my efforts toward getting out of corporate finance. I'd called the woman Natalia recommended from the investment firm that invested in woman- and minority-owned businesses and she was very interested in me. "Plus, we try to only hire analysts from Morgan or Goldman, so you'll have a great chance." She also made it clear that, as with most other firms, it was mandatory that I finish my two years at Morgan Stanley to get the position. After my experience at Morgan Stanley, the idea of helping other women and minorities succeed in business truly inspired me.

"And," I explained to Steve, "I'm taking two weeks off in between to visit my family in India." There was no precedent for taking two weeks off in a row, but why not? This request would seem small compared to the fact that I was leaving.

My sugary Dunkin' Donuts coffee tickled my lips as I spoke. I'd woken up early that morning with no desire to repeatedly press the snooze button. My day began with reading the *Wall Street Journal*'s fun tidbits from the Marketplace section and skipping Money & Investing. I walked partway to work, stopping a couple of blocks from my apartment to pick up a warm blueberry H & H bagel. There was something about these small pleasures that gave me the calmness I needed to walk into Steve's office.

Steve looked at me as if I had just asked him where to find a street that didn't exist—as if I were mistaken.

"What happened?" he asked in a tone he tried to keep controlled. "I've only been gone for a week."

"Capital markets is a better fit for me," I explained, even though I knew there wasn't a precedent for switching groups.

"You just got a great review. I told you how much the team respects and enjoys working with you. You could go so far here."

"This isn't what I want," I said firmly, putting him in uncharted territory. "I came to corporate finance because I'm aware it's the most powerful division. I expected the long hours and tons of work to be challenging, and they were, but in the end, I'm leaving because I can't believe the way people are treated here."

"But you've done so well here," he said. "You could thrive here."

"To be frank with you, at first I was appalled by the hazing culture here, but, like everything else, I got used to it. And I think that's part of the problem. The insanity has become part of being normal. I just need to get out of here to think clearly."

"I don't understand," he said.

"I know," I said. "That's the problem. No one here thinks anything is wrong," I said as I laughed. "That's precisely what's made me feel crazy from the beginning. Like there was something wrong with me for caring."

"I'm so disappointed," he said, staring at the ground. He looked back up. "We invested so much in you. Think about your long-term career. There is no better setup for a private equity firm or a hedge fund than corporate finance. Don't you want to go to business school? Harvard and Wharton MBAs clamor for these jobs, and you're already here!"

Normally all these fears would have weighed heavily on my decision, but not today. I sipped my coffee and looked at Steve as if I were casually watching a television show about other people's lives that had no effect on me.

Steve looked out the window pensively and then must have decided I was being rash. "I'll give you time to think about it," he said calmly, getting up to leave. "Take twenty-four hours and think about what you're saying." I could tell he felt more comfortable with that solution.

"I've thought about it for weeks," I shot back quickly. I could feel his nervous vibrations on my bare skin. "I'm not going to change my mind."

He sat back down and grasped the arms of his chair so

tightly that the veins on his hands twitched with the strain, conjuring a chicken's neck. "You could have come to me earlier," he said slowly.

I looked away because I could see he felt betrayed. Right then, without knocking, Larry opened the door. "Steve, I need you for a second."

Steve closed the door so I couldn't hear what they were saying. But I could tell Steve told him, since Larry played a game of looking at me and then looking away several times.

Steve came back with a newfound look of hope. "Well, we have some good news. Our group is going to be working on what could be the largest spin-off in financial history." He sat back down before he revealed more. "We have a proposal for you."

"Great," I said, starting to stroke my hair, which I was wearing partially down for the first time.

"I just checked with Larry, so you won't have to worry that it will change," he qualified before he sprang the biggest sell he knew with a winning smile. "It's really work more appropriate for a second-year analyst. But the deal is yours."

Months ago the proposal would have made me weak, but today it was the most unappealing proposition. "Thanks, but I'm really leaving. Nothing will change my mind."

Steve stood up and was now leaning over the back of his chair. I had never seen him so overwhelmed. He alternated between leaving his mouth dangling open in shock and then restraining himself by straightening his collar. His mind seemed to be racing, and then suddenly, as if he had given up, he spoke to me in a monotone voice that sounded like he was reading me my Miranda rights. He reminded me that by switching groups, I would risk losing my job since there would be so many others lined up to take my position within a week but no guarantee of another opening in the company. If I left the Morgan Stanley analyst program midway, it would raise many questions for other employers as to why I couldn't handle it.

"I know. I've already considered all these risks," I said confidently, relieved that for the first time, I didn't fear any of them. "I've already talked to a few people from my old group in capital markets, and they are working to find an open position for me."

"You spoke to Laura," he said in a knowing way. Her name carried so much power in our company his face contracted with intimidation. "You basically want to work anywhere else but corporate finance?" he said, squinting his eyes at me and lifting his fingers to his mouth as if fearing my response.

"Yes, anywhere but corporate finance. And Laura and I did speak. I'm committed to finishing my two years at Morgan Stanley," I responded, staring out the window into Times Square. I looked at him and said, "This is my choice."

"Your choice," he repeated as he nodded his head and looked lost in thought. "I'm sure you realize most analysts don't have the luxury of choosing their path. That says something about your reputation here." He raised his brows as he looked out the window. "I'll do whatever I can to support you," he said in a sad yet caring tone that reminded me how sensitive he was compared to the officers he worked for. There was something inherently genuine in him, which I appreciated. "But I'll warn you: People here aren't going to be too happy about it."

Until the end of the week on Friday, Steve kept it between us and a couple of other officers. He even put in strong recommendations for me to his business school friends across the firm. Friday, after returning from a long lunch break, I walked by Steve's office and saw Michael crumpled, sitting across from Steve. Even from afar, I could see that his eyes were wet. Steve stood over him and talked with dramatic hands. It was clear by the way Michael's defeated eyes followed me as I walked by that Steve had just told him. I could even hear part of the speech Michael was getting: "This is an opportunity for you to step up. You have done great work and now we want to help you grow even further. You could be our star analyst. I know you won't let us down . . ."

His tears surprised me. I figured Michael's biggest concern would be that his social life was about to take a huge hit. Steve must have just told him he'd be the one covering the big spin-off project they had originally offered me. A project like that would mean at least eighty-hour weeks for his whole second year. But this seemed too dramatic for him to cry about at work, which made me wonder if he felt guilty that he wasn't pulling his weight. Was it possible he was crying because he would miss me?

But I didn't spend too much time worrying about Michael. He'd get over it. Knowing that Steve was announcing my departure put a bounce in my walk—it now felt final. I walked back over to my desk area to find Luis rummaging through Michael's drawers looking for his travel-size lint roller. "Why does he have to keep so much crap? I can't find a thing."

"It's in the third drawer on the right, with his cologne and deodorant," I offered. It was clear that Luis wasn't aware I was switching groups yet.

"You're awesome," he said, looking up with a face of relief.

I placed my beeper on my desk as I looked at Luis with a radiant smile.

"What's so funny?" he asked, walking over to my desk area to come witness my joy in case it might be contagious.

"Nothing," I said, lifting my briefcase to my shoulder. "I'm just having a good day." My briefcase was practically empty—no financial reports, no laptop, no town car vouchers. The eager, innocent look frozen on Luis's face reminded me of the hundreds of Ivy League kids we'd recruit each year. They had this undying willingness to do anything they could to walk these halls. *Instead of all the scripted responses we're taught to give them with a smile, what would I say to them now?* Finance is a game of gains and losses. Think hard about what you have to gain, and harder about what you have to lose.

"If anyone is looking for me, tell them I'll be back tomorrow," I told Luis.

"Just like that?" He raised his arms in a baffled gesture and laughed.

"Just like that," I said, laughing, appreciating the melodic sound I had forgotten.

Acknowledgments

The first draft of this was written because I had the honor of crossing paths with two brilliant writers at Dartmouth who inspired me, Brock Brower and Thomas Powers. They challenged my values and reminded me what was meaningful in life. Had Brock not said again and again, "Tell me more...," this would not have been written. His smile gave me the courage to write about experiences I had mentally shoved into narrow, inaccessible crevices. Tom planted the seed that this was worth publishing and reminded me that if I believed in it and kept working hard, it would happen. They both supported me throughout the publishing process with solid advice, clever quips, and literary references I had to look up on Google.

Thanks to my brilliant agent, Susan Ginsburg, for her enthusiasm and encouragement, and for keeping the process enjoyable. Throughout, she brought vision and support. She's a master at navigating the publishing process. Thanks to Lauren LeBlanc at Atlas & Co. for being such a fabulous editor. She has an empathetic, fresh perspective on life that is refreshing. Without her genuine passion, this might not have been published. Through her keen judgment, she taught me to be a better writer. Thanks to Nicole Villeneuve, my incredible publicist, for navigating the media maze, and to James Atlas for successfully running a firm that commits itself to a bigger vision. A big thank-you to the rest of the Atlas & Co. team—Ariel Kouvaras, Nataša Lekić, Peter Desrochers, and Lukas Volger.

Thanks to my mom, dad, sisters, and husband for their constant support and loving me at my best and worst. To my extended family all over the world, for overwhelming me with love. My gratitude to friends who became readers: Amy Dahm, Anna Francis-Chang, Deanna Dyer, Michael Chang, Reshma Kapadia Gardner, Thi Luu, Melissa Nguyen, and Catherine Wittkower. To friends from my many networks that have been supportive: Zoroastrian Associations, Leadership Austin, the Op-Ed Project, 85 Broads, Writers' League of Texas, Wharton, Dartmouth, and the University of Texas.

Thanks to my beautiful husband. I'm still not surprised that on our first dinner date my fortune cookie read, "The love of your life is right in front of you." It only took one of your wide Russian smiles to captivate me.

Finally, to my meditation teachers around the world who taught me to hear my own music.